Citroën AX Owners Workshop Manual

I M Coomber

Models covered
All Citroën AX three and five-door models
AX 10, AX 11 & AX 14 (inc. GT), including special and
limited editions
954 cc, 1124 cc and 1360 cc petrol engines

Does not cover Diesel engine models

ABCDE
FGHIJ
KLMNO
PQRST

THE
BOOK

Haynes Publishing Group
Sparkford Nr Yeovil
Somerset BA22 7JJ England

Haynes Publications, Inc
861 Lawrence Drive
Newbury Park
California 91320 USA

H50 016 201 5

Acknowledgements

Thanks are due to the Champion Sparking Plug Company Limited, who supplied the illustrations showing the spark plug conditions, and to Duckhams Oils, who provided lubrication data. Certain other illustrations are the copyright of Citroën Cars Ltd, and are used with their permission. Thanks are also due to Sykes-Pickavant, who provided some of the workshop tools, and all the staff at Sparkford who helped in the production of this manual.

© **Haynes Publishing Group 1990**

A book in the **Haynes Owners Workshop Manual Series**

Printed by J. H. Haynes & Co. Ltd, Sparkford, Nr Yeovil, Somerset BA22 7JJ, England

ISBN 1 85010 470 0

British Library Cataloguing in Publication Data
Coomber, Ian, *1943*
   Citroën AX petrol owner's workshop manual.
   1. Cars. Maintenance & repair
I. Title   II. Series
629.2872
ISBN 1-85010-470-0

Contents

4

Citroën AX 11 TRE

Citroën AX GT

About this manual

Its aim

The aim of this manual is to help you get the best value from your vehicle. It can do so in several ways. It can help you decide what work must be done (even should you choose to get it done by a garage), provide information on routine maintenance and servicing, and give a logical course of action and diagnosis when random faults occur. However, it is hoped that you will use the manual by tackling the work yourself. On simpler jobs it may even be quicker than booking the car into a garage and going there twice, to leave and collect it. Perhaps most important, a lot of money can be saved by avoiding the costs a garage must charge to cover its labour and overheads.

The manual has drawings and descriptions to show the function of the various components so that their layout can be understood. Then the tasks are described and photographed in a step-by-step sequence so that even a novice can do the work.

Its arrangement

The manual is divided into twelve Chapters, each covering a logical sub-division of the vehicle. The Chapters are each divided into Sections, numbered with single figures, eg 5; and the Sections into paragraphs (or sub-sections), with decimal numbers following on from the Section they are in, eg 5.1, 5.2, 5.3 etc.

It is freely illustrated, especially in those parts where there is a detailed sequence of operations to be carried out. There are two forms of illustration: figures and photographs. The figures are numbered in sequence with decimal numbers, according to their position in the Chapter - eg Fig. 6.4 is the fourth drawing /illustration in Chapter 6. Photographs carry the same number (either individually or in related groups) as the Section or sub-section to which they relate.

There is an alphabetical index at the back of the manual as well as a contents list at the front. Each Chapter is also preceded by its own individual contents list.

References to the 'left' or 'right' of the vehicle are in the sense of a person in the driver's seat facing forwards.

Unless otherwise stated, nuts and bolts are removed by turning anti-clockwise, and tightened by turning clockwise.

Vehicle manufacturers continually make changes to specifications and recommendations, and these, when notified, are incorporated into our manuals at the earliest opportunity.

Whilst every care is taken to ensure that the information in this manual is correct, no liability can be accepted by the authors or publishers for loss, damage or injury caused by any errors in, or omissions from, the information given.

Project vehicle

The project vehicle used in the preparation of this manual, and appearing in the photographic sequences was a Citroën AX 11 TRE.

Introduction to the Citroën AX

The Citroën AX was introduced into the UK market in July 1987, the initial versions being three-door hatchbacks, with transverse engine and transmission driving the front wheels. The five-door version was introduced in April 1988.

Three engine sizes are offered, being 954 cc, 1124 cc or 1360 cc. All engine types are of the same water-cooled, single overhead camshaft design. A four or five-speed manual transmission is fitted.

Independent suspension is fitted front and rear, the front having MacPherson struts, the rear trailing arms and torsion bars. Higher per-formance models are fitted with an anti-roll bar to the front and rear suspension systems. All models have double-acting telescopic shock absorbers to the front and rear suspension.

The steering system is rack and pinion type, mounted high on the bulkhead to protect against damage in the event of an accident.

Although of compact external proportions, the interior is spacious and well thought out. Designed as a low maintenance vehicle, regular servicing at the specified intervals will ensure the reliable, safe and economical motoring for which it was originally built.

Jacking and towing

Jacking

The jack supplied with the car by the manufacturers is designed for use only when changing a roadwheel. The jack locates under the body sill on the side concerned at the jack point mid- way between the front and rear wheel arches. Before jacking up the car to change the road-wheel, prise free the embellisher from the wheel concerned and then loosen the wheelbolts. Ensure that the jack is securely located and standing on firm level ground. The car should be in gear and the handbrake fully applied.

The spare wheel is carried by a holder under the rear of the car and is lowered by unscrewing the securing bolt in the boot floor. Ensure that the spare tyre is inflated to the correct pressure before fitting.

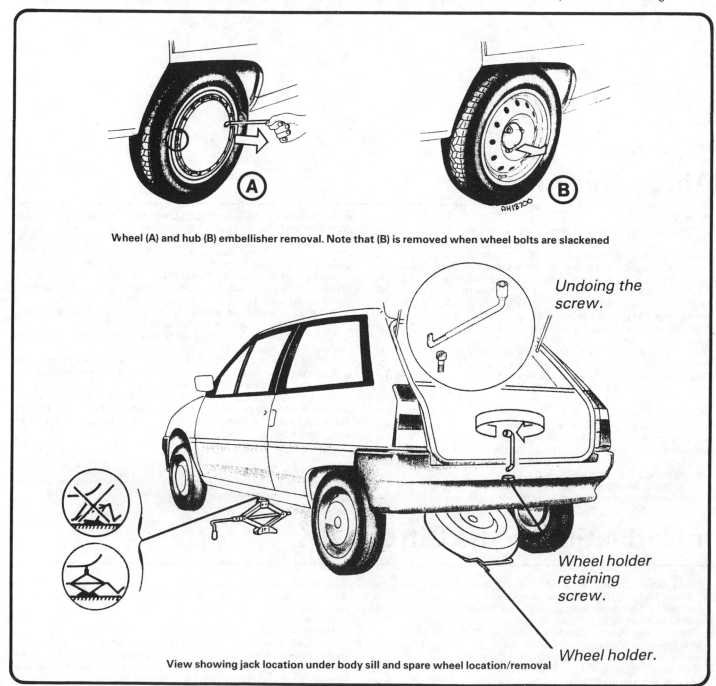

Wheel (A) and hub (B) embellisher removal. Note that (B) is removed when wheel bolts are slackened

Undoing the screw.

Wheel holder retaining screw.

Wheel holder.

View showing jack location under body sill and spare wheel location/removal

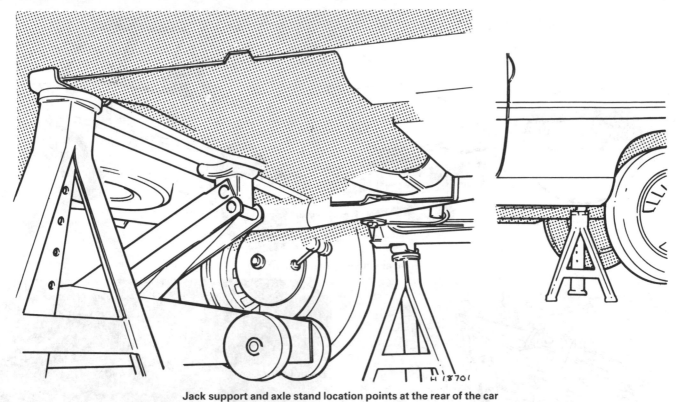

Jack support and axle stand location points at the rear of the car

Jack support bar and axle stand location points at the front end

With the car suitably raised, remove the wheel and replace it with the spare, tighten the bolts so that they are hand-tight, lower the car and then fully tighten the bolts. Locate the punctured tyre into the spare wheel support and raise it. Have the puncture repaired at the earliest opportunity.

If you are going to carry out work under the car it is preferable to position the car over an inspection pit. If this is not available use a workshop trolley or substantial screw or bottle type hydraulic jack. *Always supplement a jack with axle stands*. The sill jacking points or their adjacent re-inforced areas should be used as jacking points for raising the car. A beam may be placed transversely under the inboard mounting points of the suspension arms and the front end jacked up

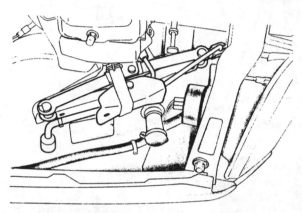

Front end towing eye locations

Jack location in the engine compartment

under that. At the rear, jack up under the side members and position the axle stands under side members just forwards of the rear wheel arch each side. If jacking centrally at the rear, fit the jack under the axle beam.

Towing

Towing eyes are fitted to the front and rear of the vehicle for attachment of a tow rope. The front towing eyes are located under the front bumper. On GT models, access to the towing eye is gained by removing a blanking plate on the front spoiler. The rear towing eye on all models is located on the rear bumper.

Front towing eye

Always turn the ignition key to position A when being towed; this allows the steering to be turned and brake lights, indicators, horn and wipers to function. Note that if the engine is not running, the battery will discharge with use of electrical equipment which should be kept to a minimum.

On no account turn the ignition key to the S position whilst being towed, because if the key is withdrawn the steering will lock.

General dimensions, weights and capacities

Dimensions
Overall length .... 3.50 m (138 in)
Overall width .... 1.56 m (61.5 in)
Overall height .... 1.35 m (53.5 in)
Wheelbase .... 2.285 m (89.9 in)
Turning circle (between kerbs):
    AX 10 and AX 11 models .... 9.23 m (30.3 ft)
    AX 14 and AX GT models .... 10.2 m (33.6 ft)

Weights

	3-door	5-door
Kerb weight:		
AX 10 E/RE	640 kg (1411 lb)	655 kg (1444 lb)
AX 11 RE/TRE	645 kg (1422 lb)	660 kg (1455 lb)
AX 14 TRS/TZS	695 kg (1532 lb)	710 kg (1566 lb)
AX GT	730 kg (1610 lb)	
Maximum roof rack load	50 kg (110 lb)	

Capacities
Engine oil (including filter) .... 3.5 litres (6.2 pints)
Transmission oil .... 2.0 litres (3.5 pints)
Cooling system .... 4.8 litres (8.4 pints)
Fuel tank:
    AX 10 and AX 11 models .... 36 litres (8.0 gals)
    AX 14 and GT models .... 43 litres (9.5 gals)
Brake hydraulic system .... 0.22 litres (0.39 pints)
Windscreen washer reservoir .... 1.5 litres (2.6 pints)
Windscreen and rear screen washer reservoir ..... 3.0 litres (5.3 pints)

Buying spare parts and vehicle identification numbers

Buying spare parts

Spare parts are available from many sources. Citroën have many dealers throughout the UK, and other dealers, accessory stores and motor factors will also stock some spare parts suitable for Citroën cars. Our advice regarding spare part sources is as follows:

Officially appointed vehicle main dealers – This is the best source for parts which are peculiar to your vehicle and are otherwise not generally available (eg. complete cylinder heads, internal transmission components, badges, interior trim, etc). It is also the only place you should buy parts if your vehicle is still under warranty. To be sure of obtaining the correct parts it will always be necessary to give the storeperson your vehicle's engine and chassis number, and if possible, to take the 'old' part along for a positive identification. Remember that many parts are available on a factory exchange scheme – any parts returned should always be clean. It obviously makes good sense to go straight to the specialist on your vehicle for this type of part, for they are best equipped to supply you.

Other dealers and auto accessory stores – These are often very good places to buy materials and components needed for the maintenance of your vehicle (eg, oil filters, spark plugs, bulbs, drivebelts, oils and greases, touch-up paint, filler paste, etc). They also sell general accessories, usually have convenient opening hours, charge lower prices and can often be found not far from home.

Motor factors – Good factors will stock all the more important components which wear out relatively quickly (eg, clutch components, pistons, valves, exhaust systems, brake cylinders/pipes/hoses/seals/shoes and pads, etc). Motor factors will often provide new or reconditioned components on a part exchange basis – this can save a considerable amount of money.

Vehicle identification numbers

Modifications are a continuing and unpublicised process in vehicle manufacture. Spare parts manuals and lists are compiled on a numerical basis, the individual vehicle numbers being essential to identify correctly the component required.

Chassis serial number: This is located on the right-hand side wing valance within the engine compartment.

Vehicle information plate: This is located on the bulkhead on the right-hand side in the engine compartment.

Engine number: This is located on the front (exhaust manifold) face of the engine, towards the transmission.

Transmission number: This is located on the top face of the transmission unit.

Body paint code: This is located on the right-hand side wing valance within the engine compartment.

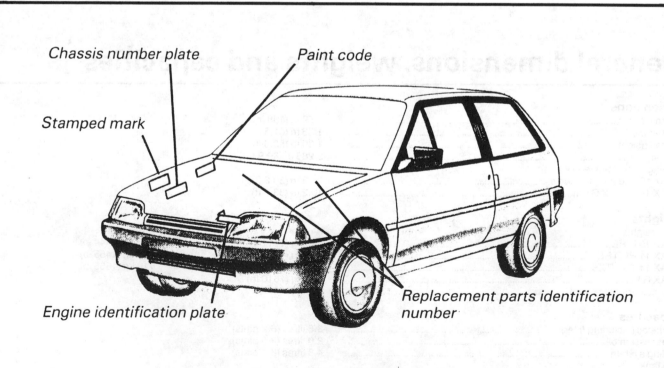

Identification plate locations

General repair procedures

Whenever servicing, repair or overhaul work is carried out on the car or its components, it is necessary to observe the following procedures and instructions. This will assist in carrying out the operation efficiently and to a professional standard of workmanship.

Joint mating faces and gaskets

Where a gasket is used between the mating faces of two components, ensure that it is renewed on reassembly, and fit it dry unless otherwise stated in the repair procedure. Make sure that the mating faces are clean and dry with all traces of old gasket removed. When cleaning a joint face, use a tool which is not likely to score or damage the face, and remove any burrs or nicks with an oilstone or fine file.

Make sure that tapped holes are cleaned with a pipe cleaner, and keep them free of jointing compound if this is being used unless specifically instructed otherwise.

Ensure that all orifices, channels or pipes are clear and blow through them, preferably using compressed air.

Oil seals

Whenever an oil seal is removed from its working location, either individually or as part of an assembly, it should be renewed.

The very fine sealing lip of the seal is easily damaged and will not seal if the surface it contacts is not completely clean and free from scratches, nicks or grooves. If the original sealing surface of the component cannot be restored, the component should be renewed.

Protect the lips of the seal from any surface which may damage them in the course of fitting. Use tape or a conical sleeve where possible. Lubricate the seal lips with oil before fitting and, on dual lipped seals, fill the space between the lips with grease.

Unless otherwise stated, oil seals must be fitted with their sealing lips toward the lubricant to be sealed.

Use a tubular drift or block of wood of the appropriate size to install the seal and, if the seal housing is shouldered, drive the seal down to the shoulder. If the seal housing is unshouldered, the seal should be fitted with its face flush with the housing top face.

Screw threads and fastenings

Always ensure that a blind tapped hole is completely free from oil, grease, water or other fluid before installing the bolt or stud. Failure to do this could cause the housing to crack due to the hydraulic action of the bolt or stud as it is screwed in.

When tightening a castellated nut to accept a split pin, tighten the nut to the specified torque, where applicable, and then tighten further to the next split pin hole. Never slacken the nut to align a split pin hole unless stated in the repair procedure.

When checking or retightening a nut or bolt to a specified torque setting, slacken the nut or bolt by a quarter of a turn, and then retighten to the specified setting.

Locknuts, locktabs and washers

Any fastening which will rotate against a component or housing in the course of tightening should always have a washer between it and the relevant component or housing.

Spring or split washers should always be renewed when they are used to lock a critical component such as a big-end bearing retaining nut or bolt.

Locktabs which are folded over to retain a nut or bolt should always be renewed.

Self-locking nuts can be reused in non-critical areas, providing resistance can be felt when the locking portion passes over the bolt or stud thread.

Split pins must always be replaced with new ones of the correct size for the hole.

Special tools

Some repair procedures in this manual entail the use of special tools such as a press, two or three-legged pullers, spring compressors etc. Wherever possible, suitable readily available alternatives to the manufacturer's special tools are described, and are shown in use. In some instances, where no alternative is possible, it has been necessary to resort to the use of a manufacturer's tool and this has been done for reasons of safety as well as the efficient completion of the repair operation. Unless you are highly skilled and have a thorough understanding of the procedure described, never attempt to bypass the use of any special tool when the procedure described specifies its use. Not only is there a very great risk of personal injury, but expensive damage could be caused to the components involved.

Tools and working facilities

Introduction

A selection of good tools is a fundamental requirement for anyone contemplating the maintenance and repair of a motor vehicle. For the owner who does not possess any, their purchase will prove a considerable expense, offsetting some of the savings made by doing-it-yourself. However, provided that the tools purchased meet the relevant national safety standard and are of good quality, they will last for many years and prove an extremely worthwhile investment.

To help the average owner to decide which tools are needed to carry out the various tasks detailed in this manual, we have compiled three lists of tools under the following headings: *Maintenance and minor repair, Repair and overhaul,* and *Special*. The newcomer to practical mechanics should start off with the *Maintenance and minor repair* tool kit and confine himself to the simpler jobs around the vehicle. Then, as his confidence and experience grow, he can undertake more difficult tasks, buying extra tools as, and when, they are needed. In this way, a *Maintenance and minor repair* tool kit can be built-up into a *Repair and overhaul* tool kit over a considerable period of time without any major cash outlays. The experienced do-it-yourselfer will have a tool kit good enough for most repair and overhaul procedures and will add tools from the *Special* category when he feels the expense is justified by the amount of use to which these tools will be put.

It is obviously not possible to cover the subject of tools fully here. For those who wish to learn more about tools and their use there is a book entitled *How to Choose and Use Car Tools* available from the publishers of this manual.

Maintenance and minor repair tool kit

The tools given in this list should be considered as a minimum requirement if routine maintenance, servicing and minor repair operations are to be undertaken. We recommend the purchase of combination spanners (ring one end, open-ended the other); although more expensive than open-ended ones, they do give the advantages of both types of spanner.

Combination spanners - 10, 11, 12, 13, 14 & 17 mm
Adjustable spanner - 9 inch
Engine sump/gearbox drain plug key (8 mm square)
Spark plug spanner (with rubber insert)
Spark plug gap adjustment tool
Set of feeler gauges
Brake adjuster spanner
Brake bleed nipple spanner
Screwdriver - 4 in long x $\frac{1}{4}$ in dia (flat blade)
Screwdriver - 4 in long x $\frac{1}{4}$ in dia (cross blade)
Combination pliers - 6 inch
Hacksaw (junior)
Tyre pump
Tyre pressure gauge
Oil can
Fine emery cloth (1 sheet)
Wire brush (small)
Funnel (medium size)

Repair and overhaul tool kit

These tools are virtually essential for anyone undertaking any major repairs to a motor vehicle, and are additional to those given in the *Maintenance and minor repair* list. Included in this list is a comprehensive set of sockets. Although these are expensive they will be found invaluable as they are so versatile - particularly if various drives are included in the set. We recommend the $\frac{1}{2}$ in square-drive type, as this can be used with most proprietary torque wrenches. If you cannot afford a socket set, even bought piecemeal, then inexpensive tubular box spanners are a useful alternative.

The tools in this list will occasionally need to be supplemented by tools from the *Special* list.

Sockets (or box spanners) to cover range in previous list
Reversible ratchet drive (for use with sockets)
Extension piece, 10 inch (for use with sockets)
Universal joint (for use with sockets)
Torque wrench (for use with sockets)
'Mole' wrench - 8 inch
Ball pein hammer
Soft-faced hammer, plastic or rubber
Screwdriver - 6 in long x $\frac{5}{16}$ in dia (flat blade)
Screwdriver - 2 in long x $\frac{5}{16}$ in square (flat blade)
Screwdriver - 1$\frac{1}{2}$ in long x $\frac{1}{4}$ in dia (cross blade)
Screwdriver - 3 in long x $\frac{1}{8}$ in dia (electricians)
Pliers - electricians side cutters
Pliers - needle nosed
Pliers - circlip (internal and external)
Cold chisel - $\frac{1}{2}$ inch
Scriber
Scraper
Centre punch
Pin punch
Hacksaw
Valve grinding tool
Steel rule/straight-edge
Allen keys (inc. splined/Torx type if necessary)
Selection of files
Wire brush (large)
Axle-stands
Jack (strong trolley or hydraulic type)

Special tools

The tools in this list are those which are not used regularly, are expensive to buy, or which need to be used in accordance with their manufacturers' instructions. Unless relatively difficult mechanical jobs are undertaken frequently, it will not be economic to buy many of these tools. Where this is the case, you could consider clubbing together with friends (or joining a motorists' club) to make a joint purchase, or borrowing the tools against a deposit from a local garage or tool hire specialist.

The following list contains only those tools and instruments freely available to the public, and not those special tools produced by the vehicle manufacturer specifically for its dealer network. You will find occasional references to these manufacturers' special tools in the text of this manual. Generally, an alternative method of doing the job without the vehicle manufacturers' special tool is given. However, sometimes, there is no alternative to using them. Where this is the case and the relevant tool cannot be bought or borrowed, you will have to entrust the work to a franchised garage.

> Valve spring compressor (where applicable)
> Piston ring compressor
> Balljoint separator
> Universal hub/bearing puller
> Impact screwdriver
> Micrometer and/or vernier gauge
> Dial gauge
> Stroboscopic timing light
> Tachometer
> Universal electrical multi-meter
> Cylinder compression gauge
> Lifting tackle
> Trolley jack
> Light with extension lead

Buying tools

For practically all tools, a tool factor is the best source since he will have a very comprehensive range compared with the average garage or accessory shop. Having said that, accessory shops often offer excellent quality tools at discount prices, so it pays to shop around.

There are plenty of good tools around at reasonable prices, but always aim to purchase items which meet the relevant national safety standards. If in doubt, ask the proprietor or manager of the shop for advice before making a purchase.

Care and maintenance of tools

Having purchased a reasonable tool kit, it is necessary to keep the tools in a clean serviceable condition. After use, always wipe off any dirt, grease and metal particles using a clean, dry cloth, before putting the tools away. Never leave them lying around after they have been used. A simple tool rack on the garage or workshop wall, for items such as screwdrivers and pliers is a good idea. Store all normal wrenches and sockets in a metal box. Any measuring instruments, gauges, meters, etc, must be carefully stored where they cannot be damaged or become rusty.

Take a little care when tools are used. Hammer heads inevitably become marked and screwdrivers lose the keen edge on their blades from time to time. A little timely attention with emery cloth or a file will soon restore items like this to a good serviceable finish.

Working facilities

Not to be forgotten when discussing tools, is the workshop itself. If anything more than routine maintenance is to be carried out, some form of suitable working area becomes essential.

It is appreciated that many an owner mechanic is forced by circumstances to remove an engine or similar item, without the benefit of a garage or workshop. Having done this, any repairs should always be done under the cover of a roof.

Wherever possible, any dismantling should be done on a clean, flat workbench or table at a suitable working height.

Any workbench needs a vice: one with a jaw opening of 4 in (100 mm) is suitable for most jobs. As mentioned previously, some clean dry storage space is also required for tools, as well as for lubricants, cleaning fluids, touch-up paints and so on, which become necessary.

Another item which may be required, and which has a much more general usage, is an electric drill with a chuck capacity of at least $\frac{5}{16}$ in (8 mm). This, together with a good range of twist drills, is virtually essential for fitting accessories such as mirrors and reversing lights.

Last, but not least, always keep a supply of old newspapers and clean, lint-free rags available, and try to keep any working area as clean as possible.

Spanner jaw gap comparison table

Jaw gap (in)	Spanner size
0.250	$\frac{1}{4}$ in AF
0.276	7 mm
0.313	$\frac{5}{16}$ in AF
0.315	8 mm
0.344	$\frac{11}{32}$ in AF; $\frac{1}{8}$ in Whitworth
0.354	9 mm
0.375	$\frac{3}{8}$ in AF
0.394	10 mm
0.433	11 mm
0.438	$\frac{7}{16}$ in AF
0.445	$\frac{3}{16}$ in Whitworth; $\frac{1}{4}$ in BSF
0.472	12 mm
0.500	$\frac{1}{2}$ in AF
0.512	13 mm
0.525	1/4 in Whitworth; $\frac{5}{16}$ in BSF
0.551	14 mm
0.563	$\frac{9}{16}$ in AF
0.591	15 mm
0.600	$\frac{5}{16}$ in Whitworth; $\frac{3}{8}$ in BSF
0.625	$\frac{5}{8}$ in AF
0.630	16 mm
0.669	17 mm
0.686	$\frac{11}{16}$ in AF
0.709	18 mm
0.711	$\frac{3}{8}$ in Whitworth; $\frac{7}{16}$ in BSF
0.748	19 mm
0.750	$\frac{3}{4}$ in AF
0.813	$\frac{13}{16}$ in AF
0.820	$\frac{7}{16}$ in Whitworth; $\frac{1}{2}$ in BSF
0.866	22 mm
0.875	$\frac{7}{8}$ in AF
0.920	$\frac{1}{2}$ in Whitworth; $\frac{9}{16}$ in BSF
0.938	$\frac{15}{16}$ in AF
0.945	24 mm
1.000	1 in AF
1.010	$\frac{9}{16}$ in Whitworth; $\frac{5}{8}$ in BSF
1.024	26 mm
1.063	$1\frac{1}{16}$ in AF; 27 mm
1.100	$\frac{5}{8}$ in Whitworth; $\frac{11}{16}$ in BSF
1.125	$1\frac{1}{8}$ in AF
1.181	30 mm
1.200	$\frac{11}{16}$ in Whitworth; $\frac{3}{4}$ in BSF
1.250	$1\frac{1}{4}$ in AF
1.260	32 mm
1.300	$\frac{3}{4}$ in Whitworth; $\frac{7}{8}$ in BSF
1.313	$1\frac{5}{16}$ in AF
1.390	$1\frac{3}{8}$ in Whitworth; $1\frac{5}{16}$ in BSF
1.417	36 mm
1.438	$1\frac{7}{16}$ in AF
1.480	$\frac{7}{8}$ in Whitworth; 1 in BSF
1.500	$1\frac{1}{2}$ in AF
1.575	40 mm; $1\frac{5}{8}$ in Whitworth
1.614	41 mm
1.625	$1\frac{5}{8}$ in AF
1.670	1 in Whitworth; $1\frac{1}{8}$ in BSF
1.688	$1\frac{11}{16}$ in AF
1.811	46 mm
1.813	$1\frac{13}{16}$ in AF
1.860	$1\frac{1}{8}$ in Whitworth; $1\frac{1}{4}$ in BSF
1.875	$1\frac{7}{8}$ in AF
1.969	50 mm
2.000	2 in AF
2.050	$1\frac{1}{4}$ in Whitworth; $1\frac{3}{8}$ in BSF
2.165	55 mm
2.362	60 mm

Conversion factors

Length (distance)
Inches (in)	X	25.4	= Millimetres (mm)	X 0.0394	= Inches (in)
Feet (ft)	X	0.305	= Metres (m)	X 3.281	= Feet (ft)
Miles	X	1.609	= Kilometres (km)	X 0.621	= Miles

Volume (capacity)
Cubic inches (cu in; in³)	X	16.387	= Cubic centimetres (cc; cm³)	X 0.061	= Cubic inches (cu in; in³)
Imperial pints (Imp pt)	X	0.568	= Litres (l)	X 1.76	= Imperial pints (Imp pt)
Imperial quarts (Imp qt)	X	1.137	= Litres (l)	X 0.88	= Imperial quarts (Imp qt)
Imperial quarts (Imp qt)	X	1.201	= US quarts (US qt)	X 0.833	= Imperial quarts (Imp qt)
US quarts (US qt)	X	0.946	= Litres (l)	X 1.057	= US quarts (US qt)
Imperial gallons (Imp gal)	X	4.546	= Litres (l)	X 0.22	= Imperial gallons (Imp gal)
Imperial gallons (Imp gal)	X	1.201	= US gallons (US gal)	X 0.833	= Imperial gallons (Imp gal)
US gallons (US gal)	X	3.785	= Litres (l)	X 0.264	= US gallons (US gal)

Mass (weight)
Ounces (oz)	X	28.35	= Grams (g)	X 0.035	= Ounces (oz)
Pounds (lb)	X	0.454	= Kilograms (kg)	X 2.205	= Pounds (lb)

Force
Ounces-force (ozf; oz)	X	0.278	= Newtons (N)	X 3.6	= Ounces-force (ozf; oz)
Pounds-force (lbf; lb)	X	4.448	= Newtons (N)	X 0.225	= Pounds-force (lbf; lb)
Newtons (N)	X	0.1	= Kilograms-force (kgf; kg)	X 9.81	= Newtons (N)

Pressure
Pounds-force per square inch (psi; lbf/in²; lb/in²)	X	0.070	= Kilograms-force per square centimetre (kgf/cm²; kg/cm²)	X 14.223	= Pounds-force per square inch (psi; lbf/in²; lb/in²)
Pounds-force per square inch (psi; lbf/in²; lb/in²)	X	0.068	= Atmospheres (atm)	X 14.696	= Pounds-force per square inch (psi; lbf/in²; lb/in²)
Pounds-force per square inch (psi; lbf/in²; lb/in²)	X	0.069	= Bars	X 14.5	= Pounds-force per square inch (psi; lbf/in²; lb/in²)
Pounds-force per square inch (psi; lbf/in²; lb/in²)	X	6.895	= Kilopascals (kPa)	X 0.145	= Pounds-force per square inch (psi; lbf/in²; lb/in²)
Kilopascals (kPa)	X	0.01	= Kilograms-force per square centimetre (kgf/cm²; kg/cm²)	X 98.1	= Kilopascals (kPa)
Millibar (mbar)	X	100	= Pascals (Pa)	X 0.01	= Millibar (mbar)
Millibar (mbar)	X	0.0145	= Pounds-force per square inch (psi; lbf/in²; lb/in²)	X 68.947	= Millibar (mbar)
Millibar (mbar)	X	0.75	= Millimetres of mercury (mmHg)	X 1.333	= Millibar (mbar)
Millibar (mbar)	X	0.401	= Inches of water (inH₂O)	X 2.491	= Millibar (mbar)
Millimetres of mercury (mmHg)	X	0.535	= Inches of water (inH₂O)	X 1.868	= Millimetres of mercury (mmHg)
Inches of water (inH₂O)	X	0.036	= Pounds-force per square inch (psi; lbf/in²; lb/in²)	X 27.68	= Inches of water (inH₂O)

Torque (moment of force)
Pounds-force inches (lbf in; lb in)	X	1.152	= Kilograms-force centimetre (kgf cm; kg cm)	X 0.868	= Pounds-force inches (lbf in; lb in)
Pounds-force inches (lbf in; lb in)	X	0.113	= Newton metres (Nm)	X 8.85	= Pounds-force inches (lbf in; lb in)
Pounds-force inches (lbf in; lb in)	X	0.083	= Pounds-force feet (lbf ft; lb ft)	X 12	= Pounds-force inches (lbf in; lb in)
Pounds-force feet (lbf ft; lb ft)	X	0.138	= Kilograms-force metres (kgf m; kg m)	X 7.233	= Pounds-force feet (lbf ft; lb ft)
Pounds-force feet (lbf ft; lb ft)	X	1.356	= Newton metres (Nm)	X 0.738	= Pounds-force feet (lbf ft; lb ft)
Newton metres (Nm)	X	0.102	= Kilograms-force metres (kgf m; kg m)	X 9.804	= Newton metres (Nm)

Power
Horsepower (hp)	X	745.7	= Watts (W)	X 0.0013	= Horsepower (hp)

Velocity (speed)
Miles per hour (miles/hr; mph)	X	1.609	= Kilometres per hour (km/hr; kph)	X 0.621	= Miles per hour (miles/hr; mph)

Fuel consumption*
Miles per gallon, Imperial (mpg)	X	0.354	= Kilometres per litre (km/l)	X 2.825	= Miles per gallon, Imperial (mpg)
Miles per gallon, US (mpg)	X	0.425	= Kilometres per litre (km/l)	X 2.352	= Miles per gallon, US (mpg)

Temperature

Degrees Fahrenheit = ($^{\circ}$C x 1.8) + 32

Degrees Celsius (Degrees Centigrade; $^{\circ}$C) = ($^{\circ}$F - 32) x 0.56

*It is common practice to convert from miles per gallon (mpg) to litres/100 kilometres (l/100km), where mpg (Imperial) x l/100 km = 282 and mpg (US) x l/100 km = 235

Safety first!

Professional motor mechanics are trained in safe working procedures. However enthusiastic you may be about getting on with the job in hand, do take the time to ensure that your safety is not put at risk. A moment's lack of attention can result in an accident, as can failure to observe certain elementary precautions.

There will always be new ways of having accidents, and the following points do not pretend to be a comprehensive list of all dangers; they are intended rather to make you aware of the risks and to encourage a safety-conscious approach to all work you carry out on your vehicle.

Essential DOs and DON'Ts

DON'T rely on a single jack when working underneath the vehicle. Always use reliable additional means of support, such as axle stands, securely placed under a part of the vehicle that you know will not give way.

DON'T attempt to loosen or tighten high-torque nuts (e.g. wheel hub nuts) while the vehicle is on a jack; it may be pulled off.

DON'T start the engine without first ascertaining that the transmission is in neutral and the parking brake applied.

DON'T suddenly remove the filler cap from a hot cooling system – cover it with a cloth and release the pressure gradually first, or you may get scalded by escaping coolant.

DON'T attempt to drain oil until you are sure it has cooled sufficiently to avoid scalding you.

DON'T grasp any part of the engine, exhaust or catalytic converter without first ascertaining that it is sufficiently cool to avoid burning you.

DON'T allow brake fluid or antifreeze to contact vehicle paintwork.

DON'T syphon toxic liquids such as fuel, brake fluid or antifreeze by mouth, or allow them to remain on your skin.

DON'T inhale dust – it may be injurious to health (see *Asbestos* below).

DON'T allow any spilt oil or grease to remain on the floor – wipe it up straight away, before someone slips on it.

DON'T use ill-fitting spanners or other tools which may slip and cause injury.

DON'T attempt to lift a heavy component which may be beyond your capability – get assistance

DON'T rush to finish a job, or take unverified short cuts.

DON'T allow children or animals in or around an unattended vehicle.

DO wear eye protection when using power tools such as drill, sander, bench grinder etc, and when working under the vehicle.

DO use a barrier cream on your hands prior to undertaking dirty jobs – it will protect your skin from infection as well as making the dirt easier to remove afterwards; but make sure your hands aren't left slippery. Note that long-term contact with used engine oil can be a health hazard.

DO keep loose clothing (cuffs, tie etc) and long hair well out of the way of moving mechanical parts.

DO remove rings, wristwatch etc, before working on the vehicle – especially the electrical system.

DO ensure that any lifting tackle used has a safe working load rating adequate for the job.

DO keep your work area tidy – it is only too easy to fall over articles left lying around.

DO get someone to check periodically that all is well, when working alone on the vehicle.

DO carry out work in a logical sequence and check that everything is correctly assembled and tightened afterwards.

DO remember that your vehicle's safety affects that of yourself and others. If in doubt on any point, get specialist advice.

IF, in spite of following these precautions, you are unfortunate enough to injure yourself, seek medical attention as soon as possible.

Asbestos

Certain friction, insulating, sealing, and other products – such as brake linings, brake bands, clutch linings, torque converters, gaskets, etc – contain asbestos. *Extreme care must be taken to avoid inhalation of dust from such products since it is hazardous to health.* If in doubt, assume that they *do* contain asbestos.

Fire

Remember at all times that petrol (gasoline) is highly flammable. Never smoke, or have any kind of naked flame around, when working on

the vehicle. But the risk does not end there – a spark caused by an electrical short-circuit, by two metal surfaces contacting each other, by careless use of tools, or even by static electricity built up in your body under certain conditions, can ignite petrol vapour, which in a confined space is highly explosive.

Always disconnect the battery earth (negative) terminal before working on any part of the fuel or electrical system, and never risk spilling fuel on to a hot engine or exhaust.

It is recommended that a fire extinguisher of a type suitable for fuel and electrical fires is kept handy in the garage or workplace at all times. Never try to extinguish a fuel or electrical fire with water.

Note: *Any reference to a 'torch' appearing in this manual should always be taken to mean a hand-held battery-operated electric lamp or flashlight. It does NOT mean a welding/gas torch or blowlamp.*

Fumes

Certain fumes are highly toxic and can quickly cause unconsciousness and even death if inhaled to any extent. Petrol (gasoline) vapour comes into this category, as do the vapours from certain solvents such as trichloroethylene. Any draining or pouring of such volatile fluids should be done in a well ventilated area.

When using cleaning fluids and solvents, read the instructions carefully. Never use materials from unmarked containers – they may give off poisonous vapours.

Never run the engine of a motor vehicle in an enclosed space such as a garage. Exhaust fumes contain carbon monoxide which is extremely poisonous; if you need to run the engine, always do so in the open air or at least have the rear of the vehicle outside the workplace.

If you are fortunate enough to have the use of an inspection pit, never drain or pour petrol, and never run the engine, while the vehicle is standing over it; the fumes, being heavier than air, will concentrate in the pit with possibly lethal results.

The battery

Never cause a spark, or allow a naked light, near the vehicle's battery. It will normally be giving off a certain amount of hydrogen gas, which is highly explosive.

Always disconnect the battery earth (negative) terminal before working on the fuel or electrical systems.

If possible, loosen the filler plugs or cover when charging the battery from an external source. Do not charge at an excessive rate or the battery may burst.

Take care when topping up and when carrying the battery. The acid electrolyte, even when diluted, is very corrosive and should not be allowed to contact the eyes or skin.

If you ever need to prepare electrolyte yourself, always add the acid slowly to the water, and never the other way round. Protect against splashes by wearing rubber gloves and goggles.

When jump starting a car using a booster battery, for negative earth (ground) vehicles, connect the jump leads in the following sequence: First connect one jump lead between the positive (+) terminals of the two batteries. Then connect the other jump lead first to the negative (–) terminal of the booster battery, and then to a good earthing (ground) point on the vehicle to be started, at least 18 in (45 cm) from the battery if possible. Ensure that hands and jump leads are clear of any moving parts, and that the two vehicles do not touch. Disconnect the leads in the reverse order.

Mains electricity and electrical equipment

When using an electric power tool, inspection light etc, always ensure that the appliance is correctly connected to its plug and that, where necessary, it is properly earthed (grounded). Do not use such appliances in damp conditions and, again, beware of creating a spark or applying excessive heat in the vicinity of fuel or fuel vapour. Also ensure that the appliances meet the relevant national safety standards.

Ignition HT voltage

A severe electric shock can result from touching certain parts of the ignition system, such as the HT leads, when the engine is running or being cranked, particularly if components are damp or the insulation is defective. With electronic ignition the HT voltage is much higher and could prove fatal.

Routine maintenance

Maintenance is essential for ensuring safety and is desirable for the purpose of getting the best in terms of performance and economy from the car. Over the years the need for periodic lubrication – oiling and greasing – has been drastically reduced, if not totally eliminated. This has unfortunately tended to lead some owners to think that because no such action is required the components either no longer exist or will last for ever. This is a serious delusion. If anything, there are now more places, particularly in the steering and suspension, where joints and pivots are fitted. Although you do not grease them any more you still have to look at them – and look at them just as often as you may previously have had to grease them. The largest initial element of maintenance is visual examination. This may lead to repairs or renewal.

The following service schedules are a list of the maintenance requirements, and the intervals at which they should be carried out, as recommended by the manufacturers. Where applicable, these procedures are covered in greater detail throughout this manual, near the beginning of each Chapter.

Every 250 miles (400 km) or weekly – whichever comes first

Engine (Chapter 1)
Check the engine oil level using the dipstick. The oil level must be maintained between the high and low markings at all times. Top up when necessary but do not overfill

Cooling system (Chapter 2)
Check the coolant level. Top up if necessary
Check for signs of leakage, and hose security

Fuel system (Chapter 3)
Check for signs of leakage, and hose security

Transmission (Chapter 6)
Check for oil leaks

Braking system (Chapter 8)
Check the level of brake fluid in the fluid reservoir. The level must be kept between the high and low markings on the reservoir wall. Top up if necessary

Suspension (Chapter 9)
Check the tyre pressures, and examine them for wear and damage

Electrical system (Chapter 12)
Check and if necessary top up the fluid level in the windscreen/tailgate washer reservoir

After the first 1000 to 1500 miles (1600 to 2400 km)

Cars with new or overhauled components

Engine (Chapter 1)
Renew the oil and filter

Braking system (Chapter 8)
Check the brake system for any signs of leakage

Every 7500 miles (12 500 km) or six months – whichever comes first

Engine (Chapter 1)
Drain and renew the engine oil
Renew the engine oil filter

Driveshafts (Chapter 7)
Inspect the driveshaft bellows for signs of damage and/or leaks
Check the joints for excessive wear

Suspension and steering (Chapters 9 and 10)
Inspect the steering balljoint gaiters and the rack bellows for signs of leakage, damage or perishing

Electrical components (Chapter 12)
Check all exterior lights for satisfactory operation

Every 15 000 miles (25 000 km) or 12 months – whichever comes first

Engine (Chapter 1)
Check and if necessary, adjust the valve clearances

Fuel system (Chapter 3)
Renew the air filter element
Renew the fuel filter (in-line)

Ignition system (Chapter 4)
Check and adjust or replace the spark plugs

Clutch (Chapter 5)
Check the clutch pedal height

Brakes (Chapter 8)
Check the disc pad linings
Check the front brake discs for excessive wear
Make a provisional check of the rear brake linings

Under bonnet view (air cleaner ducting removed for clarity)

1	Battery	6	Coolant filler cap	11 Car jack and wheelbrace
2	Headlamp beam adjuster	7	Engine oil filler cap	12 Suspension strut upper mounting
3	Air intake temperature control unit	8	Engine oil dipstick	13 Accelerator cable
4	Cooling fan	9	Headlight wiring connection	14 Choke cable
5	Bonnet lock	10	Windscreen/tailgate washer	15 Carburettor
			reservoir filler cap	

16 Air cleaner
17 Fuel pump
18 Ignition module
19 Brake master cylinder/reservoir

View of front underside

1 Gearshift rod
2 Suspension arm
3 Engine sump drain plug
4 Windscreen/tailgate window washer reservoir

5 Alternator drivebelt adjuster
6 Alternator
7 Engine oil filter
8 Exhaust pipe

9 Radiator
10 Transmission
11 Horn
12 Driveshaft

13 Front brake calliper
14 Stabilizer
15 Brake pipes

View of rear underside

1 Torsion bar
2 Rear brake drum
3 Shock absorber
4 Handbrake cable (to right-hand rear brake)
5 Fuel tank
6 Handbrake cable equalizer
7 Exhaust pipe
8 Heat shield
9 Handbrake cable (to left-hand rear brake)
10 Axle arm mounting (front)
11 Axle arm mounting (rear)
12 Exhaust silencer
13 Spare wheel and holder
14 Rear axle

Bodywork (Chapter 11)
    Check that all of the body drain channels are clear
    Lubricate the door/tailgate hinges and locks
    Examine the body for signs of corrosion (particularly in structural
mounting areas)

Electrical system (Chapter 12)
    Check the alternator drivebelt for condition and adjustment

Brakes (Chapter 8)
    Drain and renew the brake system hydraulic fluid.

Suspension and steering (Chapters 9 and 10)
    Check the wheel bearings for wear and damage
    Check the steering and suspension balljoints for wear and
damage
    Check the shock absorbers for operation and leaks

Every 30 000 miles (50 000 km) or 24 months – whichever comes first

Cooling system (Chapter 2)
    Check the density of the antifreeze in the engine coolant.
    Drain and renew if necessary.

Every 36 000 miles (58 000 km)

Engine (Chapter 1)
    Renew the camshaft drivebelt. **Note:** *Although not specified by the manufacturers, the author advises renewal as a precautionary measure against possible high mileage failure*

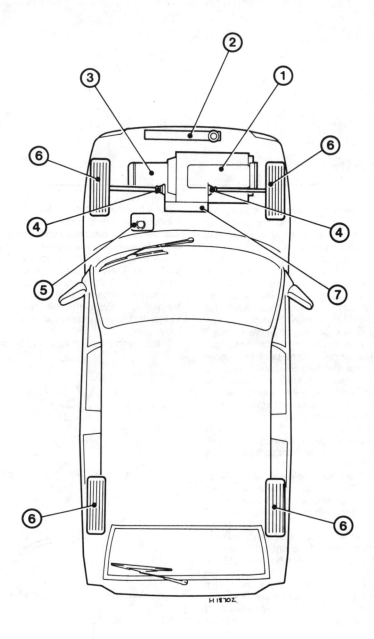

Recommended lubricants and fluids

Component or system	Lubricant type/specification	Duckhams recommendation
Engine (1)	Multigrade engine oil, viscosity SAE 10W/40 or 15W/40	Duckhams QXR, Hypergrade, or 10W/40 Motor Oil
Cooling system (2)	Ethylene glycol based antifreeze	Duckhams Universal Antifreeze and Summer Coolant
Manual transmission (3)	Gear oil, viscosity 75W/80	Duckhams Hypoid PT 75W/80
Driveshaft CV joints (4)	Special lubricant supplied in repair kit	
Brake fluid reservoir (5)	Hydraulic fluid to DOT 4	Duckhams Universal Brake and Clutch Fluid
Hub/wheel bearings (6)	Multi-purpose lithium based grease	Duckhams LB 10
Steering rack (7)	Multi-purpose lithium based grease	Duckhams LB 10

Fault diagnosis

Introduction

The vehicle owner who does his or her own maintenance according to the recommended schedules should not have to use this section of the manual very often. Modern component reliability is such that, provided those items subject to wear or deterioration are inspected or renewed at the specified intervals, sudden failure is comparatively rare. Faults do not usually just happen as a result of sudden failure, but develop over a period of time. Major mechanical failures in particular are usually preceded by characteristic symptoms over hundreds or even thousands of miles. Those components which do occasionally fail without warning are often small and easily carried in the vehicle.

With any fault finding, the first step is to decide where to begin investigations. Sometimes this is obvious, but on other occasions a little detective work will be necessary. The owner who makes half a dozen haphazard adjustments or replacements may be successful in curing a fault (or its symptoms), but he will be none the wiser if the fault recurs and he may well have spent more time and money than was necessary. A calm and logical approach will be found to be more satisfactory in the long run. Always take into account any warning signs or abnormalities that may have been noticed in the period preceding the fault – power loss, high or low gauge readings, unusual noises or smells, etc – and remember that failure of components such as fuses or spark plugs may only be pointers to some underlying fault.

The pages which follow here are intended to help in cases of failure to start or breakdown on the road. There is also a Fault Diagnosis Section at the end of each Chapter which should be consulted if the preliminary checks prove unfruitful. Whatever the fault, certain basic principles apply. These are as follows:

Verify the fault. This is simply a matter of being sure that you know what the symptoms are before starting work. This is particularly important if you are investigating a fault for someone else who may not have described it very accurately.

Don't overlook the obvious. For example, if the vehicle won't start, is there petrol in the tank? (Don't take anyone else's word on this particular point, and don't trust the fuel gauge either!) If an electrical fault is indicated, look for loose or broken wires before digging out the test gear.

Cure the disease, not the symptom. Substituting a flat battery with a fully charged one will get you off the hard shoulder, but if the underlying cause is not attended to, the new battery will go the same way. Similarly, changing oil-fouled spark plugs for a new set will get you moving again, but remember that the reason for the fouling (if it wasn't simply an incorrect grade of plug) will have to be established and corrected.

Don't take anything for granted. Particularly, don't forget that a 'new' component may itself be defective (especially if it's been rattling round in the boot for months), and don't leave components out of a fault diagnosis sequence just because they are new or recently fitted. When you do finally diagnose a difficult fault, you'll probably realise that all the evidence was there from the start.

Electrical faults

Electrical faults can be more puzzling than straightforward mechanical failures, but they are no less susceptible to logical analysis if the basic principles of operation are understood. Vehicle electrical wiring exists in extremely unfavourable conditions – heat, vibration and chemical attack – and the first things to look for are loose or corroded connections and broken or chafed wires, especially where the wires pass through holes in the bodywork or are subject to vibration.

All metal-bodied vehicles in current production have one pole of the battery 'earthed', ie connected to the vehicle bodywork, and in nearly all modern vehicles it is the negative (–) terminal. The various electrical components – motors, bulb holders etc – are also connected to earth, either by means of a lead or directly by their mountings. Electric current flows through the component and then back to the battery via the bodywork. If the component mounting is loose or corroded, or if a good path back to the battery is not available, the circuit will be incomplete and malfunction will result. The engine and/or gearbox are also earthed by means of flexible metal straps to the body or subframe; if these straps are loose or missing, starter motor, generator and ignition trouble may result.

Assuming the earth return to be satisfactory, electrical faults will be

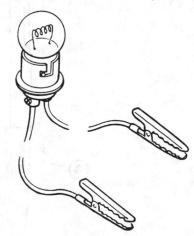

A simple test lamp is useful for tracing electrical faults

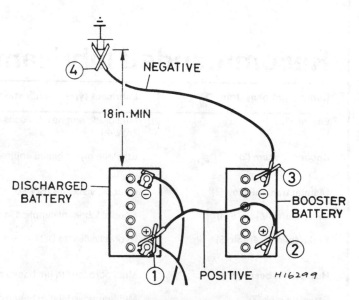

Jump start lead connections for negative earth vehicles – connect leads in order shown

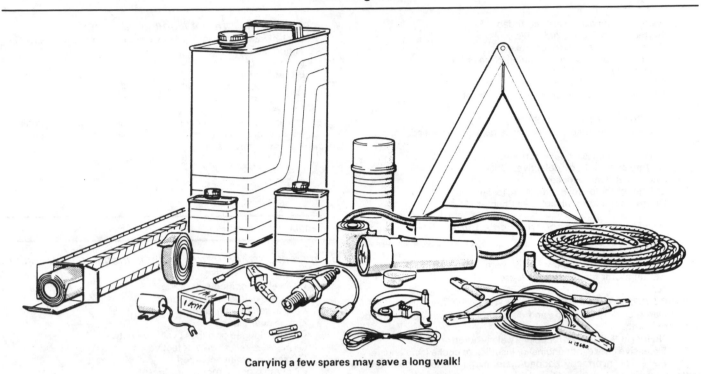

Carrying a few spares may save a long walk!

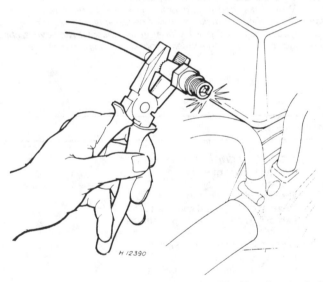

Crank engine and check for spark. Note use of insulated tool to hold plug lead

due either to component malfunction or to defects in the current supply. Individual components are dealt with in Chapter 12. If supply wires are broken or cracked internally this results in an open-circuit, and the easiest way to check for this is to bypass the suspect wire temporarily with a length of wire having a crocodile clip or suitable connector at each end. Alternatively, a 12V test lamp can be used to verify the presence of supply voltage at various points along the wire and the break can be thus isolated.

If a bare portion of a live wire touches the bodywork or other earthed metal part, the electricity will take the low-resistance path thus formed back to the battery: this is known as a short-circuit. Hopefully a short-circuit will blow a fuse, but otherwise it may cause burning of the insulation (and possibly further short-circuits) or even a fire. This is why it is inadvisable to bypass persistently blowing fuses with silver foil or wire.

Spares and tool kit

Most vehicles are supplied only with sufficient tools for wheel changing; the *Maintenance and minor repair* tool kit detailed in *Tools and working facilities,* with the addition of a hammer, is probably sufficient

for those repairs that most motorists would consider attempting at the roadside. In addition a few items which can be fitted without too much trouble in the event of a breakdown should be carried. Experience and available space will modify the list below, but the following may save having to call on professional assistance:

Spark plugs, clean and correctly gapped
HT lead and plug cap – long enough to reach the plug furthest from the distributor
Drivebelt(s) – emergency type may suffice
Spare fuses
Set of principal light bulbs
Tin of radiator sealer and hose bandage
Exhaust bandage
Roll of insulating tape
Length of soft iron wire
Length of electrical flex
Torch or inspection lamp (can double as test lamp)
Battery jump leads
Tow-rope
Ignition waterproofing aerosol
Litre of engine oil
Sealed can of hydraulic fluid
Emergency windscreen
Worm drive clips
Tube of filler paste

If spare fuel is carried, a can designed for the purpose should be used to minimise risks of leakage and collision damage. A first aid kit and a warning triangle, whilst not at present compulsory in the UK, are obviously sensible items to carry in addition to the above.

When touring abroad it may be advisable to carry additional spares which, even if you cannot fit them yourself, could save having to wait while parts are obtained. The items below may be worth considering:

Clutch and throttle cables
Cylinder head gasket
Alternator brushes
Tyre valve core

One of the motoring organisations will be able to advise on availability of fuel etc in foreign countries.

Engine will not start

Engine fails to turn when starter operated

Flat battery (recharge, use jump leads, or push start)

Battery terminals loose or corroded
Battery earth to body defective
Engine earth strap loose or broken
Starter motor (or solenoid) wiring loose or broken
Ignition/starter switch faulty
Major mechanical failure (seizure)
Starter or solenoid internal fault (see Chapter 12)

Starter motor turns engine slowly

Partially discharged battery (recharge, use jump leads, or push start)
Battery terminals loose or corroded
Battery earth to body defective
Engine earth strap loose
Starter motor (or solenoid) wiring loose
Starter motor internal fault (see Chapter 12)

Starter motor spins without turning engine

Flat battery
Starter motor pinion sticking on sleeve
Flywheel gear teeth damaged or worn
Starter motor mounting bolts loose

Engine turns normally but fails to start

Damp or dirty HT leads and distributor cap (crank engine and check for spark)
No fuel in tank (check for delivery at carburettor)
Excessive choke (hot engine) or insufficient choke (cold engine)
Fouled or incorrectly gapped spark plugs (remove, clean and regap)
Other ignition system fault (see Chapter 4)
Other fuel system fault (see Chapter 3)
Poor compression (see Chapter 1)
Major mechanical failure (eg camshaft drive)

Engine fires but will not run

Insufficient choke (cold engine)
Air leaks at carburettor or inlet manifold
Fuel starvation (see Chapter 3)
Ballast resistor defective, or other ignition fault (see Chapter 4)

Engine cuts out and will not restart

Engine cuts out suddenly – ignition fault

Loose or disconnected LT wires
Wet HT leads or distributor cap (after traversing water splash)
Coil or condenser failure (check for spark)
Other ignition fault (see Chapter 4)

Engine misfires before cutting out – fuel fault

Fuel tank empty
Fuel pump defective or filter blocked (check for delivery)
Fuel tank filler vent blocked (suction will be evident on releasing cap)
Carburettor needle valve sticking
Carburettor jets blocked (fuel contaminated)
Other fuel system fault (see Chapter 3)

Engine cuts out – other causes

Serious overheating
Major mechanical failure (eg camshaft drive)

Engine overheats

Ignition (no-charge) warning light illuminated

Slack or broken drivebelt – retension or renew (Chapter 12)

Ignition warning light not illuminated

Coolant loss due to internal or external leakage (see Chapter 2)
Thermostat defective
Low oil level
Brakes binding
Radiator clogged externally or internally
Electric cooling fan not operating correctly
Engine waterways clogged
Ignition timing incorrect or automatic advance malfunctioning
Mixture too weak **Note:** *Do not add cold water to an overheated engine or damage may result*

Low engine oil pressure

Gauge reads low or warning light illuminated with engine running

Oil level low or incorrect grade
Defective gauge or sender unit
Wire to sender unit earthed
Engine overheating
Oil filter clogged or bypass valve defective
Oil pressure relief valve defective
Oil pick-up strainer clogged
Oil pump worn or mountings loose
Worn main or big-end bearings **Note:** *Low oil pressure in a high-mileage engine at tickover is not necessarily a cause for concern. Sudden pressure loss at speed is far more significant. In any event, check the gauge or warning light sender before condemning the engine.*

Engine noises

Pre-ignition (pinking) on acceleration

Incorrect grade of fuel
Ignition timing incorrect
Distributor faulty or worn
Worn or maladjusted carburettor
Excessive carbon build-up in engine

Whistling or wheezing noises

Leaking vacuum hose
Leaking carburettor or manifold gasket
Blowing head gasket

Tapping or rattling

Incorrect valve clearances
Worn valve gear
Worn timing belt
Broken piston ring (ticking noise)

Knocking or thumping

Unintentional mechanical contact (eg fan blades)
Worn drivebelt
Peripheral component fault (generator, water pump etc)
Worn big-end bearings (regular heavy knocking, perhaps less under load)
Worn main bearings (rumbling and knocking, perhaps worsening under load)
Piston slap (most noticeable when cold)

Chapter 1 Engine

Contents

Specifications

General

Four-cylinder, in-line, overhead camshaft. All alloy with wet cylinder liners. Mounted transversely and inclined 6° to the front. Transmission mounted on left-hand end of engine.

Engine type	TU
Application and code/displacement:	
AX 10 models	C1A 954 cc
AX 11 models	H1A 1124 cc
AX 14 models (up to 1988)	K1A 1360 cc
AX 14 models (from 1988-on)	K1G 1360 cc
AX GT models	K2A 1360 cc
Bore x stroke:	
954 cc	70 x 62 mm
1124 cc	72 x 69 mm
1360 cc	75 x 77 mm
Compression ratio:	
954 and 1124 cc	9.4 : 1
1360 cc	9.3 : 1

Crankshaft

Number of main bearings	5
Main journal diameter	49.965 to 49.981 mm
Regrind undersize	0.30 mm
Crankpin diameter:	
954 cc	37.992 to 38.008 mm
1124 cc and 1360 cc	44.975 to 44.991 mm
Regrind undersize	0.30 mm
Maximum allowable ovality (main journal and crankpin)	0.007 mm
Endfloat	0.01 to 0.30 mm
Thrust washer thicknesses	2.40, 2.50, 2.55 and 2.60 mm

Connecting rods
Maximum weight difference on any engine .... 3 grams

Cylinder liners
Type .... Wet, removable, cast iron, matched to piston
Protrusion from block (without seal) .... 0.03 to 0.10 mm
Protrusion difference between liners (maximum) .... 0.05 mm

Pistons
Type .... Aluminium alloy, with two compression rings and one scraper matched to piston
Running clearance .... 0.85 to 1.15 mm
Maximum allowable weight difference between pistons .... 2 grams
Compression ring gap clearance (in bore) .... 0.25 to 0.45 mm

Gudgeon pin
Fit .... Clearance in piston, interference in connecting rod

Cylinder head
Material .... Aluminium alloy
Maximum distortion .... 0.05 mm
Height:
    954 cc .... 187.43 to 187.53 mm
    1124 cc and 1360 cc .... 206.93 to 207.03 mm
Number of camshaft bearings 5
Camshaft drive .... Toothed belt

Valves
Seat, combined angle:
    Inlet .... 120°
    Exhaust .... 90°
Valve clearances (cold):
    Inlet – all models .... 0.20 mm (0.008 in)
    Exhaust – all models except K2A engine .... 0.40 mm (0.016 in)
    Exhaust – K2A engine .... 0.30 mm (0.012 in)

Valve timing (at nominal clearance of 0.7 mm (0.028 in)):

	C1A	H1A	K1A	K1G	K2A
Inlet opens (BTDC)	9° 16′	5°19′	5° 55′	7° 14′	7° 28′
Exhaust opens (BBDC)	31° 21′	43° 49′	44° 25′	54° 30′	56°
Inlet closes (ABDC)	11° 10′	32° 58′	32° 22	39° 45′	41° 02′
Exhaust closes (ATDC)	-6° 55′*	-0° 6′*	0° 42′	0° 45′	7° 27′

* (BTDC)

Valve stem diameter:
    Inlet .... 6.97 to 6.98 mm
    Exhaust .... 6.95 to 6.96 mm
Valve head diameter:
    Inlet:
        C1A .... 34.7 mm
        All other engines .... 36.7 mm
    Exhaust:
        C1A .... 27.7 mm
        All other engines .... 29.2 mm

Lubrication system
Oil pump type .... Two gears, chain driven from crankshaft
Filter type .... Disposable cartridge
Sump capacity:
    With filter change .... 3.5 litres (6.2 pints)
    Without filter change .... 3.2 litres (5.6 pints)
Difference between minimum and maximum marks on dipstick .... 1.5 litres (2.5 pints)
Minimum oil pressure at 90°C (194°F):
    650 rpm .... 1.5 bar (21.8 lbf/in^2)
    4000 rpm .... 4.0 bar (58.0 lbf/in^2)
Oil pressure warning light operating pressure:
    Up to September 1987 .... 0.8 bar (11.6 lbf/in^2)
    From September 1987 .... 0.5 bar (7.3 lbf/in^2)
Lubricant type/specification .... Multigrade engine oil, viscosity SAE 10W/40 or 15W/40 (Duckhams QXR, Hypergrade, or 10W/40 Motor Oil)

Torque wrench settings

	Nm	lbf ft
Crankshaft pulley	110	81
Camshaft sprocket	80	59
Big-end bearing cap	40	30

Torque wrench settings (continued)

	Nm	lbf ft
Flywheel	65	48
Distributor/fuel pump housing	8	6
Camshaft thrust fork	16	12
Thermostat housing	8	6
Main bearing cap casting main bearing bolts:		
Stage 1	20	15
Stage 2	Tighten a further 45°	Tighten a further 45°
Oil pump	8	6
Sump	8	6
Sump drain plug	30	22
Connecting rod	40	30
Valve rocker adjuster locknut	18	13
Main bearing cap casting to block	8	6
Water pump housing:		
8 mm bolts	30	22
6 mm bolts	50	37
Cylinder head bolts:		
Stage 1	20	15
Stage 2	Tighten a further 240°	Tighten a further 240°
Timing belt tensioner:		
Initial	15	11
Final	23	17
Timing cover	8	6
Valve cover	5	4
Dipstick tube	15	11
Oil pressure switch	28	21
Oil filter	15	11
Engine to transmission bolts	45	33
Engine/transmission mountings	Refer to Figs. 1.20 and 1.21	
Engine/transmission torque stay	Refer to Fig. 1.22	

1 General description

The engine, which has four cylinders and an overhead camshaft, is mounted transversely, driving the front wheels, and it is inclined to the front by 6°, with the exhaust manifold towards the radiator and the inlet manifold and carburettor on the bulkhead side of the engine.

The engine has four wet liner cylinders, a five-bearing crankshaft and an overhead camshaft.

Camshaft drive is by toothed belt. The belt is tensioned by a spring-loaded wheel and also drives the coolant pump. The camshaft operates directly on to the rocker arms, adjustment being by ballstud and locknut. The distributor is driven directly from the tail of the camshaft.

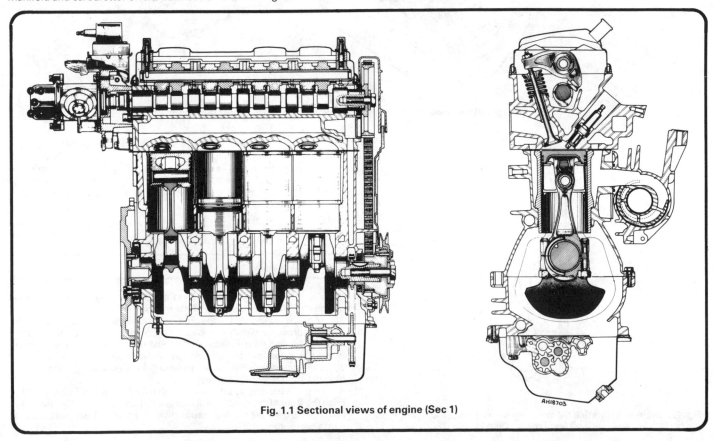

Fig. 1.1 Sectional views of engine (Sec 1)

AH18703

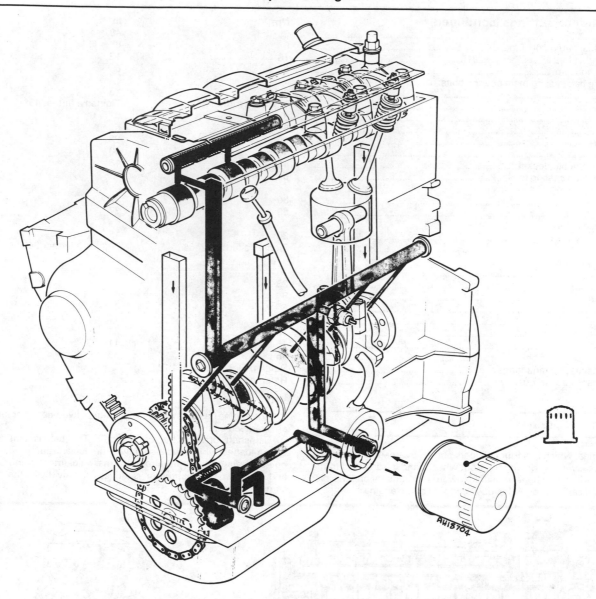

Fig. 1.2 Cutaway view of the engine showing lubrication circuit (Sec 1)

The oil pump is located in the sump and is chain driven from the crankshaft. A forced feed lubrication system is employed. Oil from the pump passes to the oil filter then to the oil gallery, crankshaft and camshaft. The valve stems are lubricated by oil returning from the camshaft to the sump. The oil pump chain and sprockets are lubricated by oil in the sump.

2   Routine maintenance

Carry out the following procedures at the intervals given in *Routine maintenance* at the beginning of the manual.
1   The oil level should be checked preferably when the engine is cold.
2   Withdraw the dipstick, wipe it clean, re-insert it and then withdraw it for the second time. The oil level should be between the high and low marks. If it is too low, top up through the filler cap (photo).
3   The quantity of oil required to raise the oil level from the low to the high mark is 1.5 litres (2.5 pints).
4   To drain the engine oil it is preferable for the engine to be hot. First raise the front of the car on ramps or with a jack. Unscrew the drain plug in the sump, remove the filler cap and allow the oil to drain into a suitable container (photo).

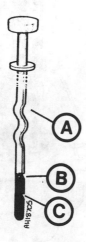

Fig. 1.3 Engine oil dipstick (A) showing Maximum (B) and Minimum (C) oil level marks (Sec 2)

2.2 Topping up the engine oil level

2.4 Engine sump drain plug

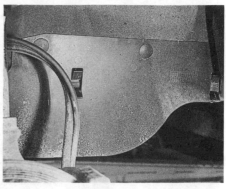
5.3 Side access panel showing retaining clips

5   When the oil has drained, wipe clean the drain plug then refit and tighten it.
6   The oil filter is of disposable cartridge type and is renewed as described in Section 9. The filter must be replaced at the intervals specified in *Routine maintenance* at the beginning of the manual.
7   Lower the car to the ground then fill the engine with the specified quantity and grade of oil.
8   Start the engine. There will be a short delay before the oil warning lamp goes out. This is normal and is caused by the new filter (if fitted) having to fill with oil.
9   Switch off the engine, wait ten minutes and check the oil level and top up if necessary.
10   Periodically check around the engine for signs of excessive oil or coolant leaks.

3   Major operations possible with engine in car

1   The following components can be removed and refitted with the engine in the car:

(a)   Cylinder head and rocker gear
(b)   Camshaft (having removed the cylinder head)
(c)   Timing belt and tensioner
(d)   Sump and oil pump
(e)   Big-end bearings
(f)   Pistons, connecting rods and liners

2   In most instances, no special tools are required to remove and refit the above items, but when refitting the timing belt, a special tensioning tool will be necessary, (refer to Section 5 for details). A torque wrench will be required when reassembling most fittings, and reference should be made to the Specifications at the start of this Chapter for the respective setting requirements.

4   Major operations requiring engine removal

The following operations can only be carried out with the engine removed from the car:

(a)   Main bearings renewal
(b)   Crankshaft removal and refitting

5   Timing belt – removal and refitting

Note: *When refitting the timing belt, a special Citroën adjustment tool No. 4507-TJ will be required to ensure that the belt is correctly tensioned. If the Citroën tool is not available, a similar tool can be fabricated as described to ensure correct adjustment. Failing this,a temporary adjustment can be made as described in paragraph 12. This will allow provisional use of the car until belt adjustment can be checked/adjusted at a Citroën garage.*

Fig. 1.4 Underside view showing crankshaft pulley bolts (6), alternator mounting bolts (8 and 9) and adjuster bolt (7) (Sec 5)

1   Disconnect the battery earth lead.
2   Apply the handbrake, then raise and support the car at the front so that the front roadwheels are clear of the ground.
3   Remove the front roadwheel on the right-hand side, then unclip and remove the side access panel (photo).
4   Loosen off the alternator mounting and adjustment bolts and remove the drivebelt.
5   Undo the three crankshaft pulley retaining bolts, remove the pulley, then unbolt and remove the upper, centre and lower timing covers (photo).
6   Remove the sparking plugs to ease turning the engine over by hand.
7   Turn the engine over by hand, using a spanner on the crankshaft sprocket retaining nut, to set the crankshaft at the TDC position. At this point, the TDC holes of the flywheel and the appropriate TDC hole in the engine flywheel flange are in alignment, as are those of the camshaft sprocket and the corresponding hole in the front face of the cylinder head. Insert twist drills or bolts of suitable diameter and length into these holes to lock the engine in position (photos).
8   Unscrew the timing belt tensioner nut to release the tensioner (photo), then disengage the belt from the timing sprockets, but note its direction of fitting which is indicated by arrows. If the belt is likely to be re-used, do not handle it (or the sprockets and tensioner) with oily or wet hands.
9   If the belt is old or has covered a high mileage, shows signs of excessive wear or deterioration, it must be renewed.
10   To refit the timing belt, first check that the engine is set at the TDC position. Fit the belt over the sprockets so that it is correctly orientated, (arrows pointing in normal direction of travel). Engage the timing belt with the crankshaft sprocket then, keeping it taut, feed it onto the camshaft sprocket, around the tensioner pulley, and onto the water pump sprocket. Loosen the nut and turn the tensioner roller anti-

5.5 Remove the timing covers (engine removed for clarity)

5.7A Locking the engine at TDC: Insert bolt through camshaft sprocket (arrowed) ...

5.7B ... and into flywheel through flange at rear of block (arrowed)

5.8 Timing belt tensioner nut (arrowed)

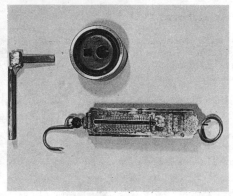

5.11A Timing belt tensioner, tool and a spring balance

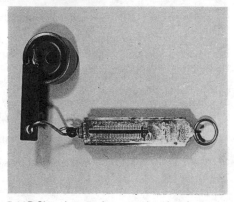

5.11B Showing tensioner, tool and spring balance when in engagement

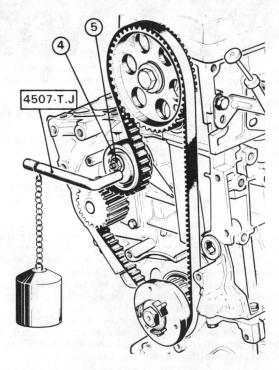

Fig. 1.5 Adjusting the timing belt tension using Citroen tool 4507-TJ with tensioner (4) and its retaining nut (5) (Sec 5)

clockwise by hand. Tighten the nut.
11   Citroën garages use the special tool shown in Fig. 1.5 to tension the timing belt. A similar tool may be fabricated using an 8.0 cm (3.2 in) long arm and a 1.5 kg (3.3 lb) weight (or a spring gauge, photos). The torque applied to the roller will approximate 12 kgf cm (10.5 lbf in). Pre-tension

the timing belt with the tool and tighten the nut, then remove the timing pins and rotate the crankshaft through two complete turns. Loosen the nut and allow the roller to re-position itself. Tighten the nut.
12   If the special tool is not available, an approximate setting may be achieved by turning the roller hub anti-clockwise, until it is just possible to turn the timing belt through 90° by finger and thumb midway between the crankshaft and camshaft sprockets. The square in the roller hub should then be directly below the adjustment nut, and the deflection of the belt in the midway position should be approximately 6.0 mm (0.24 in). If using this method, the tension should be re-checked by a Citroën garage at the earliest opportunity.
13   Refit the timing covers, the spark plugs and the crankshaft pulley.
14   Refit the alternator and its drivebelt as described in Chapter 12.
15   Refit the access panel and the roadwheel then lower the vehicle to the ground.

6   Camshaft – removal and refitting

The camshaft can only be removed and refitted from the cylinder head when the latter is removed from the engine. To remove the cylinder head, refer to Section 7. To remove the camshaft from the cylinder head, refer to Section 22. Refit the camshaft and cylinder head as described in Section 37.

7   Cylinder head – removal (engine in car)

1   Disconnect the battery earth lead.
2   Drain the cooling system as described in Chapter 2.
3   Remove the air cleaner unit and its intake ducting as described in Chapter 3.
4   Disconnect the coolant hoses from the cylinder head and position them out of the way.
5   Disconnect the fuel feed pipe hose from the fuel pump. Allow for

7.10A Removing the valve cover nuts

7.10B Removing the valve cover gasket

7.11A Remove the spacers (arrowed) ...

7.11B ... and baffle plate

7.12A Unscrew the bolts ...

7.12B ... and remove the upper timing cover ...

7.12C ... intermediate cover ...

7.12D ... and lower cover

7.13 Camshaft sprocket set at TDC

fuel spillage as the hose is detached, and plug it to prevent further leakage of fuel. Detach the servo vacuum hose from the manifold.

6   Disconnect the accelerator cable and the choke cable from the carburettor as described in Chapter 3.

7   Disconnect the following wiring leads and position the respective wires out of the way:

(a)   *The TDC connector from the support bracket*
(b)   *The ignition coil harness*
(c)   *The engine coolant thermal switch wire*
(d)   *The wiring harness connector from the socket next to the distributor*

8   Unbolt and detach the engine dipstick locating bracket from the exhaust side of the cylinder head.

9   Undo the retaining nuts and detach the exhaust downpipe from the manifold.

10   Unscrew the nuts and remove the valve cover. Remove the rubber gasket from the cover (photos).

11   Remove the two spacers and baffle plate from the studs (photos).

12   Unbolt and remove the crankshaft pulley, then unbolt and remove the upper, intermediate and lower timing covers.

13   Turn the engine clockwise, using a socket on the crankshaft pulley bolt, until the small hole in the camshaft sprocket is aligned with the corresponding hole in the cylinder head. Insert the shank of a close-fitting twist drill (eg a 10 mm drill) into the holes (photo).

14   Align the TDC holes in the flywheel and cylinder block rear flange and insert a further twist drill or long bolt (photo 5.7).

15   Loosen the timing belt tensioner roller nut (photo), turn the tensioner clockwise using a screwdriver or square drive in the special hole, then re-tighten the nut.

16   Mark the normal direction of rotation on the timing belt, if not already marked, then remove it from the camshaft, water pump, and crankshaft sprockets.

17   Unscrew the tensioner nut and remove the tensioner roller.

18   Progressively loosen the cylinder head bolts using the reverse sequence to that shown in Fig. 1.19 the remove all the bolts.

19   Lift off the rocker arm assembly (photo).

20   Rock the cylinder head to free it from the block, then lift it from the location dowels (photo). Two angled metal rods, shown in Fig. 1.7 may be used for this purpose.

7.15 Loosening the timing belt tensioner roller nut

7.19 Removing the rocker arm assembly

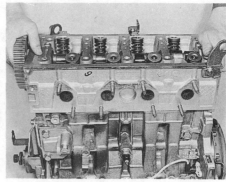

7.20 Lifting the cylinder head from the block

Fig. 1.6 Cylinder head removal showing items to be detached (Sec 7)

9   Fuel hose
10 Ignition coil harness
11 TDC connector at support

12 Electrical harness
13 Coolant hoses at outlet housing
14 Thermal switch wire

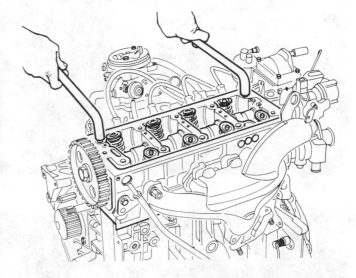

Fig. 1.7 Using two angled metal rods to free the cylinder head from the block (Sec 7)

21   Remove the cylinder head gasket from the block.
22   Fit cylinder liner clamps, or large washers secured with nuts and bolts, to keep the liners in position (Fig. 1.8). *If the liners are disturbed the engine will have to be removed for new seals to be fitted.*

Fig. 1.8 Cylinder liner clamps (8.1132 T/A1) fitted to Secure the liners whilst the cylinder head is removed (Sec 7)

8   Engine oil seals – renewal (engine in car)

Camshaft and crankshaft front oil seals

1   Before starting to remove the timing belt covers and sprockets, refer to the special note at the start of Section 5 for special tool requirements when refitting and adjusting the timing belt.
2   Proceed as described in Section 5, paragraphs 1 to 7 inclusive.
3   With the engine locked at the TDC position, loosen off the camshaft and/or crankshaft pulley/sprocket retaining bolt(s).
4   Loosen off the timing belt tensioner and remove the timing belt.
5   Prise free and remove the camshaft and/or crankshaft sprocket(s). Remove the crankshaft thrust flange using a pair of screwdrivers as levers if necessary.
6   Withdraw the appropriate oil seal by pushing it from its housing using screwdrivers as levers or a suitable hooked tool, but take care not

to damage the housing(s) (photos). As they are removed, note the direction of fitting.
7   Never re-use an old seal once it has been removed. Ensure that the seal housing is clean before fitting the new seal into position. Lubricate

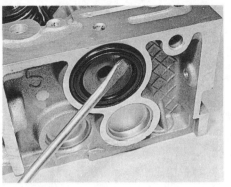

8.6A Prising out the camshaft oil seal

8.6B Prising out the crankshaft oil seal

9.1 Oil filter removal using a chain wrench

the lips of the seal to ease fitting. Carefully tap the seal into position using a tubular drift, or socket of suitable diameter.

8   When the oil seal(s) are fitted, relocate the sprockets and refit the timing belt as described in Section 5. Ensure that the key is in position on the crankshaft when fitting its sprocket and thrust flange.

Crankshaft rear oil seal

9   Access to this seal is obtained by separating the engine from the gearbox, and then unbolting the clutch and flywheel. Refer to the appropriate Sections in Chapters 1, 5 and 6 for their removal procedure.

10   The oil seal can be extracted by prising it free using a pair of screwdrivers or failing this method, using Citroën tool No. 4507-TD (Fig. 1.9). A similar flat plate type of puller can be fabricated, having two holes drilled in it at diagonally opposed points an equal distance from the centre. Suitable self-tapping screws are then inserted through each hole and into the oil seal. The puller can then withdraw the oil seal. **Note:** *Do not drill beyond the depth of the seal.*

11   Carefully drive the new oil seal into position using a suitable tubular drift, or if available, Citroën tool No 4507-TG, (Fig. 1.10).

12   Refit the flywheel. New securing bolts must be used and their threads smeared with a suitable thread-locking compound. Tighten the bolts to the specified torque wrench setting.

13   Refit the clutch (Chapter 5) and refit the engine to the gearbox, (Chapter 1 or 6 as applicable).

Fig. 1.9 Crankshaft rear oil seal removal (5) using Citroën tool No 4507-TD with two self-tapping screws (6) (Sec 8)

9   Oil filter – removal and refitting

1   The oil filter is of disposable cartridge type. Unscrew it with an oil filter wrench, but have some rag to hand to soak up the oil which will be spilt (photo). If a proper wrench is not available a large worm drive hose clip can be fitted to the filter and the screw used as a gripping point. If all else fails, a screwdriver can be driven right through the cartridge and this used as a lever to unscrew it.

2   It is very important to purchase and fit the correct type of filter.

3   Clean the filter mounting ring on the crankcase and apply engine oil to the rubber seal on the cartridge. Do not use grease as it may make the filter difficult to unscrew (photo).

4   Check that the threaded sleeve is tight on the crankcase, offer up the new filter and screw it on using hand pressure only.

5   Top up the engine oil, run the engine and check for any signs of oil leakage from the filter seal.

10   Valve clearances – checking and adjustment

1   The valve clearances must be checked with the engine cold; therefore do not run the engine for a minimum period of two hours prior to making the checks.

2   Disconnect the crankcase ventilation hose from the valve cover.

3   Unscrew the nuts and remove the valve cover.

4   Remove the two spacers and baffle plate from the studs.

5   Prepare to rotate the crankshaft, either by jacking up one front wheel and turning the wheel with 4th or 5th gear engaged, or by using a

Fig. 1.10 Inserting the crankshaft rear oil seal (5) using Citroën Tool No 4507-TG (Sec 8)

spanner on the crankshaft pulley bolt. Rotation will be easier if the spark plugs are first removed.

6   Rotate the crankshaft until No 1 exhaust valve (flywheel end) is fully open. No 3 inlet valve and No 4 exhaust valve clearances may now be

9.3 Clean the filter mounting surface on the crankcase

10.7 Adjusting the valve clearances

12.6 Disconnect the accelerator cable from the carburettor

checked and adjusted.

7   Insert a feeler blade of the correct thickness between the rocker arm and valve stem. It should be a firm sliding fit if the clearance is correct. If adjustment is necessary, loosen the adjuster nut with a ring spanner, turn the adjuster as required with a screwdriver, then retighten the nut (photo).

8   Adjust the valve clearances in the following sequence:

Valve fully open	Adjust valve
No 1 Exhaust	No 3 Inlet and No 4 Exhaust
No 3 Exhaust	No 4 Inlet and No 2 Exhaust
No 4 Exhaust	No 2 Inlet and No 1 Exhaust
No 2 Exhaust	No 1 Inlet and No 3 Exhaust

9   When all the valve clearances have been adjusted, refit the baffle plate with its edge pointing downwards, followed by the two spacers.
10   Check that the rubber gasket is re-usable, then refit the valve cover and tighten the nuts.
11   Reconnect the crankcase ventilation hose.

11   Engine removal methods

Although it is possible to remove the engine and/or the gearbox separately, they would both need to be lowered in order to allow separation. It is therefore more convenient to remove the two as a unit and then to separate them.

The engine and gearbox are removed from the car by lowering them from their mountings and withdrawing them from underneath the car at the front. In view of this the car will need to be raised at the front end sufficiently enough to provide the necessary clearance to allow the units to be removed.

A suitable hoist (or trolley jack) will be needed to support the engine as it is lowered and withdrawn. Where a hoist is to be used, it is preferable that the engine be lowered onto a suitable trolley to ease withdrawal from under the front of the car and prevent damaging the

sump. It will also be beneficial in positioning the engine under the car when refitting.

Apart from these items, no specialised tools are required, but the aid of an assistant during some operations, particularly the actual removal and refitting operations will be most beneficial.

12   Engine and gearbox – removal

1   Disconnect and remove the battery (Chapter 12).
2   Drain the engine cooling system (Chapter 2).
3   Drain the engine oil (Section 2) and the gearbox oil (Chapter 6).
4   Unclip and remove the jack from its location on the right-hand side of the engine compartment.
5   Remove the air cleaner unit and the air intake ducting (Chapter 3).
6   Disconnect the accelerator cable and the choke cable from the carburettor (Chapter 3) (photo).
7   Disconnect the clutch cable from the operating lever and the support bracket above the clutch housing (Chapter 5).
8   Disconnect the speedometer cable from the gearbox by extracting the rubber retainer and pulling the cable clear.
9   Although not absolutely essential, it is advisable to remove the radiator and cooling fan as described in Chapter 2. This allows additional access to the engine components and prevents possible damage to them during the actual removal and refitting operations.
10   Disconnect the fuel feed hose from the fuel pump, plug it and move it out of the way.
11   Disconnect the remaining coolant hoses from the engine. Apart from the top and bottom hoses, these include the expansion hose from the radiator (if still fitted), the coolant hose to the carburettor, and the heater hoses at the thermostat, and at the retainer on the inlet manifold and intermediate connector.
12   Detach the servo vacuum hose from the inlet manifold.
13   Detach the multi-plug wiring connectors from the harness attachment point beneath the fuel pump. Also detach the leads from the starter motor, the earth leads and the reversing light switch leads from the gearbox (photos).
14   Ensure the handbrake is applied, loosen off the front roadwheel

12.13A Detach the wiring harness connectors, ...

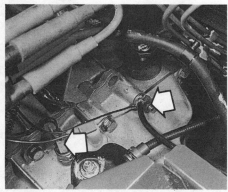

12.13B ... the earth leads and the reversing light switch leads from the gearbox (arrowed)

12.16 Disconnect the gearshift control rods at their balljoints (arrowed)

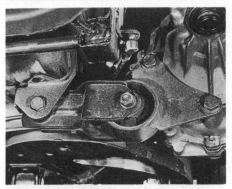

12.18 Engine/gearbox torque stay

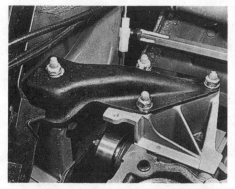

12.21 Right-hand engine mounting

12.22 View showing left-hand mounting with centre bolt removed

12.23 Engine and transmission removal

13.2 Remove the engine-to-gearbox bolts ...

13.3 ... then separate the two units

bolts, then raise and support the car at the front on axle stands. Allow a clearance under the front of the car of approximately 80 cm (30 inches) to the ground for engine removal. Remove the two front roadwheels.

15   Remove the complete exhaust system (Chapter 3).

16   Prise free the three gearshift control rods at their balljoint connections to the gearbox (photo). Do not alter the balljoint settings on the rods.

17   Detach the front anti-roll bar (where fitted) with reference to Chapter 9.

18   Unbolt and detach the engine/gearbox torque stay (photo).

19   Remove the right and left-hand driveshafts as described in Chapter 7.

20   Check around the engine and gearbox to ensure that all attachments are disconnected and out of the way for removal. Attach the support sling to the engine lift brackets and take the weight of the combined engine/gearbox unit with the hoist.

21   Unscrew and remove the three retaining bolts from the right- hand engine mounting (photo).

22   Unscrew the single through-bolt from the left-hand mounting (photo).

23   Carefully lower the unit from the engine compartment. As it is lowered, take care not to damage the carburettor and fittings on the steering box. An assistant is useful here to assist in guiding the engine and gearbox clear of the surrounding components as they are lowered from the car. When fully lowered, release the support sling and withdraw the power unit from under the front of the car (photo).

24   **Note:** *Do not move the car whilst the driveshafts are removed.* If the car must be moved, temporarily refit the driveshafts into their hubs and suspend the inboard end of each shaft with a length of wire or cord.

13   Engine and gearbox – separation

1   Unbolt and remove the starter motor. Note that the outboard bolt also secures the air cleaner mounting bracket.

2   Unscrew and remove the engine-to-gearbox mounting bolts (photo).

3   Support the engine and pull the gearbox from it (photo). Do not allow the weight of the gearbox to rest on the input shaft during separation. Remove any loose location dowels.

14   Ancillary engine components – removal

1   Before engine dismantling begins, it is necessary to remove the externally mounted ancillary components. The extent and sequence of their removal is dependent on the amount to which the engine is being dismantled. If the engine is being fully dismantled, remove the following items:

   (a)   *Inlet manifold and carburettor (Chapter 3)*
   (b)   *Exhaust manifold (Chapter 3)*
   (c)   *Fuel pump (Chapter 3)*
   (d)   *Distributor ignition coil unit and HT leads (Chapter 4)*
   (e)   *Clutch unit (Chapter 5)*
   (f)   *Thermostat (Chapter 2)*
   (g)   *Alternator and mounting bracket (Chapter 12)*
   (h)   *Engine oil filter (Section 9 in this Chapter)*
   (i)   *Oil pressure switch, coolant temperature sensor switch*

2   With the major ancillary items removed, the engine sub-assemblies can now be dismantled as required by referring to the appropriate Sections that follow.

15   Engine dismantling – general

1   As the engine is stripped, clean each part in a bath of paraffin.

2   Never immerse parts with oilways in paraffin (eg crankshaft and rocker shaft). To clean these parts, wipe down carefully with a petrol-dampened rag. Oilways can be cleaned out with wire. If an air line is available, all parts can be blown dry and the oilways blown through as an added precaution.

16.3A Unscrew the crankshaft pulley bolt ...

16.3B ... and remove the hub/sprocket ...

16.3C ... and oil seal flange

3   Re-use of old gasket or oil seals is false economy. To avoid the possibility of trouble after the engine has been reassembled always use new items throughout.

4   Do not throw away the old gasket, for sometimes it happens that an immediate replacement cannot be found and the old gasket is then very useful as a template. Hang up the gaskets as they are removed.

5   If this is the first time that you have dismantled your engine/transmission unit then special attention should be given to the location of the various components and sub-assemblies. This is especially necessary due to the slightly unconventional layout of the model.

6   Many of the component casings are manufactured in aluminium alloy and special care must therefore be taken not to knock, drop or put any unnecessary pressure on these components.

7   Whenever possible, refit nuts, bolts and washers from where they were removed in order not to mix them up. If they cannot be reinstalled lay them out in such a way that it is clear where they came from.

8   Do not remove or disturb the timing plate on the clutch housing if this can be avoided. To reset, refer to Chapter 4.

16   Timing belt and associated components – removal (engine out of car)

1   Refer to Section 5, observe the preliminary notes and then proceed as described in paragraphs 5 to 8 and remove the timing belt.

2   With the timing drivebelt removed, unscrew the retaining bolt and remove the tension adjuster.

3   Have an assistant hold the flywheel stationary with a wide-bladed screwdriver inserted between the starter ring gear teeth, then unscrew the crankshaft pulley bolt and remove the hub/sprocket and oil seal flange (photos).

4   Using a screwdriver, prise the front oil seal from the block and main bearing casting with reference to Section 8.

17   Cylinder head – removal (engine out of car)

Remove the appropriate engine ancillary components and then the cylinder head as described in Section 7, paragraphs 10 to 22 inclusive.

18   Flywheel – removal

1   Unbolt and remove the clutch unit from the flywheel. To prevent the flywheel from turning, jam the starter ring gear.

2   Unbolt and remove the flywheel. Note that the flywheel retaining bolts will need to be renewed during reassembly.

3   Remove the crankshaft rear oil seal as described in Section 8 if this is to renewed.

19   Sump and oil pump – removal

1   If the engine is still in the car, drain the sump oil as described in Section 2.

2   If the engine is removed from the car, invert the engine and make it secure.

3   Unscrew the retaining bolts and nuts and remove the sump. It will probably stick to the jointing compound and be reluctant to be removed, in which case carefully prise it free taking care not to damage or distort the sump pan (photos).

4   Unbolt the oil pump and tilt it to disengage the pump sprocket from the drive chain (photos).

20   Connecting rods, pistons and liners – removal

1   If the engine is in the car, remove the timing belt (Section 5), the cylinder head (Section 7) and the sump (Section 19).

2   If the engine is out of the car, remove the previously mentioned components and support the block on its flywheel end.

3   Mark the liners for position, starting with No 1 (at the flywheel end). Similarly mark the big-end bearing caps.

4   Temporarily refit the crankshaft pulley bolt (if previously removed) and turn the crankshaft so that Nos 1 and 4 pistons (No 1 at flywheel end) are at bottom dead centre (BDC).

5   Unscrew the nuts and remove the big-end bearing caps (photo). Remove the lower big-end shells, keeping them identified for position.

6   Remove the clamps and withdraw the liners, complete with pistons, from the block (photo).

7   Remove the liner bottom O-rings (photo).

8   Repeat the procedure for Nos 2 and 3 pistons and liners.

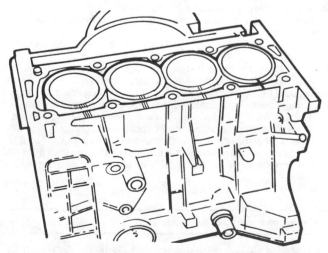

Fig. 1.11 **Mark the liners in numerical sequence of fitting in the cylinder block (Sec 20)**

H.20120

19.3A Unscrew the retaining nuts and bolts ...

19.3B ... and remove the sump

19.4A Unscrew the retaining bolts ...

19.4B ... and remove the oil pump from the chain

20.5 Removing a big-end bearing cap

9　Withdraw the pistons and connecting rods from the bottom end of each liner for inspection and renovation, but keep each liner and piston/connecting rod together.

21 Crankshaft and main bearings – removal

1　With the engine inverted, unscrew the bolts securing the main bearing cap casting to the neck (photos).
2　Progressively unscrew the main bearing bolts, and lift the main bearing cap casting from the block. Gently tap it with a wooden or soft-headed mallet to release it. Prise out the main bearing shells, keeping them identified for location.
3　Remove the oil pump chain from the crankshaft (photo).
4　Lift the crankshaft from the block and remove the main bearing shells, keeping them identified for location. Also remove the endfloat rings from No 2 main bearing location (photos).

22 Cylinder head – dismantling

1　If the following ancillary items are still attached to the cylinder head, remove them. Refer to the appropriate Chapters for details if necessary.

(a)　Inlet manifold (with carburettor), exhaust manifold and the fuel pump (Chapter 3)
(b)　Spark plugs and ignition distributor (Chapter 4)
(c)　Coolant outlet housing and thermostat (Chapter 2)

2　The camshaft can be withdrawn from the head with the sprocket attached but if it is to be removed from the camshaft, hold the sprocket stationary using an oil filter stop wrench or tool as shown (photo). Unscrew the bolt and remove the sprocket (photos).
3　Unbolt and remove the camshaft thrust fork (photo).
4　Carefully withdraw the camshaft from the cylinder head (photo). As it is withdrawn, support the camshaft and ensure that the cam lobes do not damage the bearing surfaces in the cylinder head. Extract the oil seal from the cylinder head at the timing belt end.
5　Before removing the valves from the cylinder head, clean and prepare a suitable area on the workbench.
6　Remove each valve and spring assembly using a valve spring compressor. Extract the split collets from between the spring retaining cup washer and valve stem (photo).
7　Progressively release the tension of the compressor until it can be removed, the spring and retainer withdrawn, and the valve extracted from the guide (photos).
8　As the valves are removed, keep them in order by inserting them in a card having suitable holes punched in it, numbered from 1 to 8. Discard the valve stem oil seals.

23 Engine components – examination for wear

When the engine has been stripped down and all parts properly cleaned, decisions have to be made as to what needs renewal. The following Sections tell the examiner what to look for. In any border-line case it is always best to decide in favour of a new part. Even if a part may still be serviceable, its life will have to be reduced by wear and the degree of trouble needed to renew it in future must be taken into consideration. However, these things are relative and it depends on whether a quick 'survival' job is being done or whether the car as a whole is being regarded as having many thousands of miles of useful and economical life remaining.

24 Camshaft and rocker assemblies – examination and renovation

1　The camshaft lobes should be examined for signs of flats or scoring or any other form of wear or damage. At the same time the rocker arms should also be examined, particularly on the faces where they bear against the camshaft, for signs of wear. Very slight wear may be

20.6 Removing a liner and piston assembly

20.7 Liner showing bottom O-ring (arrowed)

21.1A Unscrew the main bearing cap casting front bolts ...

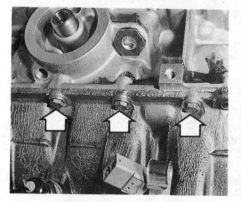

21.1B ... and side bolts (arrowed)

21.3 Remove the oil pump chain

21.4A Lift out the crankshaft and ...

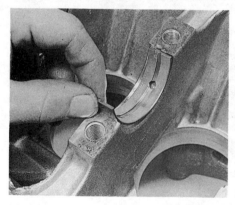

21.4B ... remove the main bearing shells ...

21.4C ... and endfloat rings from the crankcase

22.2A Using a home made tool to secure the camshaft sprocket when removing/refitting the retaining bolt

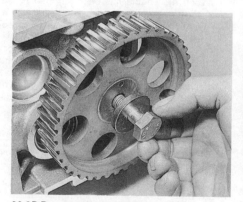

22.2B Remove the retaining bolt and washer ...

22.2C ... then withdraw the camshaft sprocket. Note the location peg and cut-out (arrowed)

22.3 Camshaft thrust fork (arrowed)

22.4A Camshaft withdrawal from the cylinder head

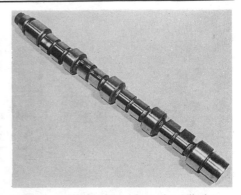

22.4B Camshaft removed from the cylinder head

22.6 Compress the valve spring and extract the collets ...

22.7A ... followed by the retainer ...

22.7B ... spring ...

22.7C ... spring seat ...

22.7D ... and valve

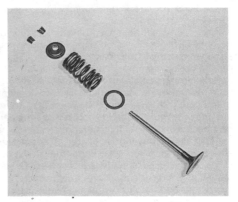

22.7E Valve components removed from cylinder head

24.5 Rocker shaft components removal

24.6A Remove the stud from the end bearing ...

24.6B ... for access to the retaining grub screw

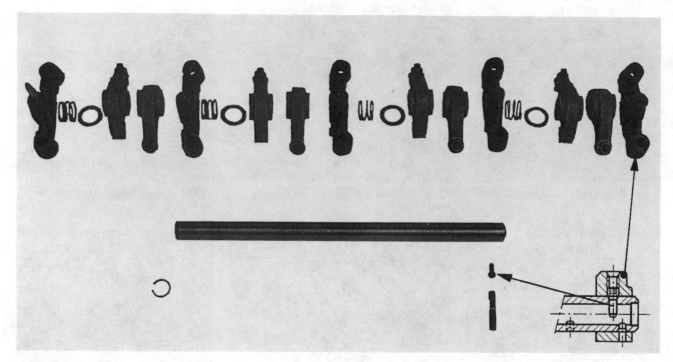

Fig. 1.12 Rocker shaft assembly dismantled to show the order and orientation of components and the end bearing retaining method (shown in Sectional view) (Sec 24)

removed by rubbing with an oilstone but maintain the original contour.

2   The camshaft bearing journals should be in good condition and show no signs of pitting or scoring as they are relatively free from stress.

3   If the bearing surfaces are scored or discoloured it is possible that the shaft is not running true, and in this case it will have to be renewed. For an accurate check get your Citroën agent to inspect both the camshaft and cylinder head.

4   Worn camshaft bearings in the cylinder head can only be rectified by renewal of the head, an expensive business, as the bearings are machined directly in the head.

5   The rocker assembly can be dismantled on removing the circlip from the timing belt end of the rocker shaft (photo).

6   When removing the various rocker components from the shaft, take careful note of the sequence in which they are removed. In particular note that the No 2 and No 4 rocker bearings are identical, keep the components in order as they are removed from the shaft for inspection. The final rocker bearing is secured to the rocker shaft by the rocker cover stud, or an Allen screw under that stud (photos).

7   Check the rocker shaft for signs of wear. Check it for straightness by rolling it on a flat surface. It is unlikely to be bent but if this is the case it must either be straightened or renewed. The shaft surface should be free of wear ridges caused by the rocker arms. Check the oil feed holes and clear them out if blocked or sludged-up.

8   Check each rocker arm for wear on an unworn part of the shaft. Check the end of the adjuster screw and the face of the rocker arm where it bears on the camshaft. Any signs of cracks or serious wear will necessitate renewal of the rocker arm.

25   Cylinder head, valves and piston crowns – decarbonising, examination and renovation

1   Wash the cylinder head clean and carefully scrape away the carbon build-up in the combustion chambers and exhaust ports, using a scraper which will not damage the surfaces to be cleaned. If a rotary wire brush and drill is available this may be used for removing the carbon.

2   The valves may also be scraped and wire-brushed clean in a similar manner.

3   With the cylinder head cleaned and dry, examine it for cracks or damage. In particular inspect the valve seat areas for signs of hairline cracks, pitting or burning. Check the head mating surfaces for distortion,

the maximum permissible amount being 0.05 mm (0.002 in).

4   The makers state that no machining of the cylinder head surface is permitted. A warped head must therefore be renewed.

5   Factory exchange cylinder heads may have had 0.2 mm machined off the mating face. These heads are identified by the letter 'R' stamped on the mating face adjacent to the No 3 cylinder. A gasket 0.2 mm thicker than normal must be used with such a head; the thicker gasket is identified by a cut-out in the tab at the clutch end.

6   Minor surface wear and pitting of the valve seats can probably be removed when the valves are reground. More serious wear or damage should be shown to your Citroën dealer or a competent automotive engineer who will advise you on the action necessary.

7   Carefully inspect the valves, in particular the exhaust valves. Check the stems for distortion and signs of wear. The valve seat faces must be in reasonable condition and if they have covered a high mileage they will probably need to be refaced on a valve grinding machine; again, this is a job for your Citroën dealer or local garage/automotive machine shop.

8   Insert each valve into its respective guide and check for excessive side play. Worn valve guides allow oil to be drained past the inlet valve stem causing a smoky exhaust, while exhaust leakage through the exhaust valve guide can overheat the valve guide and cause sticking valves.

9   If the valve guides are to be renewed this is a job best left to your Citroën agent who will have the required specialist equipment.

10   Assuming the valves and seats are in reasonable condition they should be reseated by grinding them using valve grinding carborundum paste. The grinding process must also be carried out when new valves are fitted.

11   The carborundum paste used for this job is normally supplied in a double-ended tin with coarse paste at one end and fine at the other. In addition, a suction tool for holding the valve head so that it may be rotated is also required. To grind in the valve, first smear a trace of the coarse paste onto the seat face and fit the suction grinder to the valve head. Then with a semi- rotary motion grind the valve head into its seat, lifting the valve occasionally to redistribute the grinding paste. When a dull matt continuous line is produced on both the valve seat and the valve then the paste can be wiped off. Apply a little fine paste and finish off the grinding process, then remove all traces of the paste. If a light spring is placed over the valve stem behind the head this can often be of assistance in raising the valve from time to time against the pressure of the grinding tool so as to redistribute the paste evenly round the job. The width of the line which is produced after grinding indicates the seat width, and this width should not exceed about 2 mm (0.08 in). If, after a

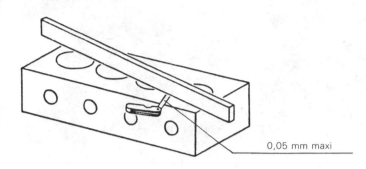

Fig. 1.13 Check the cylinder head surface for distortion (Sec 25)

moderate amount of grinding, it is apparent that the seating line is too wide, it probably means that the seat has already been cut back one or more times previously, or else the valve has been ground several times. Here again, specialist advice is best sought.

12 Examine all the valve springs to make sure that they are in good condition and not distorted. If the engine has covered 30 000 miles (45 000 km) then fit new springs at reassembly. Renew the valve stem oil seals.

13 At the same time renew the valve spring seating washers which sit directly on the cylinder head. These wear fairly quickly.

14 Before reassembling the valve and springs to the cylinder head make a final check that everything is thoroughly clean and free from grit, then lightly smear all the valve stems with engine oil prior to reassembly.

15 When the engine is in the car, certain precautions must be taken when decarbonising the piston crowns in order to prevent dislodged pieces of carbon falling into the interior of the engine which could cause damage to the cylinder bores, piston and rings, or if allowed into the water passages, damage to the water pump. Turn the engine so that the piston being worked on is at the top of its stroke and then mask off the adjacent cylinder bores and all surrounding orifices with paper and adhesive tape. Press grease into the gap all round the piston to keep the carbon particles out and then scrape all carbon away. When completed, carefully clear out the grease around the rim of the piston with a matchstick or something similar – bringing any carbon particles with it. Repeat the process on the other piston crown. It is not recommended that a ring of carbon is left round the edge of the piston on the theory that it will aid oil consumption. This was valid in the earlier days of long stroke, low revving engines but modern engines, fuels and lubricants cause less carbon deposits anyway, and any left behind tends merely to cause hot spots.

26 Timing belt, tensioner and sprockets – examination and renovation

1 Renew the timing belt as a matter of course unless it is in perfect condition and is known to have covered only a nominal mileage.

2 Inspect the sprockets and renew them if they are damaged.

3 Examine the drivebelt tensioner for signs of excessive wear or damage and renew it if required.

27 Oil pump, drive chain and sprockets – examination and renovation

1 Remove the bolts which hold the two halves of the oil pump together. Separate the halves, being prepared for the release of the relief valve spring and plunger (photos).

2 Inspect the rotors and their housing for wear and damage. No wear limits are published for this pump; any visible wear on the moving parts suggests that renewal is necessary. With the exception of the relief valve spring and plunger, individual components are not available.

3 Lubricate the pump components well before reassembly. Bolt the two halves together, being careful not to trap the spring.

4 If the pump is to be renewed it is wise to renew the chain and the crankshaft sprocket also.

5 Examine the teeth of both sprockets for wear. Each tooth on a sprocket is an inverted V-shape and wear is apparent when one side of the tooth becomes more concave in shape than the other. When badly worn, the teeth become hook-shaped and the sprockets must be renewed.

6 If the sprockets need to be renewed then the chain will have worn also and should be renewed as well. If the sprockets are satisfactory, examine the chain and look for play between the links. When the chain is held out horizontally, it should not bend appreciably. Remember, a chain is only as strong as its weakest link, and being a relatively cheap item, it is worthwhile fitting a replacement anyway.

28 Crankshaft, main and big-end bearings – examination and renovation

1 With careful servicing and regular oil and filter changes, bearings will last for a very long time. But they can still fail for unforeseen reasons. With big-end bearings, an indication is a regular rhythmic loud knocking from the crankcase. The frequency depends on engine speed and is particularly noticeable when the engine is under load. This symptom is accompanied by a fall in oil pressure although this is not normally noticeable unless an oil pressure gauge is fitted. Main bearing failure is usually indicated by serious vibration, particularly at higher engine revolutions, accompanied by a more significant drop in oil pressure and a 'rumbling' noise.

2 Big-end bearings can be removed with the engine still in the car. If the failure is sudden and the engine has a low mileage since new or overhaul, this is probably worth doing. Bearing shells in good condition have bearing surfaces with a smooth, even matt silver/grey colour all over. Worn bearings will show patches of a different colour when the bearing metal has worn away and exposed the underlay. Damaged bearings will be pitted or scored. It is always well worthwhile fitting new shells as their cost is relatively low. If the crankshaft is in good condition, it is merely a question of obtaining another set of standard size shells

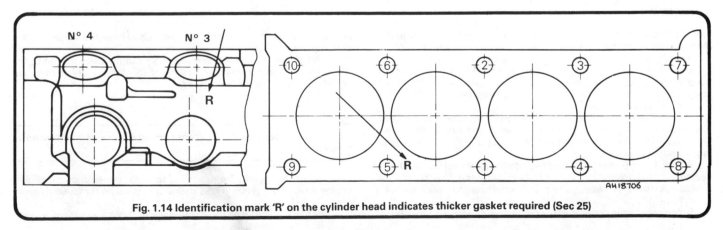

Fig. 1.14 Identification mark 'R' on the cylinder head indicates thicker gasket required (Sec 25)

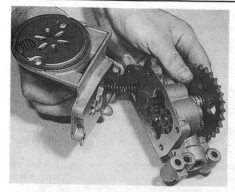

27.1A Separate the oil pump half bodies

27.1B Relief valve spring and plunger location

28.4 Measuring a crankshaft journal for wear using a micrometer

30.6 Measuring a cylinder liner protrusion

32.3 Oiling the main bearing shells

32.7A Apply jointing compound to the mating surfaces ...

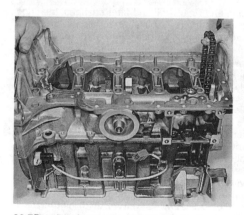

32.7B ... then lower the main bearing cap casting into position

32.8A Torque tighten the main bearing bolts ...

32.8B ... then angle-tighten a further 45°

(but see below). A reground crankshaft will need new bearing shells as a matter of course. When renewing the big-end bearing shells on AX 10 models, observe the modification note at the end of Section 29.

3   Look at the main bearing journals and the crankpins. If there are any deep scratches or score marks, the shaft will need regrinding. Such conditions will nearly always be accompanied by similar deterioration in the matching bearing shells.

4   Each bearing journal must also be perfectly round and can be checked with a micrometer (photo) or caliper gauge around the periphery at several points. If there is more then 0.007 mm (0.0003 in) ovality, regrinding is necessary.

5   A main Citroën agent or motor engineering specialist will be able to decide to what extent regrinding is necessary and also supply the special oversize shell bearings to match whatever may need grinding off.

6   Before taking the crankshaft for regrinding, check also the cylinder

bore and pistons as it may be advantageous to have the whole engine done at the same time.

7   If the crankshaft is not being reground, but the bearings are to be renewed, take the old shells along to your supplier and check that you are getting the correct size bearings.

29   Cylinder liners, pistons and connecting rods – examination and renovation

1   The liner bores may be examined for wear either in or out of the engine block; the cylinder head must, of course, be removed in each case.

2   First of all examine the top of the cylinder about a quarter of an inch

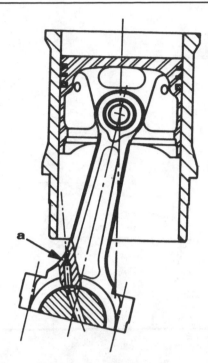

Fig. 1.15 Oil passage location in connecting rod of modified AX 10 engine (Sec 29)

7   New Citroën rings are supplied with their gaps already preset, but if you intend to use other makes the gaps should be checked and adjusted if necessary. Before fitting the new rings on the pistons, each should be inserted approximately 75 mm (3 in) down the cylinder bore and the gap measured with a feeler gauge. This must be as specified. It is essential that the gap should be measured at the bottom of the ring travel, as if it is measured at the top of a worn bore and gives a perfect fit, it could easily seize at the bottom. If the ring gap is too small, rub down the ends of the ring with a very fine file until the gap, when fitted, is correct. To keep the rings square in the bore for measurement, line each up in turn by inserting an old piston in the bore upside down, and use the piston to push the ring down. Remove the piston and measure the piston ring gap.
8   The gudgeon pins float in the piston and are an interference fit in the connecting rods. This interference fit between gudgeon pin and connecting rod means that heat is required (230 to 250°C/446° to 500°F) before a pin can be satisfactorily fitted in the connecting rod. If it is necessary to renew either the piston or connecting rod, we strongly recommend that the separation and assembly of the two be entrusted to someone with experience. Misapplied heat can ruin one, or all, of the components very easily.

Modification note: AX 10 engines from July 1988

From engine number 207 902, (AX 10 models), the connecting rods incorporate a 2 mm (0.08 in) diameter oil lubrication port in the thrust side of the big-end (Fig. 1.15). The function of this oil port is to provide additional lubrication to the cylinder walls. The big-end shells were modified to suit and it is therefore important to ensure that the correct bearing shells are obtained according to type. Ensure that the oil port is clear in each rod before assembling the engine.
To confuse matters, some models produced prior to this date also had the later type of connecting rod fitted to the No 1 cylinder only. Where this is the case, the existing type connecting rods and bearing shells should be used.

---

30 Cylinder liner protrusion – checking

1   The protrusion of the cylinder liners when assembled to the block must be within prescribed limits so that a gastight seal can be achieved when the head is bolted on. One liner protruding too much or not enough will, despite the cylinder head gasket, make it impossible to secure a gas or watertight joint.
2   An O-ring seal is fitted between each liner mating flange and the cylinder block. These seals compress when the cylinder head is tightened down to effect a watertight seal (Fig. 1.16).
3   Although the actual liner protrusion check method is the same, the procedure differs if the engine is assembled or dismantled.
4   If the cylinder head has been removed with the engine *in situ* the liners must be held under compression with the use of liner clamps. Remove the dowels from the cylinder block top face to allow the clamps to be fitted, if necessary.
5   If the engine is dismantled, check that the seal mating surfaces of the liners and the cylinder block are clean, then insert each liner into its respective position in the cylinder block without its seal.
6   Check each liner protrusion in turn measuring the distance between the top face of the liner and the top face of the cylinder block. Use a dial test indicator if available but, failing this, use a metal rule and feeler gauges to assess the protrusion (photo).
7   As the protrusion of each liner in turn is checked, ensure that it is squarely located in the cylinder block. The protrusion of each liner should be within the limits specified (see Specifications at the start of this Chapter). New liners can be rotated half a turn (180°), and/or fitted in a different position in the block, to bring protrusion within tolerance. Old liners which will not produce the desired results are best scrapped. Consult a Citroën dealer for advice.
8   Finally check the difference in height between adjacent liners. Use the dial test indicators or rule and feeler gauges to measure the difference in height, if any, between adjacent liners at a point on each lying along the centre axis parallel with the crankshaft on the top face. Each difference in level must not exceed the maximum specified.
9   If the checks reveal a discrepancy on an installed engine it will be necessary to renew the liner O-rings or even one or more liners.
10   Once the checks have shown the liners to be within limits of

below the top of the liner and with a finger feel if there is any ridge running round the circumference of the bore. In a worn cylinder bore a ridge will develop at the point where the top ring on the piston comes to the uppermost limit of its stroke. An excessive ridge indicates that the bore below the ridge is worn. If there is no ridge, it is reasonable to assume that the cylinder is not badly worn. Measurement of the diameter of the cylinder bore both in line with the piston gudgeon pin and at right angles to it, at the top and bottom of the cylinder, is another check to be made. A cylinder is expected to wear at the sides where the thrust of the piston presses against it. In time this causes the cylinder to assume an oval shape. Furthermore, the top of the cylinder is likely to wear more than the bottom of the cylinder. It will be necessary to use a proper bore measuring instrument in order to measure the differences in bore diameter across the cylinder, and variations between the top and bottom ends of the cylinder. As a general guide it may be assumed that any variation more than 0.25 mm (0.010 in) indicates that the liners should be renewed. Provided all variations are less than 0.25 mm (0.010 in) it is probable that the fitting of new piston rings will cure the problem of piston-to-cylinder bore clearances. Once again it is difficult to give a firm ruling on this as so much depends on the amount of time, effort and money which the individual owner is prepared, or wishes to spend, on the task. Certainly if the cylinder bores are obviously deeply grooved or scored, the liners must be renewed, regardless of any measurement differences in the cylinder diameter.
3   If new liners are to be fitted, new pistons will be required also, as they are supplied as matched sets.
4   Examine the piston surface and look for signs of any hairline cracks especially round the gudgeon pin area. Check that the oil drain holes below the oil control ring groove are clear, and, if not, carefully clean them out using a suitably sized drill, but don't mark the piston.
5   If any of the pistons are obviously badly worn or defective they must be renewed. A badly worn top ring band may be machined to accept a wider, stepped ring, the step on the outer face of this type of ring being necessary to avoid fouling the unworn ridge at the top of the cylinder bore.
6   Providing the engine has not seized up or suffered any other severe damage, the connecting rods should not require any attention other than cleaning. If damage has occurred or the piston/s show signs or irregular wear it is advisable to have the connecting rod alignment checked. This requires the use of specialised tools and should therefore be entrusted to a Citroën agent or a competent automotive engineer, who will be able to check and realign any defective rods.

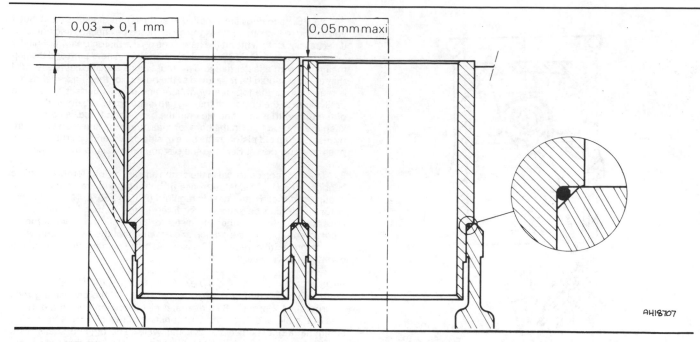

Fig. 1.16 Cylinder liner protrusion and O-ring seal location (inset) (Sec 30)

protrusion and squareness reassembling can continue or, if appropriate, temporary retainer clamps/straps should be fitted to hold them in position. *Don't turn the crankshaft if the liners are not restrained from movement.* Cover the exposed engine internal parts if there is likely to be delay before completing reassembly.

11   With new liners, once correctly located, mark their sequence in the block and withdraw them so that their piston/rods can be fitted.

31 Engine reassembly – general

1   It is during the process of engine reassembly that the job is either made a success or a failure. From the word go there are certain basic rules which is folly to ignore, namely:

(a)   *Absolute cleanliness. The working area, the components of the engine and the hands of those working on the engine must be completely free of grime and grit. One small piece of carborundum dust or swarf can ruin a big-end in no time, and nullify all the time and effort you have spent.*

(b)   *Always, no matter what the circumstances may be, use new gaskets, locking tabs, seats, nyloc (self-locking) nuts and any other parts mentioned in the Sections in this Chapter. It is pointless to dismantle an engine, spend considerable money and time on it and then waste all this for the sake of something as small as a failed oil seal. Delay the rebuilding if necessary.*

(c)   *Don't rush it. The most skilled and experienced mechanic can easily make a mistake if he is rushed.*

(d)   *Check that all nuts and bolts are clean and in good condition and ideally renew all spring washers, lockwashers and tab washers as a matter of course. A supply of clean engine oil and clean cloths (to wipe excess oil off your hands) and a torque wrench are the only things which should be required in addition to all the tools used in dismantling the engine.*

(e)   *The torque wrench is an essential requirement when reassembling the engine (and transmission) components. This is because the various housings are manufactured from aluminium alloy and whilst this gives the advantage of less weight, it also means that the various fastenings must be accurately tightened as specified to avoid distortion and/or damage to the components.*

2   Assuming that the engine has been completely stripped for reconditioning and that the block is now bare, before any reassembly takes place it must be thoroughly cleaned both inside and out.

3   Clean out the oilways using a bottle brush, wire or other suitable implement, and blow through with compressed air. Squirt some clean engine oil through to check that the oilways are clear.

4   If the core plugs are defective and show signs of weeping, they must be renewed at this stage. To remove, carefully drive a punch through the centre of the plug and use the punch to lever the plug out. Clean the aperture thoroughly and prior to fitting the new plug, smear the orifice with sealant. Use a small-headed hammer and carefully drive the new core plug into position with the convex side inwards. Check that it is correctly seated on completion.

5   As the components are assembled, lubricate them with clean engine oil and use a suitable sealant where applicable.

6   Make sure that all blind tapped holes are clean, with any oil mopped out of them. This is because it is possible for a casting to fracture when a bolt is screwed in owing to hydraulic pressure.

32 Crankshaft and main bearings – refitting

1   With the block upside-down on the bench, press the main bearing upper shells into position. Note that the grooved bearings are fitted to positions No 2 and 4.

2   Smear a little grease on the endfloat rings and locate them each side of No 2 bearing with their grooves facing outwards.

3   Oil the bearings and lower the crankshaft into position (photo).

4   Check that the crankshaft endfloat is as given in the Specifications, using a feeler blade between an endfloat ring and the crankshaft web. The rings are available in four thicknesses.

5   Fit the oil pump sprocket and chain to the front of the crankshaft, locating the sprocket on the Woodruff key.

6   Press the main bearing lower shells into position in the main bearing cap casting, noting that the grooved bearings are fitted to positions No 2 and 4.

7   Apply jointing compound to the mating face, then lower the main bearing cap casting into position over the crankshaft. At the same time feed the oil pump chain through the aperture (photos).

8   Insert the main bearing bolts dry, then tighten them evenly to the initial torque wrench setting. Angle-tighten the bolts by a further 45° (photos).

9   Refit the bolts securing the main bearing cap casting to the block and tighten them to the specified torque.

33 Connecting rods, pistons and liners – reassembly and refitting

1   Fit the piston rings to the pistons. Always fit the rings from the piston crown end. Use three old feeler blades equally spaced behind the

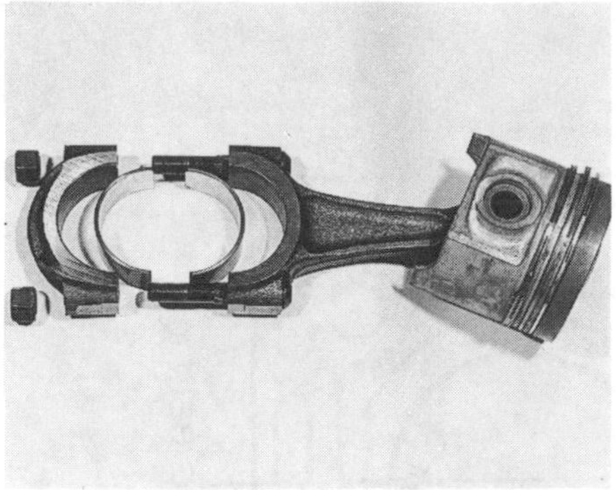

33.6A Piston and connecting rod assembly

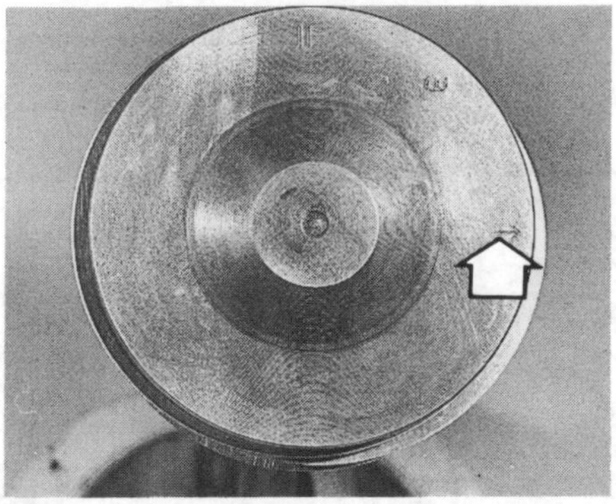

33.6B Piston crown showing direction of fitting arrow (arrowed)

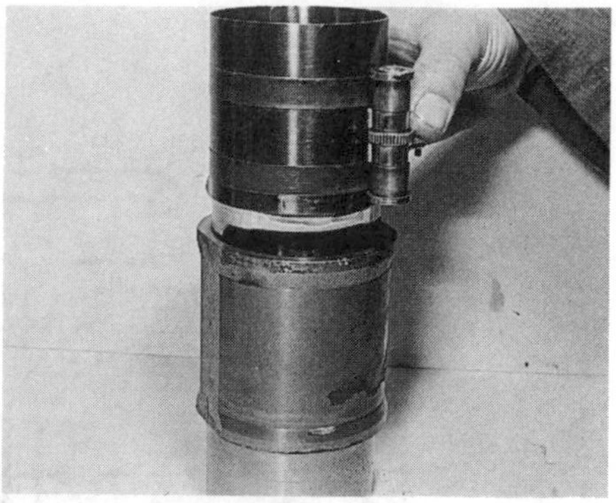

33.8A Fit compressor and lower the piston into the liner

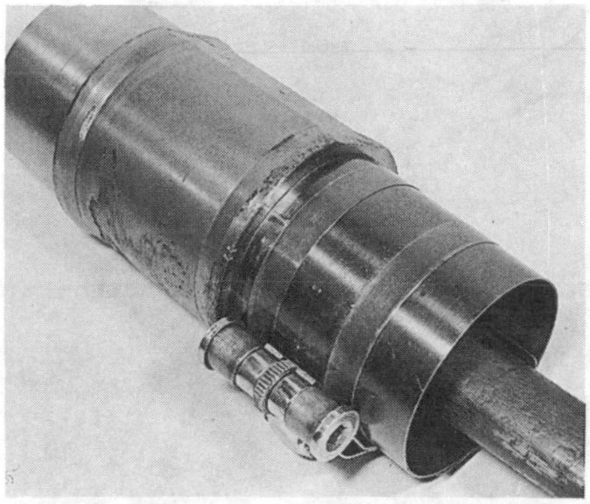

33.8B Use a hammer handle to push the piston into its liner

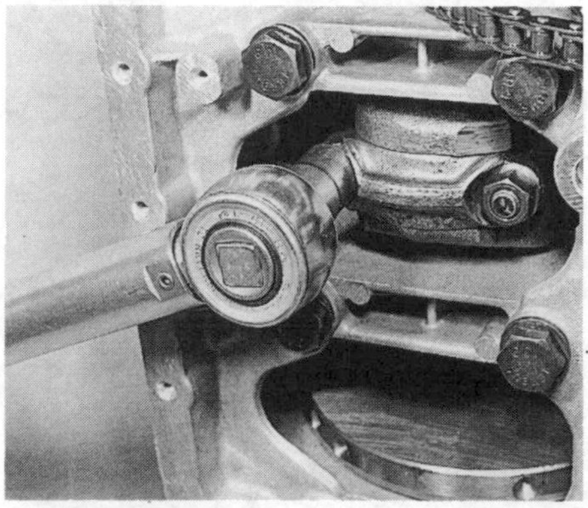

33.16 Tightening the big-end bearing cap nuts

ring so that it will slide down to the lower grooves without dropping into the higher ones.

2 Make sure that the rings are correctly located and the right way up. If genuine Citroën piston rings are being used, refer to Fig. 1.17. If special proprietary rings are being fitted, follow the manufacturer's instructions.

3 Twist the piston rings so that the gap in the oil control ring expander aligns with the gudgeon pin and the gaps in the rails are offset from the gudgeon pin by between 20.0 and 50.0 mm (0.79 and 1.97 in). The gaps in the top two compression rings should be equally spaced (120°) from the gap in the oil control expander around the piston.

4 If new piston/liner assemblies have been supplied, the identification marks on the piston and liner should be:

Piston	**Liner**
A	*One file mark on rim*
B	*Two file marks on rim*
C	*Three file marks on rim*

5 All four pistons should be of the same grading.

6 Fit the liners to the piston/connecting rod assemblies so that when installed in the cylinder block, the rim mark on the liner will be towards the oil gallery side and the arrow on the piston crown facing towards the timing cover end of the engine (photos). Piston-to-rod relationship is only important on AX 10 models that have had a connecting rod modification (Section 29).

7 Oil the piston rings liberally and fit a compressor to the piston and compress the rings fully. When fitted, the top edge of the ring compressor should be 4 to 5 mm below the crown of the piston.

8 Lubricate the bore of the liner and insert the piston. As this is done, the compressor will be pushed off (photos).

9 Push the piston down so that the piston crown is level with or just below the top edge of the liner.

10 With the pistons and liners reassembled, fit a new O-ring seal over the bottom end of each liner in turn, ensuring that the seals are not twisted as they are fitted.

11 Remove the big-end caps, wipe the recesses in the rod and cap absolutely clean and fit the bearing shells. If the original shells are being used again, make sure that they are being returned to their original locations.

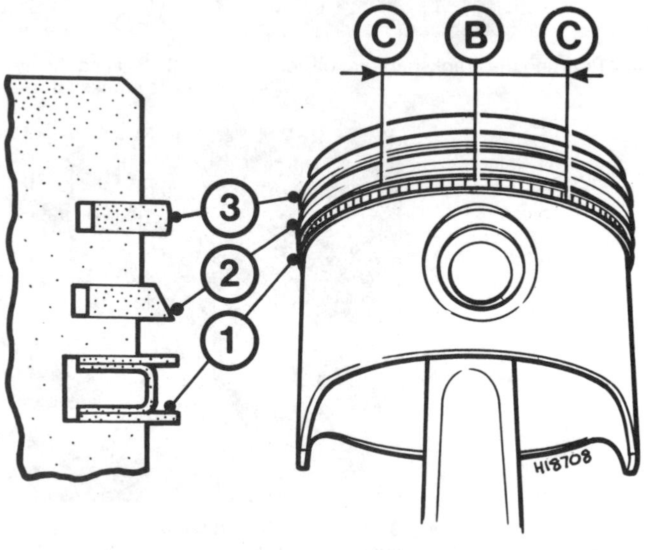

Fig. 1.17 Positioning the piston ring gaps on assembly (Sec 33)

1 Scraper ring
(b) Expander gap on axis of gudgeon pin hole
(c) Scraper rings gaps on alternate sides of gudgeon pin axis within 20 to 50 mm (0.79 to 1.96 in)

2 Tapered face ring gap 120° from gudgeon pin axis

3 Curved face ring gap 120° from gudgeon pin axis in opposite direction

FRONT OF VEHICLE

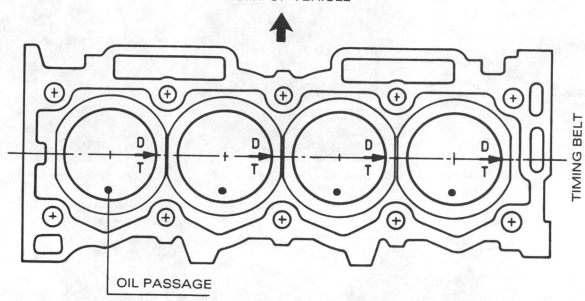

OIL PASSAGE

Fig. 1.18 Piston rod fitting direction. The connecting rod oil passage hole in later AX 10 models must be as indicated (Sec 33)

34.4 Refitting the crankshaft rear oil seal

34.5 Using the flywheel and four bolts to fit the crankshaft rear oil seal

35.1A Apply locking fluid to the flywheel bolts ...

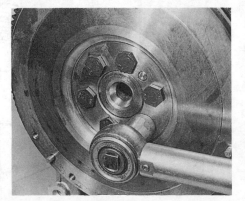

35.1B ... then fit and tighten them to the specified torque

36.1 Locate new seals over the valves guides

12   Push the liner/rod assemblies into the block, without disturbing the seals and aligning the location marks.

13   Fit clamps to hold the liners in the block.

14   Support the block on its flywheel end.

15   Check that the crankshaft rotates freely, then position it so that the No 1 and 4 crankpins are positioned at bottom-dead-centre (BDC). Lubricate the crankpin journals with clean engine oil.

16   Press the No 1 piston down its liner and guide the connecting rod big-end over the crankpin journal. Refit the big-end bearing cap and tighten the retaining nuts evenly to the specified torque wrench setting (photo).

17   Check that the crankshaft rotates freely, (the liner still being secured by its clamp). The pulley bolt can be temporarily fitted to enable the crankshaft to be rotated.

18   Repeat the procedure to fit the remaining connecting rods onto their respective crankshaft journals.

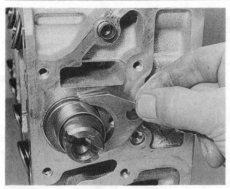

37.2 Fit the camshaft thrust fork

37.3 Fit the camshaft oil seal

37.6 Cylinder head gasket located on the block

37.8 Camshaft sprocket set at TDC

37.9 Lowering the cylinder head into position (with manifolds)

37.10 Refitting the rocker assembly

34 Oil pump and sump – refitting

1 Support the block upside-down on the bench.
2 Check that the oil pump location pin is fitted to the main bearing casting, then refit the oil pump while tilting it to engage the drive sprocket with the chain. Insert and tighten the bolts.
3 Apply jointing compound to the mating faces of the sump and main bearing casting. Refit the sump, insert the bolts and tighten them to the specified torque.
4 Dip the new crankshaft rear oil seal in oil and locate it over the rear of the crankshaft (photo).
5 Citroën garages use their special tool (4507-TG) to fit the oil seal, however it may be fitted by using the flywheel. Temporarily locate the flywheel on the crankshaft using four bolts, then tighten the bolts evenly until the flywheel contacts the rear flange (photo). Remove the flywheel and use a metal tube or block of wood to drive the oil seal fully into position.

35 Flywheel – refitting

1 Apply locking fluid to the threads of the flywheel bolts, locate the flywheel on the crankshaft dowel, then insert the new retaining bolts and tighten them to the specified torque while holding the flywheel in the manner employed during its removal (photos).
2 The clutch unit can be refitted at this stage by referring to Chapter 5.

36 Valves – refitting

1 Place new oil seals over the valve guides (photo).
2 Liberally lubricate the valve stems and then insert them into the valve guides from which they were removed.
3 Refit the lower spring seat, valve spring and spring cup over the

valve stem and then position the spring compressor over the assembly.
4 Compress the spring sufficiently to allow the cotters to be slipped into place in the groove machined in the top of the valve stem. Now release the spring compressor.
5 Repeat this operation until all eight valves have been assembled into the cylinder head.
6 With all the valves installed, gently tap the top of the valve stems once or twice, using a soft-faced mallet, to seat the cotters and centralise the components.

37 Cylinder head and camshaft – refitting

1 Oil the camshaft bearings and insert the camshaft into the cylinder head.
2 Refit the camshaft thrust fork and tighten the bolt (photo).
3 Dip the new oil seal in oil, and press it into the cylinder head until flush, using a metal tube or large socket and hammer (photo).
4 Refit the camshaft sprocket so that the location peg enters the cut-out. Insert and tighten the bolt while holding the sprocket stationary using either method described in paragraph 2 of Section 22.
5 Remove the cylinder liner clamps, then clean the cylinder head and block joint faces thoroughly. Also clean the cylinder head bolt holes.
6 Locate the new cylinder head gasket on the block dowels as shown (photo).
7 Align the TDC holes in the flywheel and block rear flange, and insert a twist drill or long bolt.
8 Align the small hole in the camshaft sprocket with the hole in the cylinder head and insert a twist drill or bolt (photo).
9 Lower the cylinder head onto the block so that it engages the two dowels (photo).
10 Refit the rocker arm assembly, engaging it over the dowels (photo).
11 Lubricate the cylinder head bolt threads and heads with molybdenum disulphide grease or engine oil. Insert them and tighten to the initial torque using the sequence given in Fig. 1.19 (photo).

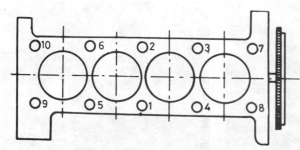

Fig. 1.19 Cylinder head bolt tightening sequence (Sec 37)

12   Using the same sequence, angle-tighten the bolts by 240° (photo).
13   If the engine is in the car, refit the timing belt (Section 5) and adjust the valve clearances (Section 10), then refit the remaining associated components to the cylinder head (Section 39).

38   Timing belt and associated components – refitting

1   Support the engine upright on the bench.
2   Dip the crankshaft front oil seal in oil, locate it over the front of the crankshaft, and drive it in flush with the front of the block using a metal tube or socket (photo). There is no seating, so take care not to drive it in too far.
3   Fit the oil seal flange, followed by the hub/sprocket. Insert the pulley bolt and spacer, and tighten the bolt to the specified torque while holding the flywheel stationary (photo).
4   Refit the water pump housing together with a new O-ring, and tighten the bolts to the specified torque (photo).
5   Refit the timing belt tensioner roller, turn it clockwise, and tighten the nut.
6   Refit and adjust the tension of the timing belt as described in Section 5, (paragraphs 10 to 13 inclusive).

39   Ancillary engine components – refitting

1   Adjust the valve clearances as described in Section 10.
2   Refit the baffle plate with its edges pointing downwards, followed by the two spacers.
3   Fit the rubber gasket to the valve cover, locate the cover in position and tighten the nuts.
4   Apply a little sealant to the end of the engine oil dipstick holder, and insert it in the main bearing cap casting. Insert and tighten the mounting bolt.
5   Insert and tighten the oil pressure switch (photo).
6   Smear a little oil on the sealing ring, and tighten the oil filter into position by hand only.
7   Refit the timing plate and tighten the bolts.
8   Refit the TDC sensor and tighten the bolt. Fix the lead in the plastic clip on the timing plate. Note that the main body of the TDC sensor should be 1.0 mm (0.04 in) from the flywheel.
9   Apply jointing compound to the distributor mounting flange, then refit it to the cylinder head, and tighten the bolts.
10   Apply jointing compound to the thermostat housing, then refit it to the cylinder head, and tighten the bolts.
11   Refit the thermostat with reference to Chapter 2.
12   Refit the distributor with reference to Chapter 4.
13   Refit the exhaust manifold together with new gaskets. Refit the nuts and washers and tighten the nuts.
14   Refit the exhaust manifold hot air shroud and tighten the bolts.
15   Locate the coil and bracket over the distributor and tighten the bolts.
16   Position the pulley on the front of the crankshaft. Insert and tighten the bolts.
17   Refit the alternator and insert the pivot and adjustment bolts. Slip the drivebelt onto the pulleys and tighten the tension bolt until the deflection of the belt midway between the pulleys is approximately 6.0 mm (0.24 in) under firm thumb pressure. Tighten the pivot and adjustment bolts.
18   Refit the fuel pump together with a new gasket and tighten the bolts.

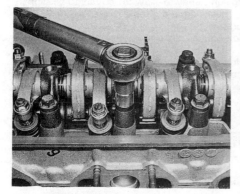

37.11 Tighten the cylinder head bolts to the initial torque

37.12 Angle-tighten the cylinder head bolts by 240°

38.2 Locate the crankshaft front oil seal

38.3 Tighten the crankshaft pulley bolt

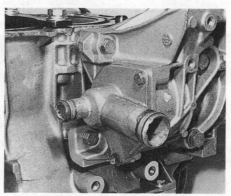

38.4 Water pump housing and retaining bolts

39.5 Oil pressure switch

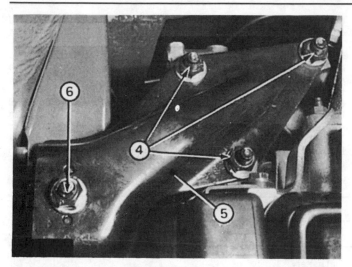

Fig. 1.20 Right-hand engine mounting bolt torque settings (Sec 41)

4   50 Nm (37 lbf ft)   6   35 Nm (26 lbf ft)
5   Mounting

Fig. 1.21 Engine/transmission mounting torque settings (Sec 41)

1   17 Nm (12.5 lbf ft)   3   Mounting
2   50 Nm (37 lbf ft)

19   Thoroughly clean the mating faces of the inlet manifold and cylinder head, and apply jointing compound.
20   Refit the inlet manifold complete with carburettor and tighten the nuts.
21   Reconnect the hose between the fuel pump and carburettor, and tighten the clips.
22   Reconnect the vacuum hose between the distributor and carburettor.
23   Refit and tighten the spark plugs.
24   Refit the HT leads and distributor cap.

40   Engine – reconnection to gearbox

1   Check that the clutch release bearing is correctly fitted to the release fork. To prevent the bearing being disconnected while fitting the gearbox to the engine, tie the external release arm in the released position.
2   Lubricate the input shaft splines, clutch release bearing sleeve and fork fingers with molybdenum disulphide grease.
3   Refit any location dowels removed, then offer the gearbox to the engine so that the input shaft enters the clutch friction disc and engages the splines.
4   Push the gearbox fully onto the engine location dowels.
5   Insert and tighten the gearbox-to-engine bolts, noting that the air cleaner mounting bracket is secured by the outboard bolt on the starter motor side.
6   Refit the starter motor (Chapter 12).

41   Engine and gearbox – refitting

1   If the driveshafts were refitted to move the car when the engine and gearbox were removed, they must be withdrawn from the front hubs.
2   Raise the car at the front end and support it on axle stands at the required height.
3   Move the engine/gearbox unit carefully into position underneath the front of the car and attach the lifting hoist and sling.
4   Check that the various cables, wiring harnesses and associated engine components are positioned out of the way so that they will not get snagged or damaged as the power unit is raised into position.
5   Carefully raise the engine and gearbox up through the engine compartment, and engage with the mountings each side. As the unit is raised, an assistant should be at hand to help in guiding the unit into position, and in particular, to ensure that the carburettor is not damaged

on the bulkhead fittings.
6   With the engine/gearbox unit located in the mounting points, refit the right-hand mounting support and initially hand tighten the retaining nuts, then fit the gearbox carrier bolt and nuts. Tighten the respective fastenings to their torque wrench settings with reference to Figs. 1.20 and 1.21.
7   Detach the engine/gearbox lift sling and hoist.
8   Reconnect the gearshift linkages.
9   Refit the engine torque stay and tighten the retaining bolts to the specified torque settings with reference to Fig. 1.22.
10   Refit the right and left-hand drive shafts as described in Chapter 7.
11   Reconnect the remaining engine/gearbox ancillary items by reversing the removal procedures given in Section 14. Renew any hose retaining clips and hoses that show signs of deterioration and ensure that all hose and wiring connections are securely made.
12   Do not reconnect the battery until all of the other ancillary items are attached.
13   Refill the cooling system as described in Chapter 2.
14   If not already fitted, locate and hand tighten the new oil filter and refill with the specified engine oil as described in Section 2.
15   Top up the gearbox oil level as described in Section 2 of Chapter 6.
16   Check that all of the associated fittings are reconnected before removing the axle stands and lowering the car.

Fig. 1.22 Engine/transmission torque stay torque settings (Sec 41)

7   60 Nm (44 lbf ft)   8   90 Nm (66 lbf ft)

42 Engine – initial start-up after overhaul

1   Make sure that the battery is fully charged and that all lubricants, coolant and fuel are replenished.
2   It will require several revolutions of the engine on the starter motor to pump the petrol up to the carburettor.
3   As soon as the engine fires and runs, keep it going at a fast tickover only (no faster) and bring it up to the normal working temperature.
4   As the engine warms up there will be odd smells and some smoke from parts getting hot and burning off oil deposits. The signs to look for are leaks of water or oil which will be obvious if serious. Check also the exhaust pipe and manifold connections, as these do not always 'find'

their exact gastight position until the warmth and vibration have acted on them, and it is almost certain that they will need tightening further. This should be done with the engine stopped.
5   Road test the car to check that the timing is correct and that the engine is giving the necessary smoothness and power. Do not race the engine – if new bearings and/or pistons have been fitted it should be treated as a new engine and run in at a reduced speed.
6   Renew the engine oil at 1000 miles (1500 kms), then at the normal intervals specified in the *Routine maintenance* Section at the start of the manual.
7   It should be noted that the cylinder head bolts do not require further tightening, nor does the timing belt require further tensioning after an initial mileage has been covered.

43 Fault diagnosis – engine

Symptom	Reason(s)
Engine will not turn over when starter switch is operated	Flat battery Bad battery connections Bad connections at solenoid switch and/or starter motor Starter motor jammed Defective solenoid Starter motor defective
Engine turns over normally but fails to fire and run	No sparks at plugs No fuel reaching engine Too much fuel reaching engine (flooding)
Engine starts but runs unevenly and misfires	Ignition and/or fuel system faults Incorrect valve clearance Burnt out valves Blown cylinder head gasket, dropped liners Worn out piston rings Worn cylinder bores
Lack of power	Ignition and/or fuel system faults Incorrect valve clearance Burnt out valves Blown cylinder head gasket Worn out piston rings Worn cylinder bores
Excessive oil consumption	Oil leaks from crankshaft oil seal, rocker cover gasket, crankcase joint Worn piston rings or cylinder bores resulting in oil being burnt by engine (smoky exhaust is an indication) Worn valve guides and/or defective valve stem oil seals
Excessive mechanical noise from engine	Wrong valve clearance Worn crankshaft bearings Worn cylinders (piston slap)

Chapter 2 Cooling system

Contents

Specifications

General

System type	Pressurised with front mounted radiator, electric cooling fan, water pump and thermostat
System capacity..	4.8 litres (8.5 pints)
Pressure cap setting...	1 bar (14.5 lbf/in^2)
System warning lamp switch operating temperature.....................	110°C (230°F)
Electric cooling fan operating temperature..................................	90 to 95°C (194 to 203°F)
Thermostat starts to open	88°C (190°F)
Thermostat minimum full travel opening	7 mm (0.28 in)
Antifreeze mixture:	
Protection to -15°C (5°F)...	27% antifreeze
Protection to -35°C (-31°F)	50% antifreeze
Antifreeze type/specification	Ethylene glycol based antifreeze (Duckhams Universal Antifreeze and Summer Coolant)

Torque wrench settings

	Nm	lbf ft
Water pump upper stud	16	12
Water pump lower bolt	7	5
Housing inlet elbow..	7	5
Housing to block:		
8 mm bolts	30	22
10 mm bolts	50	37
Thermal sensor switch	14	10
Cooling fan thermo-switch	28	21
Cylinder block drain plug...	30	22

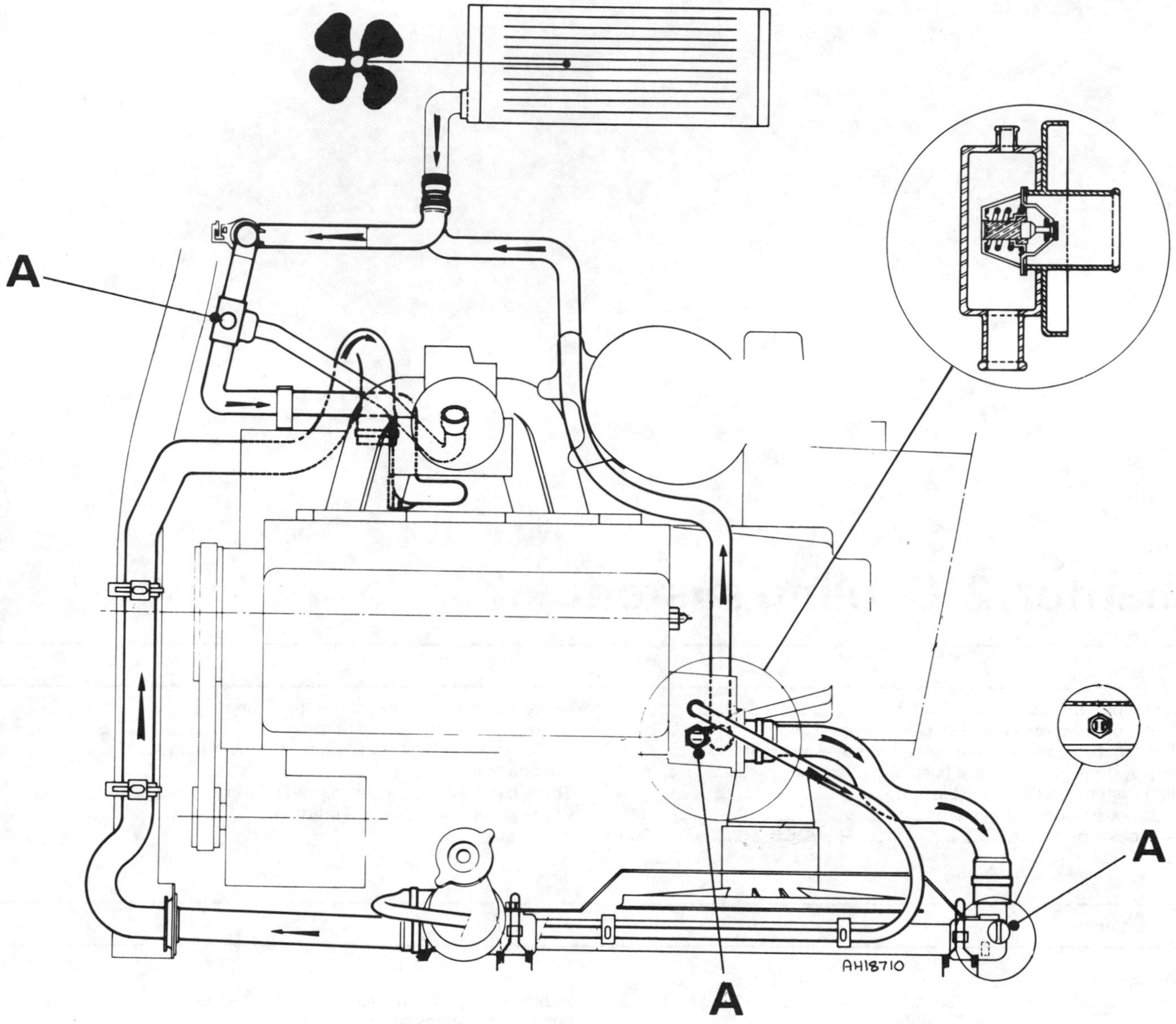

A

A

A

AH18710

Fig. 2.1 Cooling system circuit – up to September 1987 (Sec 1)

A = System bleed points

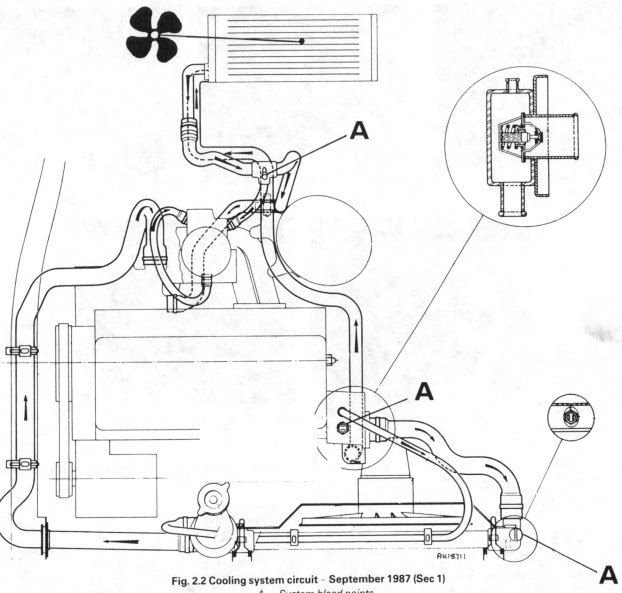

Fig. 2.2 Cooling system circuit – September 1987 (Sec 1)
A = System bleed points

1 General description

The cooling system is of pressurised type and consists of a front-mounted cross-flow radiator, thermoswitch controlled electric cooling fan, water pump and thermostat. The car interior heater matrix is supplied with a continuous supply of coolant since there is no water valve and the hot air supply is controlled by an air flap. The water pump is driven by the engine camshaft drivebelt.

The cooling system functions in the following way. After a cold start the thermostat valve is shut and coolant circulation is restricted to the engine and heater matrix. When the coolant reaches the normal engine operating temperature the thermostat starts to open and coolant circulation also flows through the radiator. The engine temperature is then controlled by the thermostat and the electric cooling fan located on the front of the radiator.

2 Routine maintenance

Carry out the following procedures at the intervals given in *Routine maintenance* at the beginning of this manual.

1   Check the level of coolant in the tank on the right-hand side of the radiator. The level is visible without removing the filler cap and should be between the filler neck and the low level warning switch housing (Fig. 2.3).

2   If the coolant level has dropped below this level, wait until the engine has cooled (about ten minutes) before removing the filler cap. Unscrew it to the safety catch position first, and pause momentarily to allow any remaining steam pressure to escape from the system, then further unscrew the cap and remove it. Do not unscrew the filler cap when the engine has just been run and is still hot, as there is a danger of scalding.

3   Top up the coolant level as required, but if it is still hot, do not add any more than 0.5 litre (1 pint) (photo). The coolant added should contain an antifreeze solution of the required ratio (Section 5). Refit the filler cap.

4   The need for regular topping up of the cooling system indicates a leak in the cooling system and this must be investigated and repaired as soon as possible.

5   Periodically inspect the system hoses and connections for condition and security.

3 Cooling system – draining and flushing

System draining

1   With the engine cold, remove the filler cap from the radiator in the sequence described in Section 2.

2.3 Topping up the coolant level

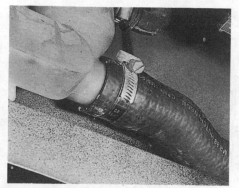

3.2 Radiator bottom hose connection

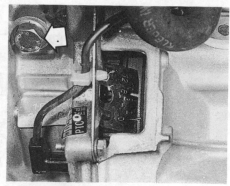

3.3 Cylinder block drain plug location (arrowed)

4.1 Bleed valve in heater coolant hose

6.3 View showing radiator, cooling fan unit, top hose and the thermostat housing (arrowed)

2   Position a suitable container beneath the bottom hose connection to the radiator. Unscrew the retaining clip and detach the hose from the radiator, then drain the coolant into the container (photo).
3   Drain the cylinder block by unscrewing the drain plug and removing it from the side of the block (photo).

System flushing

4   Provided the coolant has been renewed at the specified intervals there should be no need to flush the system. If the system has been neglected and the coolant contains excessive amounts of sediment, disconnect the radiator top hose and use cold water to flush the radiator until the water runs clear from the radiator and cylinder block.
5   In severe cases, remove the radiator and reverse flush it, or alternatively use a proprietary chemical cleaner.
6   With the system clean, reconnect the hoses and refit the cylinder block drain plug, then top up the cooling system as described in the following Section.

4   Cooling system – refilling and bleeding

1   Loosen off and remove the bleed screws from the radiator and the heater hose. Unscrew and remove the thermal switch or plug from the top of the thermostat unit and loosen the other bleed screws shown in Figs. 2.1 and 2.2 (photo).
2   Refill the cooling system through the radiator filler neck in a slow, progressive manner. The coolant must contain the correct ratio of antifreeze-to-water to ensure that the system is protected. As the coolant works its way through the system and exits from the bleed holes, refit the screws, switch or plug (as applicable). The sensor switch must be tightened to the specified torque wrench setting.
3   Continue to top up the radiator to the point where coolant overflows from the top of the filler neck. Refit the cap and then start the engine and run it at a fast idle speed to the point where the cooling fan cuts into operation. Stop the engine.
4   Allow an interval of ten minutes to pass (engine switched off), then

recheck the level of coolant in the radiator side tank and if necessary, top it up as described in Section 2.

5   Coolant mixture – general

1   Plain water should never be used in the cooling system. Apart from giving protection against freezing, an antifreeze mixture protects the engine internal surfaces and components against corrosion. This is very important in an alloy engine.
2   Always use a top quality glycol-based antifreeze which is recommended for alloy engines.
3   Ideally a 50% mixture of antifreeze and soft or demineralised water should be used to maintain maximum protection against freezing and corrosion. On no account use less than 25% antifreeze.
4   Renew the coolant at the specified intervals as the inhibitors contained in the antifreeze gradually lose their effectiveness.
5   Even when operating in climates where antifreeze is not required never use plain water, but add a corrosion inhibitor to it.

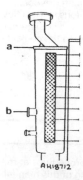

A41B712

Fig. 2.3 Coolant level must be maintained between the filler neck (a) and the low level warning switch (b) (Sec 2)

7.10A Water pump housing and bolts

7.10B Water pump housing O-ring seal

7.11A Water pump removal from the housing

7.11B Water pump O-ring (arrowed)

8.4 Disconnecting the coolant temperature switch wires

8.5 Cooling fan switch wire connector

6 Thermostat – removal, testing and refitting

1   The thermostat housing is located on the cylinder head adjacent to the distributor. Remove the air intake duct from the air cleaner and manifold for access (Chapter 3).
2   Drain the cooling system as previously described.
3   Disconnect the radiator top hose from the thermostat housing (photo).
4   Unscrew and remove the two thermostat housing cover bolts and remove the cover. This may need a little persuasion with a wooden or plastic-faced hammer.
5   Remove the thermostat. If it is stuck, do not lever it out under its bridge piece, but cut around its edge with a sharp knife.
6   Remove the rubber ring(s) and clean the mating faces of the housing and cover.
7   If the thermostat is suspected of being faulty, suspend it in a container of water which is being heated. Using a thermometer, check that the thermostat starts to open at the specified temperature.
8   Remove the thermostat from the water and allow it to cool. The valve plate should close smoothly.
9   If the unit fails to operate as described or is stuck open or shut, renew it with one of similar temperature rating.
10   Fit the thermostat and new rubber ring(s). Bolt on the cover.
11   Reconnect the coolant hose and refill and bleed the system, as described in Section 4.

bolt until the small hole in the camshaft sprocket is aligned with the corresponding hole in the cylinder head. Insert a close-fitting twist drill or bolt into the holes.
4   Align the TDC holes in the flywheel and cylinder block rear flange and insert a further twist drill or long bolt.
5   Loosen the timing belt tensioner roller nut, turn the tensioner clockwise using a screwdriver or square drive in the special hole, then re-tighten the nut.
6   Release the timing belt from the water pump sprocket.
7   Unscrew the nut from the right-hand engine mounting.
8   Using a trolley jack and block of wood, lift the right-hand side of the engine as far as possible.
9   Unscrew the nuts and remove the mounting bracket from the water pump housing.
10   Disconnect the hoses from the housing, then unbolt the housing from the block. Remove the O-ring seal (photos).
11   Unbolt the water pump from the housing and remove the O-ring (photos). If necessary, similarly remove the inlet elbow.
12   Refitting is a reversal of removal, but note the following points:

(a) Renew the O-rings
(b) Make sure that the housing-to-block location dowels are in position
(c) Tighten all nuts and bolts to the specified torque
(d) Refit and tension the timing belt with reference to the appropriate Section in Chapter 1
(e) Refill and bleed the cooling system as described in Section 4

7 Water pump – removal and refitting

1   Drain the cooling system as previously described.
2   Unbolt and remove the upper and intermediate timing covers, leaving the lower cover in position.
3   Turn the engine clockwise using a socket on the crankshaft pulley

8 Radiator (and cooling fan) – removal and refitting

1   Drain the cooling system as described in Section 3.
2   The radiator can only be withdrawn from underneath the car at the front. The car must therefore be raised and supported at the front end on axle stands. Allow sufficient working and removal clearance.

8.6A Loosen the retaining bolt ...

8.6B ... and lift the cooling fan unit out of its locators

8.6C Cooling fan unit removed from the car

8.9 Radiator and spring retainers (arrowed)

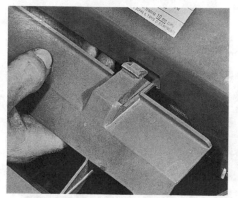

9.3A Front grille panel and retaining clip

9.3B Cooling fan relay unit

3　Disconnect the radiator top hose.
4　Detach the temperature sensor wires, noting which connector the yellow wire with the red connector is attached (photo).
5　Disconnect the cooling fan switch block connector (photo).
6　Loosen off the upper retaining bolt and remove the cooling fan unit (complete with mounting frame) (photos).
7　Disconnect the expansion hose from the thermostat housing and then release the hose from the retaining clips on the body.
8　Unscrew the two retaining bolts and detach the bonnet lock, and together with its inner cable place the lock unit out of the way.
9　Release the spring retainers from the top of the radiator (photo), then tilt the radiator towards the engine at the top and lift it clear of the bottom mountings, then lower the radiator downwards and remove it from underneath the car, taking care not to damage the core.
10　The radiator side tanks are of plastic and the radiator cannot be repaired by soldering. If the radiator is damaged or has developed a leak, a temporary repair can be made using a proprietary sealant mixed in the coolant.
11　Refitting the radiator (and cooling fan unit) is a reversal of the removal procedure. Ensure that the radiator is fully engaged in the bottom mountings before securing at the top.
12　Refill the cooling system and bleed it to complete as described in Section 4.

9　Cooling fan thermo-switch – removal and refitting

1　The thermostatically controlled switch for the cooling fan is screwed into the radiator. Before this can be removed, the system must be drained and the switch leads disconnected.
2　When refitting the switch, use a new sealing ring and tighten the switch to the specified torque wrench setting.
3　The cooling fan relay unit is mounted on the front side of the radiator cross panel. To remove the relay, detach the front grille by releasing its securing clips, then disconnect the wiring connector and withdraw the relay from its retaining clip (photos).
4　Refit in the reverse order of removal.

10　Coolant temperature warning sensor – removal and refitting

1　This sensor is located either in the end face of the cylinder head (December 1987 on), or in the coolant outlet housing (up to December 1987).
2　To remove the sensor, first drain the coolant as described in Section 3 of this Chapter.
3　Disconnect the lead from the spade connection, then unscrew the

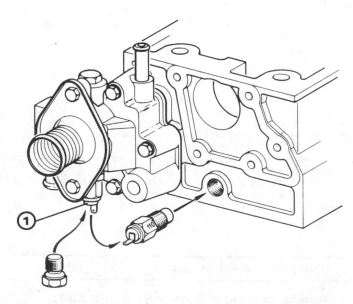

Fig. 2.4 Coolant temperature warning sensor (1) location moved from the outlet housing to the cylinder head from December 1987 on (Sec 10)

11.2 Heater control hose connections at bulkhead

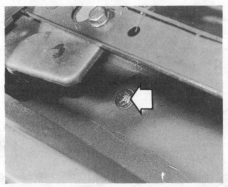

11.8 Heater unit retaining bolt on engine side of bulkhead (arrowed)

12.1 Pull free the heater and ventilation control knobs ...

12.2A ... Undo the retaining screw ...

12.2B ... and remove the panel

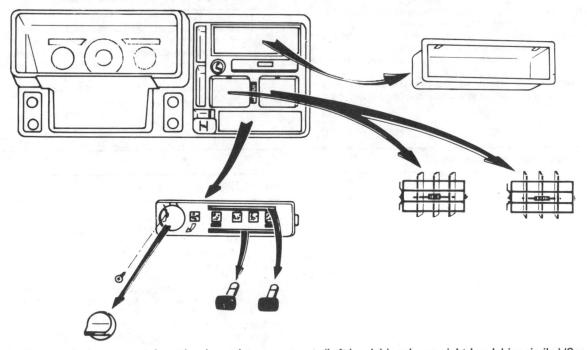

Fig. 2.5 Remove the heater control panel and associate components (Left-hand drive shown, right-hand drive similar) (Sec 11)

unit from the cylinder head or outlet housing (as applicable).

4   Refit in the reverse order of removal. Refill the cooling system and bleed it as described in Section 4.

11 Heater unit – removal and refitting

1   Drain the cooling system as described in Section 3.

2   Detach the heater feed and return hoses at the bulkhead, access to them being from underneath (photo).

3   Refer to Chapter 11, Section 22 and remove the centre console and the right and left-hand parcel shelves.

4   Remove the heater control panel as described in Section 12.

5   Disconnect the facia unit from its fixings, and then carefully pivot it upwards to allow access to the heater unit retaining nut from the underside. Support the panel in this position with a prop.

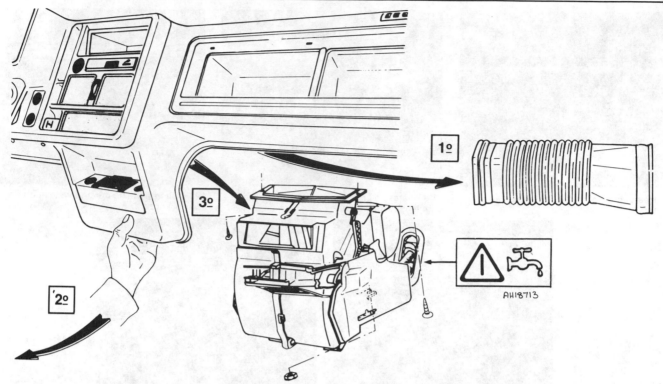

Fig. 2.6 Detach the duct (1) lift the facia (2) and remove the heater unit (3) (Sec 11)
LHD shown RHD similar

6   Remove the windscreen wiper motor arm and blade with reference to Chapter 12.

7   Unscrew the retaining nut each side, and the central screw and then remove the grille panel at the base of the windscreen.

8   Undo the single retaining bolt securing the heater unit from the engine side of the bulkhead, and the nut from the underside within the car (photo). Detach the ducts and carefully withdraw the heater from the car.

9   Refit in the reverse order of removal. Ensure that all connections are securely made and refill the cooling system as described in Section 4 of this Chapter.

12   Heater control unit – removal and refitting

1   Pull free the knobs from the heater/ventilation controls (photo).

2   Undo the retaining screw, and remove the control panel from the facia. As it is withdrawn, detach the illumination bulb wiring (photos).

3   Withdraw the control plate unit and detach the control rod and cable.

4   Refit in the reverse order of removal. Check for satisfactory operation on completion.

13   Fault diagnosis – cooling system

Symptom	Reason(s)
Overheating	Insufficient coolant in system
	Radiator blocked either internally or externally
	Thermostat not opening
	Electric cooling fan or thermoswitch faulty
	Pressure cap faulty
Overcooling	Faulty, incorrect or missing thermostat
	Electric cooling fan thermoswitch not switching off
Loss of coolant	Damaged hoses or loose clips
	Leaking water pump O-ring or gasket, as applicable

Chapter 3 Fuel and exhaust system

Contents

Specifications

General

System type	Rear mounted fuel tank, mechanical diaphragm fuel pump. Solex or Weber carburettor and a dry element air cleaner

Fuel tank capacity

AX 10 and AX 11 models	36 litres (7.9 gallons)
AX 14 and GT models	43 litres (9.5 gallons)

Fuel octane rating

	Leaded	Unleaded
Up to March 1989:		
AX 10 C1A engine	97 RON (4-star)	95 RON (No adjustment required)
AX 11 H1A engine	97 RON (4-star)	95 RON (No adjustment required)
AX 14 K1A engine	97 RON (4-star)	95 RON (Reset ignition timing to 4° at 750 rpm)
AX 14 K1G engine	97 RON (4-star)	Unsuitable
AX GT K2A engine	97 RON (4-star)	Unsuitable
From March 1989 on:		
All models	97 RON (4-star)	95 RON (Premium)

Carburettor application

AX 10 C1A engine	Weber 32 IBSH 16/100 or Solex 32 PBISA 16 REP
AX 11 H1A engine	Solex 32 PBISA 16 PSA
AX 14 K1A engine	Weber 34 TLP 3/100
AX 14 K1G engine	Solex 34 PBISA 17
AX GT K2A engine	Solex 32-34 Z2 PSA

Calibrations and settings

Weber carburettors:

	C1A	K1A
Venturi (mm)	25	26
Main jet	122	132
Air compensation jet	135	145
Emulsion tube	F112	F80
Enrichener	30	40
Fuel econostat	50	50
Air econostat	120	90
Idle jet	45	43
Idle ventilation	150	130
Accelerator pump injector	40/20	40/20
Needle valve	1.5	150
Choke valve gap (mm)	4 to 4.5	4.75
Throttle valve gap (mm)	0.8	0.8
Float lever setting (mm)	8	28
Idle speed (rpm)	750 ± 50	750 ± 50
CO percentage	0.8 to 1.2%	0.8 to 1.2%

Solex carburettors:

	C1A	H1A	K1G	K2A 1st	K2A 2nd
Venturi (mm)	25	25	26	24	27
Main jet	127	127.5	132	155	175
Air compensation jet	155	175	155	117	130
Emulsion tube	31	EM	EC	27	A2
Fuel econostat	–	40	–	–	–
Air econostat	–	150	–	–	–
Idle jet	47	46	42/46	45	(100)
Idle ventilation	135	165	–	150	
Enrichener	–	35	55	–	–
Accelerator pump injector	40	40	40	35	35
Needle valve	1.6	1.6	1.6	1.8	
Float level setting (mm)	28	–	28	35	–
Idle speed (All models)	750 ± 50 rpm				
CO percentage (All models)	0.8 to 1.2%				

Torque wrench settings

	Nm	lbf ft
Exhaust manifold/downpipe flange nuts	30	22
Exhaust pipe coupling nuts	12	9
Downpipe support clamp (K1A and K2A engines)	10	7
Exhaust manifold retaining nuts	16	12
Inlet manifold retaining nuts	8	6

1　General description

The fuel system comprises a rear mounted fuel tank, an in-line fuel filter, a fuel pump and a carburettor.

The fuel pump is a mechanical diaphragm type driven by an eccentric on the camshaft.

The carburettor is a single or twin choke downdraught type, depending on the model to which it is fitted. A dry element air cleaner is used, and this incorporates either a manual or automatic air intake temperature control device to assist in balancing the air/fuel mixture.

The inlet manifold and exhaust manifold are mounted on opposing sides of the cylinder head, and the exhaust system is a single section type from front to rear.

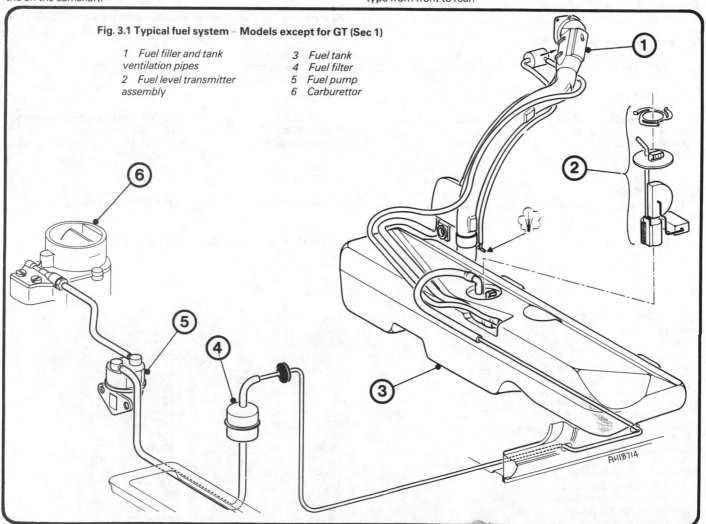

Fig. 3.1 Typical fuel system – Models except for GT (Sec 1)

1　Fuel filler and tank ventilation pipes
2　Fuel level transmitter assembly
3　Fuel tank
4　Fuel filter
5　Fuel pump
6　Carburettor

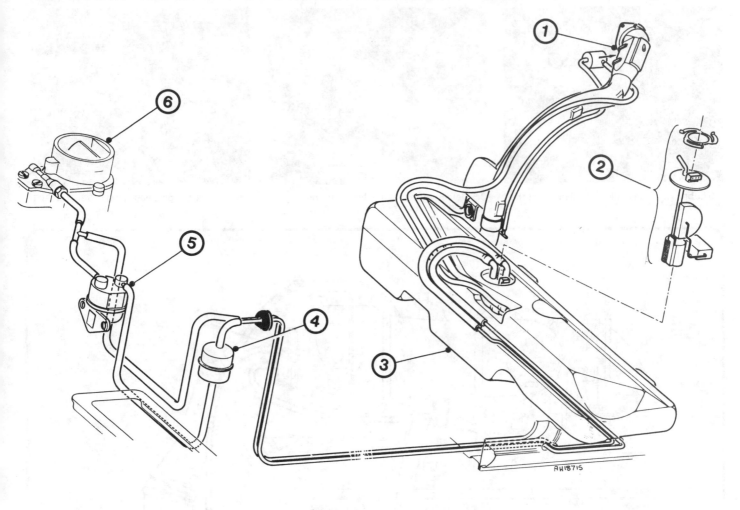

Fig. 3.2 Typical fuel system – GT models (Sec 1)

1	Fuel filler and tank ventilation pipes	2	Fuel level transmitter assembly	3	Fuel tank	5	Fuel pump
				4	Fuel filter	6	Carburettor

2 Routine maintenance

Carry out the following procedures at the intervals given in *Routine maintenance* at the beginning of the manual.

1   Check all fuel lines and hoses for damage and security, including those located on the underbody.
2   Check the accelerator pedal operation and the throttle cable for correct adjustment.
3   Renew the air filter element (Section 3).
4   Renew the in-line fuel filter (Section 6).
5   Periodically lubricate the choke and accelerator cables and the linkages (photo).
6   Inspect the exhaust system for security and leakage.

3 Air cleaner – description, removal and refitting

1   The air intake system incorporates a temperature controlled air induction system to improve the fuel mixture supplied to the engine under the varying seasonal operating temperatures.
2   On base models, a basic manual setting is made by turning the adjuster lever to the summer or winter position (marked on the intake body) as required.
3   On other models, an automatic air intake system is fitted where normal ambient air is automatically mixed as required. Warm air is drawn from the area above the exhaust manifold, and mixed with the

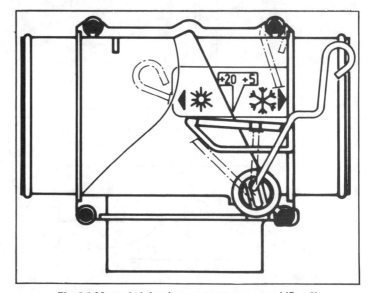

Fig. 3.3 Manual air intake temperature control (Sec 3)

ambient air in accordance with the setting of the mixer regulator valve. The valve is actuated by vacuum from the thermostat vacuum regulator unit housed in the air filter duct.

2.5 Lubricating the choke cable linkage at the carburettor

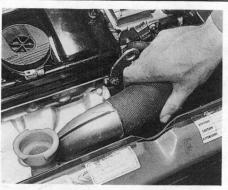

3.5 Detach the air intake duct from the exhaust manifold

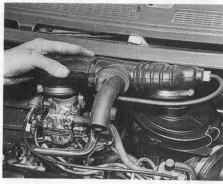

3.6 Remove the air cleaner top cover and duct unit

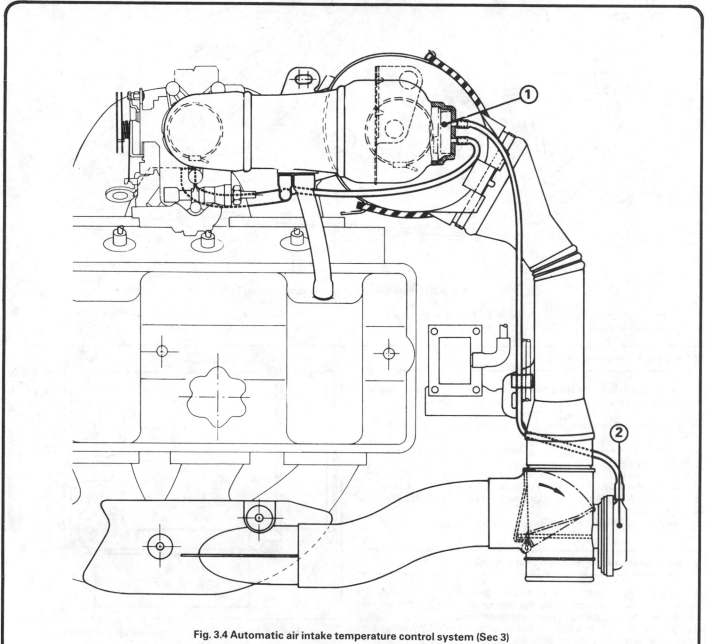

Fig. 3.4 Automatic air intake temperature control system (Sec 3)

1   *Vacuum regulator*   2   *Mixer regulator valve*

3.7 Remove the air cleaner element

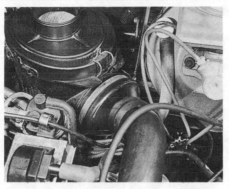

3.8A Air cleaner element refitting showing retaining clips

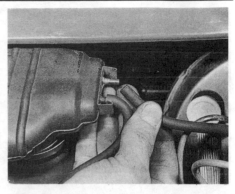

3.8B Reconnecting the air intake control vacuum hoses

5.2 Fuel pump unit

7.7 Fuel tank retaining nut, washer and insulator

8.3 Fuel level sender unit and hoses in the top of the fuel tank

4   The air cleaner element is removed and replaced together with its container as they are a combined unit.
5   To remove the cleaner unit, first detach the air intake ducting (photo).
6   Undo the two worm drive clips and lift the air cleaner upper cover and duct clear. Disconnect the air intake control vacuum hose from the cylinder head cover and the air cleaner container (photo).
7   Lift the combined element and body clear.
8   Refit in the reverse order of removal. Check that the peg of the cleaner unit engages with the bush in the cleaner support bracket. Also check that the crankcase breather hose is in good condition and clear of obstruction when refitting it (photos).

4   Fuel pump – testing

1   If the performance of the fuel pump is in doubt, first examine for fuel leaks and check that the fuel line connections are all sound.
2   Disconnect the fuel hose at the carburettor inlet connection and disconnect the ignition coil. Ensure that the tank contains fuel.
3   Direct the fuel feed hose into a suitable container and have an assistant operate the starter to crank the engine. A good spurt of fuel should be delivered on every second revolution of the engine. If not, check that the hose is not blocked. If that is clear the pump will need removal for examination or renewal.

5   Fuel pump – removal and refitting

1   Disconnect the fuel hoses from the pump. Plug the inlet hose.
2   Unscrew the pump mounting bolts and lift the pump away (photo).
3   Remove the gasket.
4   Refitting to the cylinder head is a reversal of removal, but fit a new gasket.

6   Fuel filter – removal and refitting

1   An in-line fuel filter is fitted, and is located in the engine compartment on the left-hand side between the vacuum servo unit and the wheel arch. The filter must be renewed at the specified intervals (see Routine maintenance at the start of the manual).
2   To remove the filter from the fuel line, first note its direction of fitting, then separate the filter from the hoses each side. Be prepared for fuel leakage as the hoses are detached, and plug the hose ends to prevent a continuous loss of fuel if the new filter is not being fitted immediately.
3   When fitting the new filter, ensure that it is correctly orientated as noted during removal. On completion, restart the engine and check for any signs of leakage from the filter hose connections.

7   Fuel tank – removal and refitting

1   Chock the front wheels, then raise and support the vehicle at the rear on axle stands at a height allowing a suitable working clearance underneath the car.
2   Drain or syphon any remaining fuel from the fuel tank. Empty the fuel into a suitable container for safe storage.
3   Unbolt the exhaust system at the manifold connection and remove it from the car as described in Section 18.
4   Unclip and remove the heat shield from the underside of the fuel tank.
5   Undo the retaining clips and detach the vent hose and filler hose from the connections under the right-hand rear wheel arch.
6   Unclip and detach the handbrake cables from the underside of the fuel tank.
7   Position a jack underneath the fuel tank, or ask an assistant, to support its weight, then undo the mounting nuts at the rear edge of the tank (photo).
8   Partially lower the fuel tank and detach the sender unit wires, the

9.3 Choke cable removal from carburettor
(A) Release outer cable at clamp
(B) Release inner cable from control stud

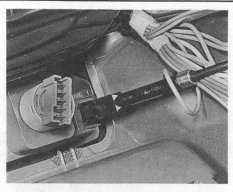

9.4A Choke cable attachment to facia panel viewed from inside

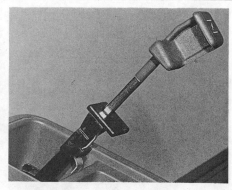

9.4B Choke cable withdrawal from facia

10.2 Accelerator cable removal from carburettor. (A) Disengage inner cable nipple, (B) Disengage outer cable from bracket

10.4A Accelerator cable to pedal clip (arrowed)

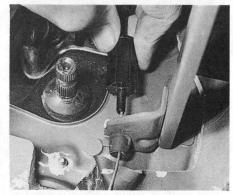

10.4B Accelerator outer cable removal from support at the pedal end

11.3 Accelerator pedal pivot and retaining nuts

13.3 Throttle stop screw on the Solex 32 PBISA 16 PSA carburettor (arrowed)

13.4 Mixture adjuster screw on the Solex 32 PBISA 16 PSA carburettor (arrowed)

supply and ventilation hose, then withdraw the fuel tank from the underside of the car.

9　If the tank is leaking or damaged it must be renewed, or if repairs are possible, entrust them to a Citroën dealer or a specialist.

10　If the tank contains sediment, wash it out with paraffin then rinse it with clean fuel.

11　Refit in the reverse order of removal. Ensure that all hose connections are securely made. If required, the sender unit wires can be reconnected by reaching down through the inspection hole in the floor located under the rear seat.

12　On completion refill the fuel tank with petrol and check for any signs of fuel leaks.

8　Fuel level sender unit – removal and refitting

1　Disconnect the battery earth lead.

2　Remove the rear seat squab and prise free the circular access cover from the floor.

3　Detach the wiring connector, the fuel line and ventilation hose from the top of the sender unit (photo).

4　Untwist the sender unit and remove it from the top of the fuel tank. Take care not to damage the unit as it is withdrawn.

5　Refitting is a reversal of the removal procedure. Renew the seal if the old one looks defective. Check for satisfactory operation on completion.

9　Choke cable – removal and refitting

1　Open and support the bonnet.

2　Disconnect the choke cable at the carburettor by loosening off the outer cable clamp bolt.

3　Disengage the cable from the support clamp, then from the stud on the choke operating lever (photo).

4　Working inside the car, pull out the choke control knob, then grip the control shaft with a pair of pliers and twist the control through 90° to

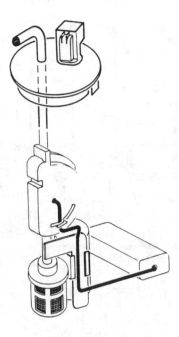

Fig. 3.5 Fuel level transmitter (Sec 8)

disengage it from the facia panel. Take care not to damage the facia. Twisting the control shaft to release it can prove difficult, and in this instance, push on the unit as it is twisted to assist in releasing the retaining clips which bear against the inside face of the facia. Once twisted free the cable can be withdrawn and the choke-on warning light wire detached (photos).

5   Refit in the reverse order of removal. When connecting the choke cable to the carburettor, ensure that a small amount of slack is present in the cable when the choke is fully released. Operate the choke to ensure satisfactory operation.

10   Accelerator cable – removal and refitting

1   Loosen the worm drive clips and remove the air intake duct from the carburettor and air cleaner unit.
2   Disconnect the cable at the carburettor by opening the throttle quadrant and detaching the inner cable nipple from it (photo).
3   Note the adjustment position of the outer cable in the support bracket, release the spring clip and withdraw the cable.
4   Remove the parcel shelf under the facia on the drivers side, then disconnect the cable from the pedal by releasing the clip (photos).
5   Pass the cable through the bulkhead and withdraw it from the engine compartment.
6   Refit in the reverse order of removal. Adjust the cable at the support bracket on the carburettor to the position noted during removal. This should remove all but a small amount of play. Fully depress the throttle pedal and check that the accelerator fully opens.
7   Refit the air cleaner intake duct.

11   Accelerator pedal – removal and refitting

1   Remove the parcel shelf from under the facia on the drivers side.
2   Disconnect the accelerator cable from the throttle pedal (see Section 10).
3   Unscrew and remove the pedal pivot retaining nuts and remove the pedal (photo).
4   Refit in the reverse order of removal. Check the action of the accelerator for satisfactory operation on completion.

12   Carburettor – description

1   A Solex or Weber carburettor is fitted, the type varies according to the model (see Specifications).
2   In all instances, the carburettor is a single choke, downdraught type except for that fitted to the K2A engine (GT models), which has a twin choke carburettor.
3   All models are fitted with a manually operated cold start choke.

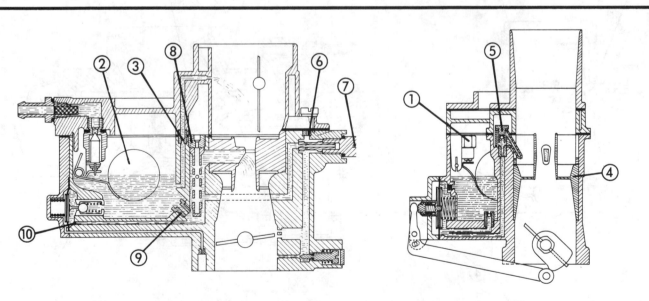

Fig. 3.6 Sectional views of the Weber 32 IBSH 16/100 carburettor fitted to the AX 10 (Sec 12)

1 Needle valve	4 Venturi	7 Idle jet	9 Main jet
2 Float	5 Accelerator pump injector	8 Emulsion tube and air	10 Enrichener
3 Petrol econostat	6 Idle ventilation	compensator jet	

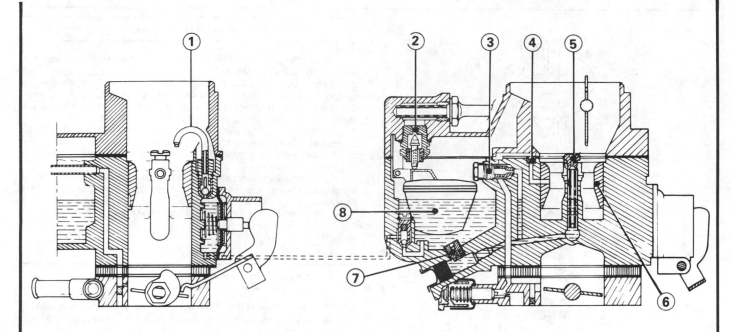

Fig. 3.7 Sectional view of the Solex 32 PBISA 16 REP carburettor fitted to the AX 10 (Sec 12)

1 Accelerator pump injector	4 Idle ventilation	6 Venturi	8 Float
2 Needle valve	5 Air compressor jet/emulsion	7 Main jet	
3 Idle jet	tube		

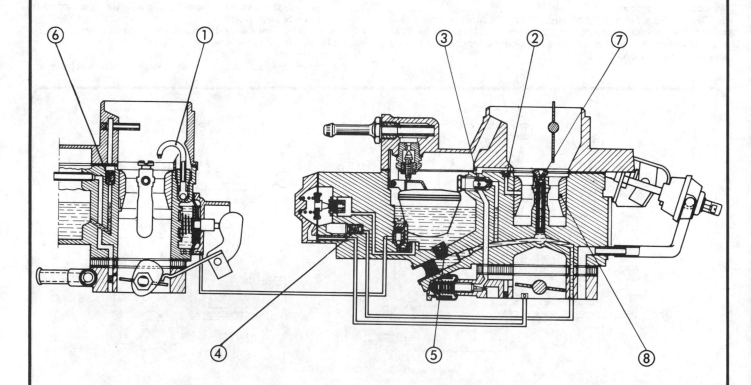

Fig. 3.8 Sectional view of the Solex 32 PBISA 16 PSA carburettor fitted to the AX 11 (Sec 12)

1 Accelerator pump injector	3 Idle jet	5 Main jet	7 Air compensator jet
2 Idle ventilator	4 Enrichener	6 Fuel econostat	8 Venturi

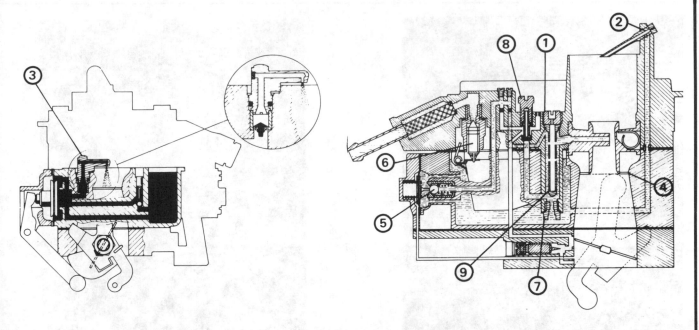

Fig. 3.9 Sectional view of the Weber 34 TLP 3/100 carburettor fitted to the AX 14 (Sec 12)

1 Air compensator jet
2 Fuel econostat
3 Accelerator pump injector

4 Venturi
5 Enrichener

6 Needle valve
7 Main jet

8 Idle jet
9 Emulsion tube

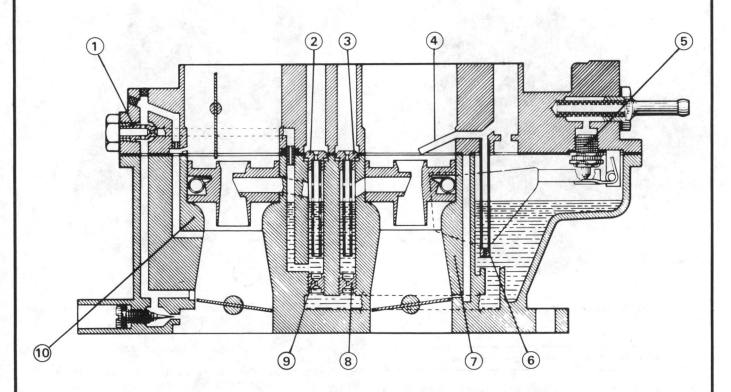

Fig. 3.10 Sectional view of the Solex 32-34 Z2 PSA carburettor fitted to the AX GT (Sec 12)

1 Idle jet
2 Air compensator jet/emulsion tube (primary)

3 Air compensator jet/emulsion tube (secondary)
4 Fuel (secondary)

5 Needle valve
6 Fuel (secondary)
7 Venturi (secondary)

8 Main jet (secondary)
9 Main jet (primary)
10 Venturi (primary)

Fig. 3.11 Throttle stop screw (A) Weber 32 IBSH 16/100 carburettor (Sec 13)

Fig. 3.12 Mixture adjuster screw (B) Weber 32 IBSH 16/100 carburettor (Sec 13)

Fig. 3.13 Throttle stop screw (A) Solex 32 PBISA 16 carburettor (Sec 13)

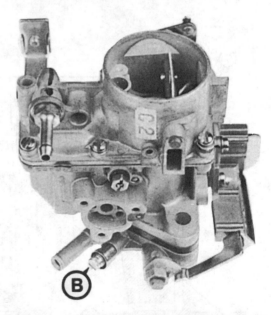

Fig. 3.14 Mixture adjuster screw (B) Solex 32 PBISA 16 carburettor (Sec 13)

13   Carburettor – idle speed and mixture adjustment

1   Before making any checks or adjustments to any of the carburettor types, the engine must have been run up to its normal operating temperature and the choke fully released. The air cleaner must be in position and the element must be clean. Finally, the ignition system must be in good order with the ignition timing correct.

2   Connect a tachometer to the engine and where necessary remove the tamperproof cap from the mixture adjustment screw.

Without an exhaust gas analyser

3   Turn the throttle stop screw to adjust the engine speed to 650 rpm.

4   Turn the mixture adjustment screw to obtain the highest idling speed.

5   Repeat the procedure given in paragraphs 3 and 4 until the engine speed is 750 rpm (ie after adjusting the mixture screw).

6   Screw in the mixture adjustment screw slightly until the engine speed starts to decrease.

With an exhaust gas analyser

7   Turn the throttle stop screw to adjust the engine speed to 750 rpm.

8   Turn the mixture adjustment screw to obtain the specified CO reading.

9   Repeat the procedure in paragraphs 7 and 8 until the idle speed is as shown in the Specifications.

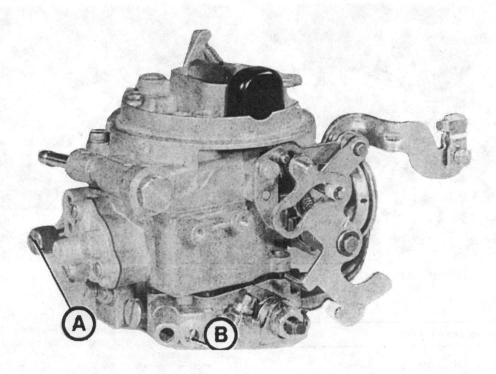

Fig. 3.15 Throttle stop screw (A) and mixture adjuster screw (B) Weber 34 TLP 3/100 carburettor (Sec 13)

Fig. 3.16 Throttle stop screw (A) Solex 32-34 Z2 PSA carburettor (Sec 13)

Fig. 3.17 Mixture adjuster screw (B) Solex 32-34 Z2 PSA carburettor (Sec 13)

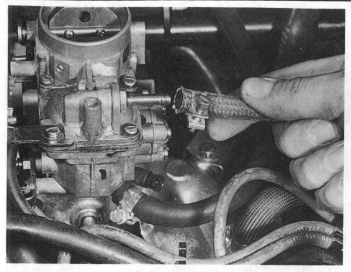

14.2 Detaching the fuel hose from the carburettor

14.7 Lifting the carburettor from the inlet manifold

14   Carburettor – removal and refitting

1   Remove the air cleaner unit as described in Section 3.
2   Detach the fuel supply hose from the carburettor and plug it to prevent fuel leakage whilst it is disconnected (photo).
3   Where applicable, partially drain the cooling system (Chapter 2) and detach the coolant hoses from the carburettor.
4   Detach the accelerator cable from the carburettor as described in Section 10.

5   Detach the choke cable from the carburettor (Section 9).
6   Detach the vacuum hose(s) from the carburettor and intermediate piece as necessary.
7   Unscrew the carburettor retaining nuts and carefully lift the carburettor clear of the manifold (photo). Try not to damage the gasket in case a replacement is not readily available, in which case the old one may possibly suffice.
8   Refit in the reverse order of removal. Fit a new gasket whenever possible. Refer to Sections 9 and 10 when refitting the choke and accelerator cables. Top up the cooling system as described in Chapter 2.

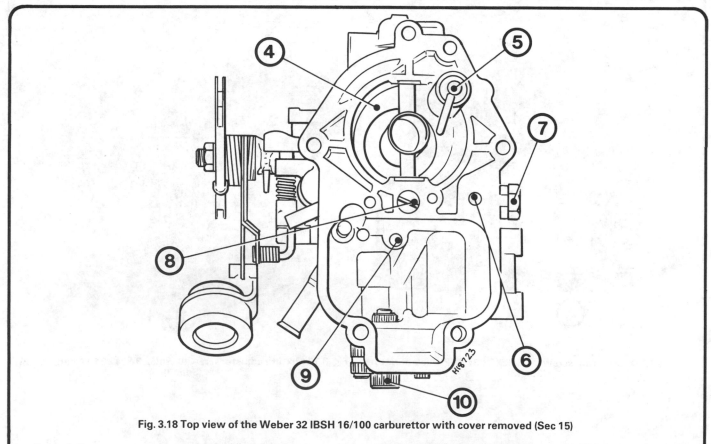

Fig. 3.18 Top view of the Weber 32 IBSH 16/100 carburettor with cover removed (Sec 15)

4 Venturi	6 Idle ventilation	8 Emulsion tube/compensator	9 Main jet
5 Accelerator pump injector	7 Idle jet	jet	10 Enrichener

Fig. 3.19 Top view of the Solex 32 PBISA 16 REP carburettor with cover removed (Sec 15)

1 Accelerator pump injector	5 Emulsion tube/compensator	6 Venturi	7 Main jet
3 Idle jet	jet		

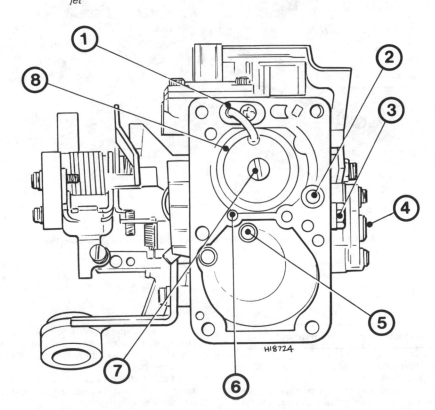

Fig. 3.20 Top view of the Solex 32 PBISA 16 PSA carburettor with cover removed (Sec 15)

1 Accelerator pump injector	3 Idle jet	5 Main jet	7 Air compensator jet
2 Idle ventilator	4 Enrichener	6 Fuel econostat	8 Venturi

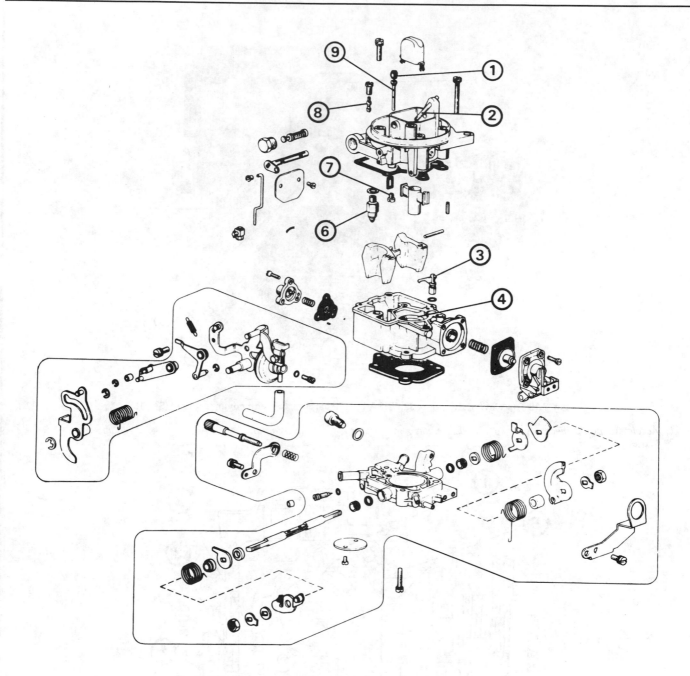

Fig. 3.21 Exploded view of the Weber 34 TLP 3/100 carburettor (Sec 15)

1 Air compensator jet	3 Accelerator pump injector	6 Needle valve	8 idle jet
2 Fuel econostat	4 Venturi	7 Main jet	9 Emulsion tube

15 Carburettor – dismantling, reassembly and adjustment

1   The carburettor should not normally need to be dismantled except for cleaning and checking the float level.

2   If the carburettor is to be dismantled, remember that it is a relatively delicate instrument and therefore requires careful handling. Use the correct tools for the job and do not interchange jets or clean them out with wire or any similar item which could damage them and interfere with their calibration.

3   Before dismantling the carburettor, or any part of it, first clean the outside and prepare a clean work area. When taking anything mechanical apart, and this applies particularly to such components as carburet-

tors, it is always sound policy to make sure that the individual parts are put back exactly where they came from, and even the same way round if it is possible to do otherwise, even though they may appear to be interchangeable.

4   To help in this procedure, mark or label items, put small parts in boxes or tins so that they don't get mixed up, and lay parts out in order of assembly on clean paper.

5   Remove the screws and lift off the float chamber cover.

6   Unscrew the air correction jet, followed by the main jet and idling fuel jet.

7   Unscrew the accelerator pump valve and remove the pump injector.

8   Remove the enrichener valve.

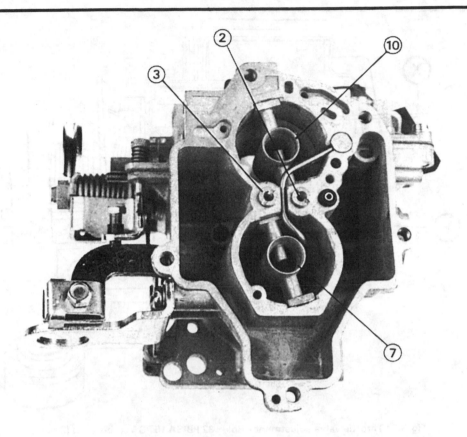

Fig. 3.22 Top view of the Solex 32-34 PSA carburettor with cover removed (Sec 15)

2   Air compensator
jet/emulsion tube (primary)

3   Air compensator
jet/emulsion tube (Secondary)

7   Venturi (Secondary)

10   Venturi (primary)

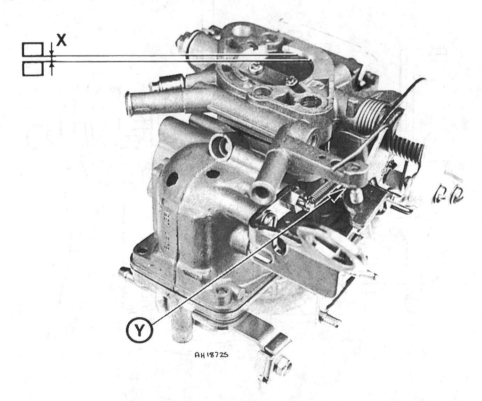

AH 18725

Fig. 3.23 Throttle valve adjustment – Solex 32 PBISA 16 REP carburettor (Sec 15)

Adjust screw Y until X = 0.8 mm (0.03 in)

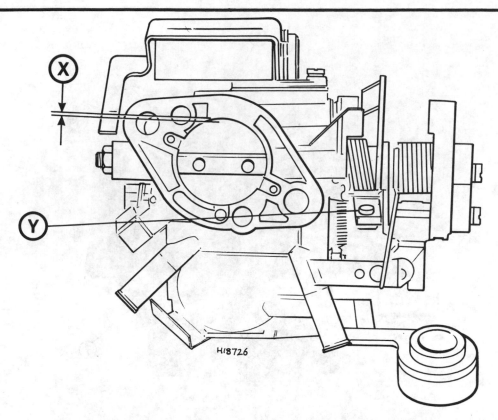

H18726

Fig. 3.24 Throttle valve adjustment – Solex 32 PBISA 16 PSA carburettor (Sec 15)

Adjust screw Y until X = 0.6 mm (0.02 in)

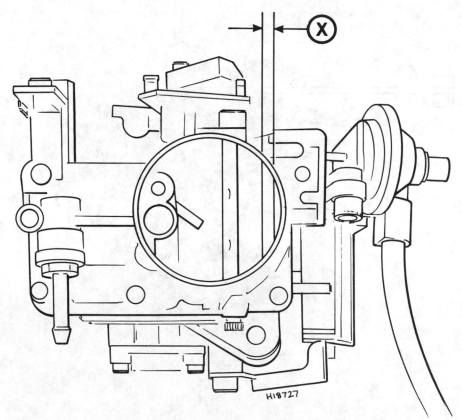

H18727

Fig. 3.25 Choke valve check (under vacuum) – Solex 32 PBISA 16 PSA carburettor (Sec 15)

X = 2.8 mm (0.11 in)   Vacuum = 350 mbar

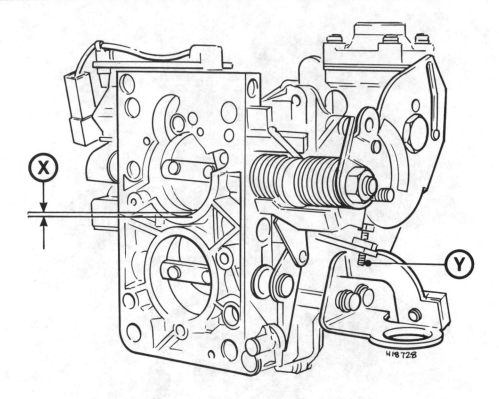

Fig. 3.26 Throttle valve adjustment – Solex 32-34 Z2 PSA carburettor (Sec 15)

Adjust screw Y until X = 0.8 mm (0.03 in)

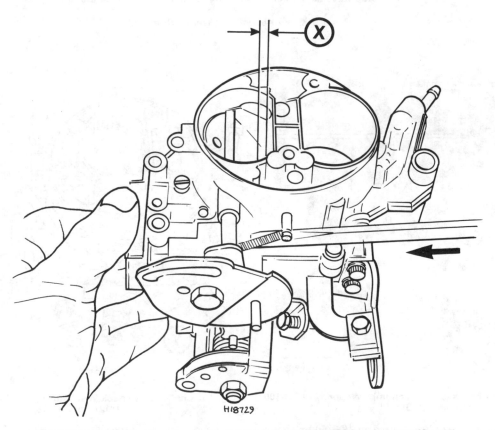

Fig. 3.27 Choke valve check (under vacuum) – Solex 32-34 Z2 PSA carburettor (Sec 15)

X = 3.0 mm (0.12 in)

Fig. 3.28 Throttle valve adjustment – Weber 34 TLP 3/100 carburettor (Sec 15)

Adjust screw Y until X = 0.8 mm (0.03 in)

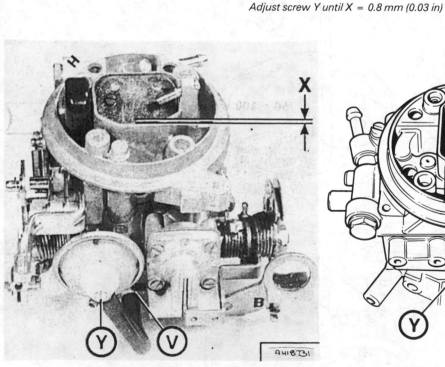

Fig. 3.29 Choke valve check (under vacuum) – Weber 34 TLP 3/100 carburettor (Sec 15)

Adjust Y   X = 4.75 mm (0.19 in)   Vacuum (V) = 500 mbar

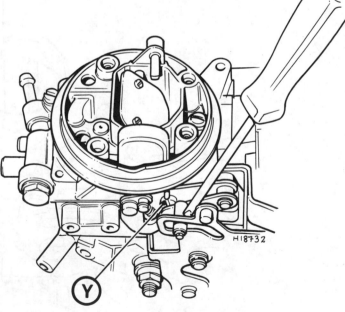

Fig. 3.30 Choke valve check (mechanical) – Weber 34 TLP 3/100 carburettor (Sec 15)

Adjustment by screw Y

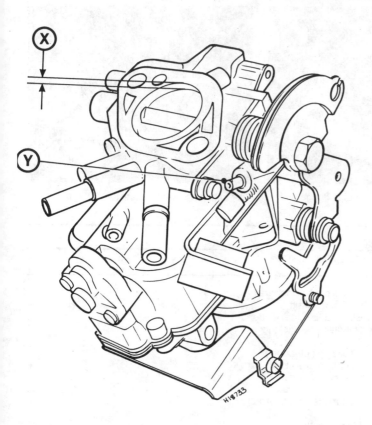

16.5 Inlet manifold and retaining nuts to the cylinder head (arrowed)

5   Unscrew the retaining nuts and remove the inlet manifold and gasket (photo).
6   Before refitting the manifold, clean off all traces of the old gasket from the manifold, carburettor and manifold flange face on the cylinder head. Always use new gaskets when reassembling.
7   Refit in the reverse order of removal. Refit and connect up the carburettor and its associate items as described in previous Sections. Tighten the retaining nuts to the specified torque wrench setting.

Fig. 3.31 Throttle valve adjustment – Weber 32 IBSH 16/100 carburettor (Sec 15)

Adjust screw Y until X = 0.8 mm (0.03 in)

9   Unscrew the needle valve.
10   Clean the float chamber and removed components with fuel and blow through the internal channels using an air line if possible.
11   Obtain a repair kit of gaskets then reassemble the carburettor in reverse order.
12   With the exception of the Solex 32 PBISA carburettor, the float level can be checked by measuring the distance between the base of the float, (when closing the needle valve under its own weight) and the underside of the cover mating flange (with the gasket fitted). It should be as shown in the specifications, if not bend the adjuster tang of the float pivot to suit. A special gauge is required to check the float adjustment on the Solex 32 PBISA carburettor, and it must therefore be checked by a Citroën dealer.
13   When the carburettor is reassembled, the throttle valve and choke valve settings should be checked. To do this, refer to the appropriate figure(s) as necessary (Figs. 3.23 to 3.31). Note that a vacuum gauge is required to check the choke opening in some instances.

16   Inlet manifold – removal and refitting

1   Remove the air cleaner unit as described in Section 3.
2   Disconnect the spark plug leads and unbolt the HT lead support bracket from the manifold.
3   Remove the carburettor as described in Section 14.
4   Disconnect the vacuum/breather hoses from the manifold.

17   Exhaust manifold – removal and refitting

1   Disconnect the hot air duct from the heat shield on top of the manifold.
2   Unbolt and remove the heat shield from the manifold.
3   Undo the retaining nuts and detach the exhaust downpipe from the manifold.
4   Undo the manifold retaining nuts and withdraw the manifold from the cylinder head. Remove the manifold gasket and clean the mating surfaces of the cylinder head and manifold before refitting begins. The gaskets must be renewed.
5   Refit in the reverse order of removal. Tighten the retaining nuts and bolts to their specified torque wrench settings.

18   Exhaust system – removal and refitting

1   The exhaust pipe is a single or two section system from the manifold to the rear of the vehicle. The complete exhaust system is easily removed by undoing the retaining nuts to the manifold, then unhooking the pipe from the suspension rings underneath the car towards the rear.
2   If the rubber suspension rings are in poor condition, they must be renewed (photo).
3   Refit the exhaust system in the reverse order of removal. Locate a new gasket between the manifold and downpipe flanges (photo).
4   Ensure that the system is clear of adjacent components and that the joint flanges are securely clamped (photo).

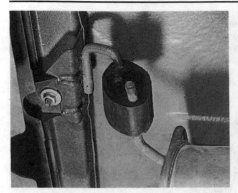

18.2 Exhaust system suspension ring

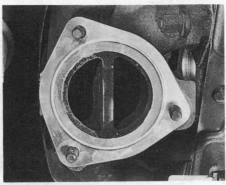

18.3 Exhaust manifold downpipe flange with new gasket fitted

18.4 Exhaust system flange joint clamp

19 Fault diagnosis – fuel and exhaust system

Symptom	Reason(s)
Difficult starting from cold	Choke control inoperative Fuel pump fault Blocked fuel line or filter Needle valve sticking
Difficult starting when hot	Choked air cleaner Choke control sticking Fuel pump faulty
Excessive fuel consumption	Mixture setting incorrect
Uneven idling	Mixture setting incorrect Air leak in intake system
Noisy or back-firing exhaust	Leak in exhaust system Ignition timing incorrect

Chapter 4 Ignition system

Contents

Specifications

System type .... Electronic (breakerless)

Distributor
Make .... Bosch or Ducellier
Rotor rotation .... Anti-clockwise
Firing order .... 1 – 3 – 4 – 2 (No 1 at clutch end)

Ignition timing (vacuum hose detached)
All models (at 750 rpm) .... 8° ± 2°

Coil
Primary resistance .... 0.8 ohms
Secondary resistance .... 6500 ohms

Spark plugs
Type:
  All models except GT .... Champion C9YCX or Eyquem FC52 LS
  GT .... Champion C7YCX or Eyquem FC62 LS
Spark plug electrode gap .... 0.6 to 0.7 mm (0.024 to 0.028 in)

Torque wrench setting

	Nm	lbf ft
Spark plugs	20 to 25	15 to 18

1 General description

The ignition system is of electronic breakerless type incorporating a control module (located near the ignition coil), pulse generator (located in the distributor), ignition coil and distributor.

In order that the engine may run correctly it is necessary for an electrical spark to ignite the fuel/air mixture in the combustion chamber at exactly the right moment in relation to engine speed and load.

Basically the ignition system functions as follows. Low tension voltage from the battery is fed to the ignition coil, where it is converted into high tension voltage. The high tension voltage is powerful enough to jump the spark plug gap in the cylinder many times a second under high compression pressure, providing that the ignition system is in good working order.

The ignition system consists of two individual circuits known as the low tension (LT) circuit and high tension (HT) circuit.

The low tension circuit (sometimes known as the primary circuit) comprises the ignition switch, primary ignition coil windings, and control module. The high tension circuit (sometimes known as the secondary circuit) comprises the secondary ignition coil windings, distributor cap, rotor arm, spark plugs and HT leads.

The primary circuit is initially switched on by the control module and a magnetic field is formed within the ignition coil. At the precise point of ignition the pulse generator causes the control module to switch off the primary circuit, and high tension voltage is then induced in the secondary circuit and fed to the spark plug via the distributor cap and rotor arm.

The ignition is advanced and retarded automatically by centrifugal weights and a vacuum capsule to ensure that the spark occurs at the correct instant in relation to engine speed and load.

Note: *When working on the ignition system remember that the high tension voltage can be considerably higher than on a conventional system and in certain circumstances could prove fatal.*

2 Routine maintenance

Carry out the following procedures at the intervals given in *Routine maintenance* at the beginning of the manual.

1 Remove the spark plugs and renew them, with reference to Section 9. Do not forget to set the electrode gaps on the new plugs.

2 The ignition timing can be checked as described in Section 7 but this

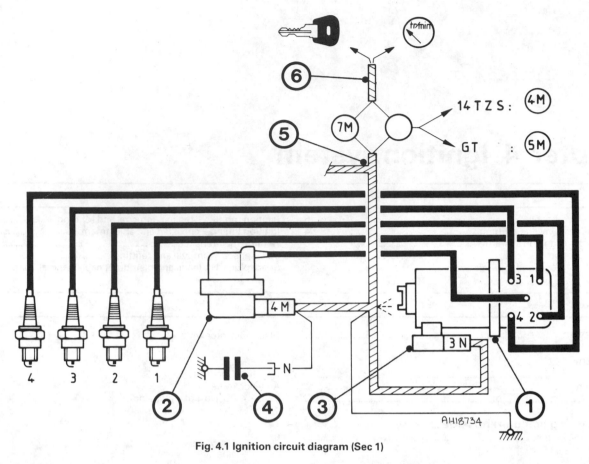

Fig. 4.1 Ignition circuit diagram (Sec 1)

1 Distributor	3 Electronic module	5 Engine
2 Ignition coil	4 Ignition capacitor	6 Instrument panel

is not normally necessary unless a malfunction in the ignition system is suspected.

3   Periodically wipe clean the HT leads and the distributor cap.

3 Ignition coil – removal and refitting

1   Remove the air cleaner intake ducting as described in Chapter 3 (photo).

2   Check that the ignition is switched off, then detach the HT lead from the coil.

3   Disconnect the LT wiring connector from the coil, then detach the wiring connector to the module unit (photo). The module unit is mounted on the side of the coil bracket and is removed with it.

4   Undo the retaining screws and remove the coil and its mounting

bracket. To detach the coil from the bracket, undo the four retaining screws and nuts (photo).

5   Refit in the reverse order of removal.

4 Distributor – removal and refitting

1   Remove the ignition coil and its mounting bracket as described in the previous Section.

2   If removing the distributor complete with its cap and leads, first identify the HT leads for position, then detach them from the plugs (pulling on the lead connectors – not the leads). Detach the leads from the support plate on the cylinder head.

3   If removing the distributor without its cap, undo the cap retaining

3.1 View showing ignition coil (1) and the air cleaner intake duct (2)

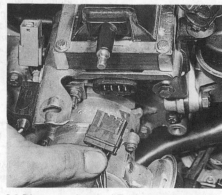

3.3 Disconnecting the LT wire connector from the coil

3.4 Ignition coil and mounting bracket

screws, detach the cap from the distributor and position it out of the way with the HT leads (photos).

4   Detach the distributor LT wiring and the vacuum hose from the diaphragm unit.

5   Mark the distributor mounting flange in relation to the distributor/fuel pump housing to provide an index mark for timing position when refitting the distributor.

6   Unscrew the mounting nuts, remove the small plates, and withdraw the distributor.

7   Check the condition of the O-ring on the mounting flange, and renew it if necessary.

8   Refitting is a reversal of removal, but turn the rotor arm as required to align the lugs with the offset slot in the camshaft. If the old distributor is being refitted, align the previously-made marks before tightening the mounting nuts. If fitting a new distributor, initially set the distributor in the middle of the slotted holes, or follow the procedure given in Section 7, then finally adjust the ignition timing.

5   Distributor – overhaul

1   Clean the exterior of the distributor.

2   Pull off the rotor arm and remove the plastic cover, where fitted (photos).

Ducellier

3   Extract the screws and remove the wiring plug.

4   Extract the three body screws. The lugs are offset so the body sections cannot be misaligned when reassembled. Separate the body sections.

5   Invert the body upper section, pull out the plastic ring and lift out the magnetic coil.

6   From the body upper section, extract the circlip and the thrustwasher.

7   Extract the vacuum unit screw and then lift out the baseplate at the same time unhooking the vacuum link (noting its engagement hole in the plate).

8   Extract the circlip and shim from the body lower section.

9   Lift out the counterweight assembly.

10   The drive dog is secured to the shaft by a pin.

11   Reassembly is a reversal of dismantling. Always renew the O-ring seal (photo).

Bosch

12   The procedure is similar to that for the Ducellier distributor but the body is in one piece. Refer to Fig. 4.3.

6   Ignition module – testing, removal and refitting

1   The ignition module is attached to the side of the coil mounting bracket. If its performance is suspect, it can be tested using a voltmeter or a 12 volt test lamp. Detach the wiring from the module and connect up a voltmeter (or test lamp) to the No 2 and 3 terminals of the module. Switch on the ignition and check that a 12 volt current passes between the terminals, then switch off the ignition. If defective, the module must be renewed.

2   Disconnect the battery earth lead.

3   Remove the air cleaner duct as described in Chapter 3.

4   Detach the wiring from the module, undo its retaining screws and remove the module.

5   Refit in the reverse order of removal. Ensure that all connections are clean and correctly made.

7   Ignition timing – checking and adjustment

Note: *The ignition timing may be checked and adjusted using the engine diagnosis socket, but the special Citroën instrument necessary will not normally be available to the home mechanic.*

1   To set the ignition timing statically so that the engine can be started, first remove No 1 spark plug (nearest clutch) and turn the engine in the

4.3A Ignition distributor showing cap and retaining screws

4.3B Ignition distributor with cap removed

5.2A Ducellier distributor showing rotor arm (1) diaphragm and retaining screw (2) and upper/lower body screws (3)

5.2B Ducellier distributor showing wiring plug location

5.11 O-ring location (arrowed) and distributor drive dog

7.2 Ignition timing plate (1) flywheel timing mark opposite O (TDC) (2) and the TDC sensor (3)

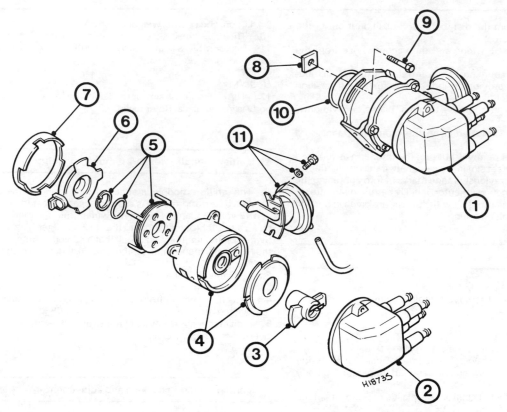

Fig. 4.2 Exploded view of the Ducellier distributor (Sec 5)

1	Distributor unit	4	Upper body and dust cap	7	Plastic ring	10	O-ring
2	Distributor cap	5	Base plate	8	Washer	11	Vacuum unit
3	Rotor arm	6	Magnetic coil	9	Screw		

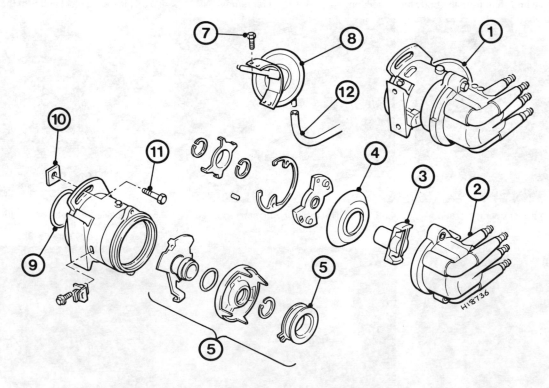

Fig. 4.3 Exploded view of the Bosch distributor (Sec 5)

1	Distributor unit	4	Seal disc	7	Screw	10	Washer
2	Cap	5	Pick up coil assembly	8	Vacuum unit	11	Screw
3	Rotor	6	Field coil	9	O-ring	12	Vacuum hose

Measuring plug gap. A feeler gauge of the correct size (see ignition system specifications) should have a slight 'drag' when slid between the electrodes. Adjust gap if necessary

Adjusting plug gap. The plug gap is adjusted by bending the earth electrode inwards, or outwards, as necessary until the correct clearance is obtained. Note the use of the correct tool

Normal. Grey-brown deposits, lightly coated core nose. Gap increasing by around 0.001 in (0.025 mm) per 1000 miles (1600 km). Plugs ideally suited to engine, and engine in good condition

Carbon fouling. Dry, black, sooty deposits. Will cause weak spark and eventually misfire. Fault: over-rich fuel mixture. Check: carburettor mixture settings, float level and jet sizes; choke operation and cleanliness of air filter. Plugs can be re-used after cleaning

Oil fouling. Wet, oily deposits. Will cause weak spark and eventually misfire. Fault: worn bores/piston rings or valve guides; sometimes occurs (temporarily) during running-in period. Plugs can be re-used after thorough cleaning

Overheating. Electrodes have glazed appearance, core nose very white – few deposits. Fault: plug overheating. Check: plug value, ignition timing, fuel octane rating (too low) and fuel mixture (too weak). Discard plugs and cure fault immediately

Electrode damage. Electrodes burned away; core nose has burned, glazed appearance. Fault: pre-ignition. Check: as for 'Overheating' but may be more severe. Discard plugs and remedy fault before piston or valve damage occurs

Split core nose (may appear initially as a crack). Damage is self-evident, but cracks will only show after cleaning. Fault: pre-ignition or wrong gap-setting technique. Check: ignition timing, cooling system, fuel octane rating (too low) and fuel mixture (too weak). Discard plugs, rectify fault immediately

normal rotational direction until pressure is felt – indicating that the piston is commencing the compression stroke. The pressure can be felt using a suitable wooden rod or piece of cork placed over the spark plug hole.

2　While looking into the timing aperture in the clutch housing/gearbox casing, continue turning the crankshaft until the single mark on the flywheel is opposite the 'O' mark on the timing plate (photo).

3　Check that the distributor rotor arm is facing the No 1 HT lead segment position in the distributor cap. To do this, remove the cap and mark the outside in line with the segment, then put it back on the distributor noting which way the rotor arm is facing.

4　If necessary, loosen the mounting nuts and turn the distributor body to bring the segment and rotor arm in line, then tighten the nuts. Refit No 1 spark plug.

5　Run the engine to normal operating temperature then stop it and connect a tachometer to it.

6　Disconnect and plug the vacuum pipe at the distributor vacuum advance unit.

7　Disconnect and remove the air cleaner inlet duct then connect a stroboscopic timing light to the engine using the HT pick-up lead connected to No 1 spark plug HT lead.

8　Set the distributor to time the ignition at 8° BTDC at the engine idle speed (750 rpm).

9　The operation of the centrifugal advance weights in the distributor can be checked by increasing the engine speed with the timing light pointing in the timing aperture and observing that the mark on the flywheel advances from its initial position.

10　To check the vacuum advance unit, run the engine at a fast idle speed and reconnect the vacuum pipe. The flywheel mark should again advance.

11　Stop the engine, disconnect the tachometer and timing light then reconnect the vacuum pipe and air cleaner inlet duct.

8　TDC sensor – removal and refitting

1　The TDC sensor (photo) is for use with the diagnostic socket located on the clutch housing. As a special instrument and adaptor are required it will normally be used only by a Citroën garage.

2　To remove the sensor, unscrew the mounting or clamp screw and withdraw the sensor unit.

3　The sensor forms part of the diagnostic socket assembly so, if it is to be completely removed, the socket must be unclipped from its bracket and the remaining wiring and earth leads disconnected.

4　Refitting is a reversal of removal, but the adjustment procedure for new and used sensors differs. New sensors have three extensions on the inner face and the unit should be inserted through the clamp until the extensions just touch the flywheel. The clamp screw is then tightened and clearance is provided as the flywheel rotates and wears the ends of the extensions. This method should not be used when refitting a used sensor. In this case, cut off the extensions completely then temporarily insert the sensor until it touches the flywheel, remove it and reposition it in the clamp 1.0 mm (0.04 in) further out.

9　Spark plugs, HT leads and distributor cap – general

1　The correct functioning of the spark plugs is vital for the correct running and efficiency of the engine, and it is therefore important to keep them clean and correctly gapped.

2　To remove the plugs, first open the bonnet and pull the HT leads from them. Grip the rubber end fitting, not the lead otherwise the lead connection may be fractured. Also remove the extensions (photo).

3　The spark plugs are deeply recessed in the cylinder head and it is recommended that dirt is removed from the recesses using a vacuum cleaner or compressed air, before removing the plugs, to prevent dirt dropping into the cylinders.

4　Unscrew the plugs using a suitable box spanner or socket.

5　Examination of the spark plugs will give a good indication of the condition of the engine. If the insulator nose of the spark plug is clean, and white, with no deposits, this is indicative of a weak mixture, or too hot a plug (a hot plug transfers heat away from the electrode slowly, a cold plug transfers heat away quickly). The plugs fitted as standard are specified at the beginning of this Chapter.

6　If the top and insulator nose are covered with hard black- looking deposits, then this is indicative that the mixture is too rich. Should the plug be black and oily, then it is likely that the engine is fairly worn, as well as the mixture being too rich.

7　If the insulator nose is covered with light tan to greyish brown deposits, then the mixture is correct and it is likely that the engine is in good condition.

8　If there are any traces of long brown tapering stains on the outside of the white portion of the plug, then the plug will have to be renewed, as this shows that there is a faulty joint between the plug body and the insulator, and compression is being allowed to leak away.

9　Before cleaning a spark plug, wash it in petrol to remove oily deposits.

10　Although a wire brush can be used to clean the electrode end of the spark plug this method can cause metal conductance paths across the nose of the insulator. It is therefore to be preferred that an abrasive powder cleaning machine is used. Such machines are available quite cheaply from motor accessory stores or you may prefer to take the plugs to your dealer who will not only be able to clean them, but also to check the sparking efficiency of each plug under compression.

11　The spark plug gap is of considerable importance as, if it is too large or too small, the size of the spark and its efficiency will be seriously impaired. For the best results the spark plug gap should be set in accordance with the Specifications at the beginning of this Chapter.

12　To set it, measure the gap with a feeler gauge, and then bend open, or close, the outer plug electrode until the correct gap is achieved. The centre electrode should never be bent, as this may crack the insulation and cause plug failure, if nothing worse.

13　Special spark plug electrode gap adjusting tools are available from most motor accessory shops.

14　Before refitting the spark plugs check that the threaded connector sleeves are tight and that the plug exterior surfaces and threads are clean.

15　Screw in the spark plugs by hand where possible, then tighten them to the specified torque. Take extra care to enter the plug threads correctly as the cylinder head is of aluminium.

16　Refit the extensions followed by the HT leads, making sure that

8.1 TDC sensor location

9.2 Removing a spark plug lead

9.18 Clean and inspect the inside of the distributor cap

the latter are in their correct order of 1-3-4-2 (No 1 nearest the clutch end of engine) in relation to the anti- clockwise direction of the rotor arm.

17   The HT leads and their connections should always be kept clean and dry and arranged neatly in the special holder. If any lead shows signs of cracking or chafing of the insulation it should be renewed.

18   Check the distributor cap whenever it is removed. If there are any very thin black lines running between the electrodes this indicates tracking and a new cap should be fitted (photo).Check the rotor arm in a similar way. Where applicable check that the spring-tensioned carbon brush in the centre of the cap is free to move and is not worn excessively.

10   Fault diagnosis – ignition system

1   If the engine fails to start and the car was running normally when it was last used, first check that there is fuel in the fuel tank. If the engine turns over normally on the starter motor and the battery is evidently well charged first check the HT (high tension) circuit.

2   A common reason for bad starting is wet or damp spark plug leads and distributor cap. Check both items and wipe dry, if necessary.

3   If the engine still fails to start, disconnect an HT lead from any spark plug and, using a nail inserted into the end fitting, hold the lead approximately 5.0 mm (0.2 in) away from the cylinder head with well-insulated pliers. While an assistant spins the engine on the starter motor, check that a regular blue spark occurs. If so the spark plugs are probably the cause of the engine's not starting and they should therefore be cleaned and regapped.

4   If no spark occurs, disconnect the main feed HT lead from the distributor cap and check for a spark as in paragraph 3. If sparks now occur, check the distributor cap, rotor arm, and HT leads, as described in Section 9 and renew them as necessary.

5   Check the security of the wiring to the ignition coil, distributor and electronic module.

6   Using an ohmmeter, check the resistance of the distributor pulse generator coil and the ignition coil windings. Renew them if the readings are not as given in the Specifications.

7   Using a voltmeter, check that there is battery voltage at the ignition coil low tension positive terminal with the ignition switched on. Connect the voltmeter across the coil LT terminals and check that the reading is zero. If it is not zero the module may be defective or the coil-to-module wire earthed.

Chapter 5 Clutch

Contents

Specifications

General

Type	Diaphragm spring, single dry plate, cable operated
Driven plate (disc) diameter:	
AX 10 and AX 11 models	160 mm (6.3 in)
AX 14 and GT models..	180 mm (7.1 in)
Clutch pedal stroke (minimum)	130 mm (5.1 in)
Pedal to bulkhead clearance (maximum)...........................	71 mm (2.8 in)
Release bearing..	Sealed ball bearing

Torque wrench settings

	Nm	lbf ft
Clutch pressure plate bolts	15	11
Engine to gearbox bolts	45	33

1 General description

The clutch is of diaphragm spring, single dry plate type with cable actuation.

The clutch pedal pivots in a bracket mounted under the facia and operates a cable to the clutch release arm (or fork). The release lever operates a thrust bearing (clutch release bearing) which bears on the diaphragm spring of the pressure plate, and releases the clutch driven plate from the flywheel. The driven plate (or disc) is splined to a shaft which transmits the drive to the gearbox.

The clutch release mechanism consists of a fork and bearing which are in permanent contact with release fingers on the pressure plate assembly. The fork pushes the release bearing forwards to bear against the release fingers, so moving the centre of the diaphragm spring inwards. The spring is sandwiched between two rings which act as fulcrum points. As the centre of the spring is pushed in, the outside of the spring is pushed out, so moving the pressure plate backwards and disengaging it from the clutch driven plate.

When the clutch pedal is released, the diaphragm spring forces the pressure plate into contact with the friction linings on the driven plate and at the same time pushes the driven plate a fraction of an inch forwards on its splines so engaging it with the flywheel. The driven plate is now firmly sandwiched between the pressure plate and the flywheel, so the drive is taken up.

As wear takes place on the driven plate friction linings the diaphragm fingers move outwards and the pedal stroke decreases; the cable mechanism incorporates an adjustment to compensate for this wear.

2 Routine maintenance

Carry out the following procedures at the intervals given in *Routine maintenance* at the beginning of the manual.

1 Depress the clutch pedal fully three times then, using a rule, measure the total stroke of the pedal pad.
2 If the stroke is not as given in the Specifications it will be necessary to adjust the cable. To do this, loosen off the locknut from the adjuster nut at the gearbox end of the cable then turn the adjuster nut as required until the specified stroke is obtained. Retighten the locknut, then fully operate the clutch pedal three times. Recheck the adjustment.
3 The clutch cable and pedal lubrication points are indicated in Fig. 5.2. These points should be lubricated whenever they are detached and reassembled. They do not require lubrication in normal service.

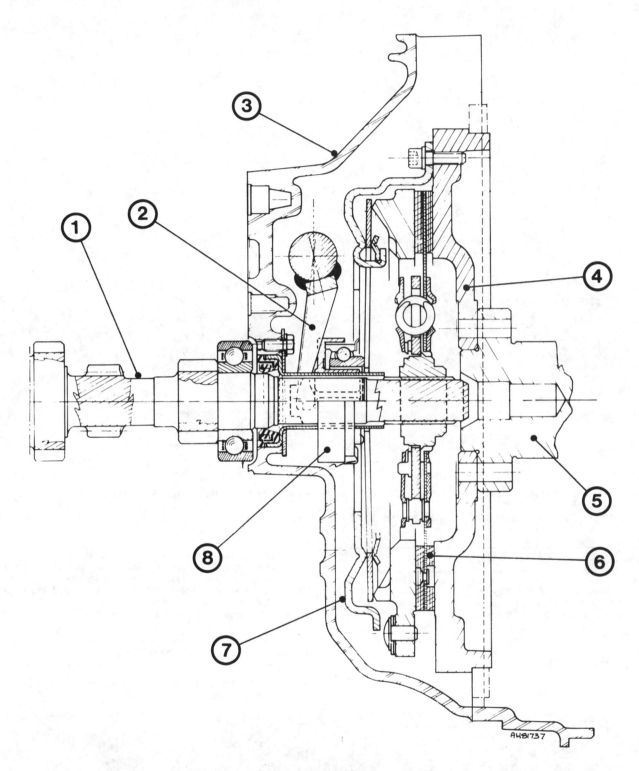

Fig. 5.1 Cross-Section view of the clutch unit (Sec 1)

1 Gearbox input shaft	3 Clutch housing unit	5 Crankshaft	7 Clutch cover
2 Clutch release lever driven plate	4 Flywheel	6 Clutch	8 Release bearing

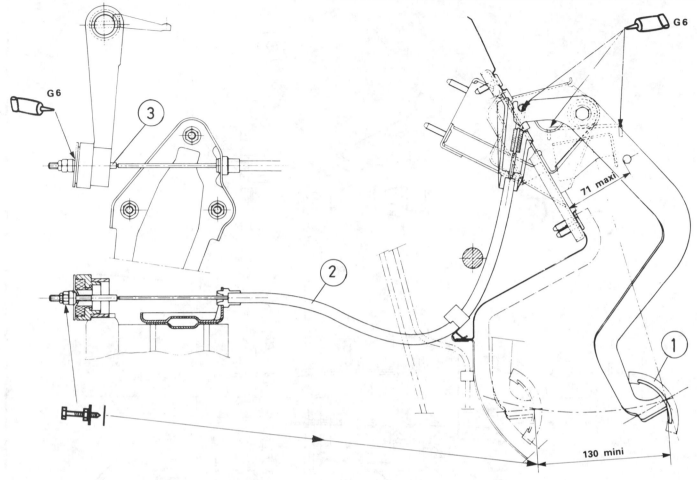

Fig. 5.2 Cross-Section view of the clutch pedal(1) cable (2) and cable connection at the release lever (3) (Sec 2)

The clearances shown are in mm Lubricate points G6 with a multi-purpose grease

3   Clutch cable – removal and refitting

1   Open and support the bonnet, then detach the cable from the release lever at the transmission end. Disconnect the outer cable from the support bracket on the top of the transmission (photo).
2   Detach and remove the parcel shelf from under the facia on the drivers side of the car. The shelf is secured by two screws on its inboard side and two press clips on the outboard side.
3   Unhook and disengage the clutch cable from the clutch pedal clevis. Both the access and the visibility are poor, and a suitable lead light will be required to see what you are doing.

4   When the cable is detached from the pedal, it can be withdrawn through the bulkhead and removed from the engine compartment side.
5   Refit in the reverse order of removal. Lightly lubricate the cable ends with grease. Ensure that the cable is correctly routed and engaged at each end. Adjust the cable as described in Section 2.
6   Check for satisfactory operation on completion.

4   Clutch pedal – removal and refitting

1   Disconnect the clutch cable from the clutch pedal as described in the previous Section.

3.1 Clutch cable attachment to operating lever (1) and mounting/support bracket (2). Also shown are the adjuster nut and its locknut (3)

4.2 General view of the pedal mounting assembly showing pivot bolt and clutch pedal return spring (arrowed)

5.3 Clutch pressure plate and driven plate removal

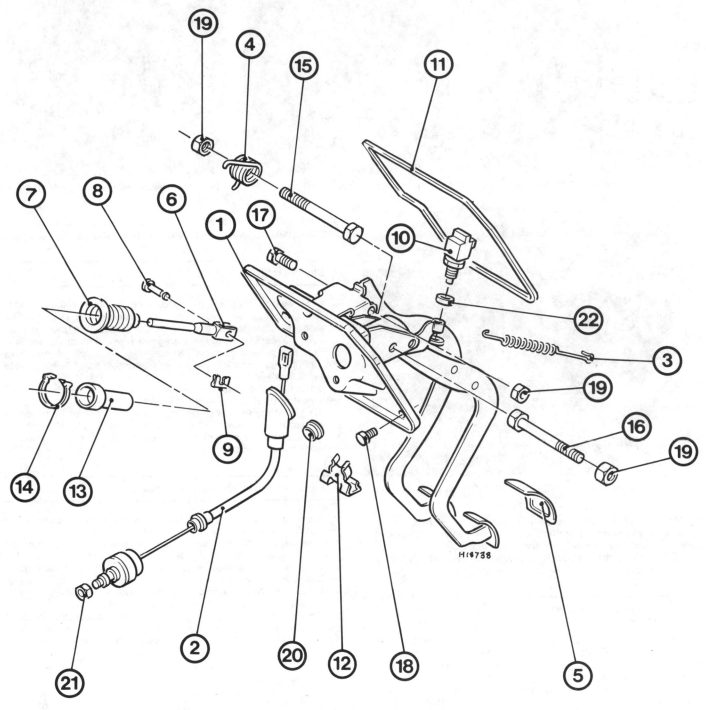

Fig. 5.3 Exploded view of the clutch and brake pedal assemblies (Sec 3)

1	Pedal bracket	7	Pushrod (boot)
2	Cable (clutch)	8	Clevis pin
3	Pedal spring	9	Clip
4	Spring	10	Stop lamp switch
5	Pedal cover	11	Gasket
6	Pushrod (brake)	12	Clip

13	Pushrod sleeve	18	Mounting screw
14	Clip	19	Nut
15	Bolt	20	Nut
16	Bolt	21	Cable locknut
17	Bolt	22	Nut

2   Unscrew the clutch pedal pivot bolt nut, slide the bolt to the side and disengage the pedal and return spring (photo).

3   Refit in the reverse order of removal. Lubricate the pivot points with multi-purpose grease.

4   Check and if necessary adjust the clutch cable/pedal stroke as described in Section 2.

5   Clutch – removal

1   Access to the clutch unit is gained after removing either the gearbox from the car as described in Chapter 6, or removing the engine and gearbox complete and then separating them as described in Chapter 1.

7.3 Using a universal clutch centralising tool

7.4 Tightening the pressure plate bolts

8.2A Clutch release bearing and guide sleeve location

8.2B Clutch release bearing and guide sleeve removal

2   Mark the clutch pressure plate in relation to the flywheel then progressively loosen the bolts. If necessary hold the flywheel stationary using a screwdriver engaged with the starter ring gear.

3   With all the bolts removed lift the pressure plate assembly from the location dowels followed by the driven plate (photo).

6   Clutch – inspection and renovation

1   The clutch driven plate should be inspected for wear and for contamination by oil. Wear is gauged by the depth of the rivet heads below the surface of the friction material. If this is less than 0.6 mm (0.024 in) the linings are worn enough to justify renewal.

2   Examine the friction faces of the flywheel and clutch pressure plate. These should be bright and smooth. If the linings have worn too much it is possible that the metal surfaces may have been scored by the rivet heads. Dust and grit can have the same effect. If the scoring is very severe it could mean that even with a new clutch driven plate, slip and juddering and other malfunctions will recur. Deep scoring on the flywheel face is serious because the flywheel will have to be removed and machined by a specialist, or renewed. If the pressure plate is worn excessively it must be renewed. If the driven plate friction linings are contaminated with oil, the plate must be renewed and the source of the oil traced and rectified.

3   If the reason for removal of the clutch has been because of slip and the slip has been allowed to go on for any length of time, it is possible that the heat generated will have adversely affected the diaphragm spring in the cover with the result that the pressure is now uneven and/or insufficient to prevent slip, even with a new driven plate. Where this occurs, the friction surfaces on the flywheel and pressure plate will often show a blue discolouration necessitating the renewal of the pressure plate.

4   With the clutch removed, the release bearing should be checked for excessive wear and noise, and renewed if necessary.

7   Clutch – refitting

1   Whenever the clutch is removed, the clutch shaft splines, release bearing guide tube and release fork ball-stud and fingers should be cleaned and lubricated with a molybdenum disulphide based grease. This will prevent clutch judder or drag which would otherwise result in difficult engagement of gears. Do not, however, apply an excessive amount of grease, which could find its way onto the clutch driven plate linings or flywheel.

2   Locate the clutch friction disc and pressure plate on the flywheel with the dowels engaged. Insert the bolts finger-tight.

3   Centralise the friction disc using a universal tool, or by making a wooden adaptor to the dimensions shown in Fig. 5.4 (photo).

4   Tighten the pressure plate bolts evenly to the specified torque wrench setting (photo).

8   Clutch release mechanism – overhaul

1   Remove the engine (Chapter 1) or gearbox (Chapter 6) for access to the clutch release mechanism components.

2   Disengage the release bearing from the lever forks and withdraw it from the input shaft sleeve (photos).

3   If required, the release lever can be removed by extracting the retaining pins and withdrawing it from the clutch housing. The nylon bushes can then be removed for inspection and replacement if required.

4   Renew any components which are excessively worn.

5   Refit in the reverse order of removal. Liberally lubricate the input shaft sleeve and those items indicated in Fig. 5.2. Do not allow any grease to come into contact with the flywheel or clutch mechanism.

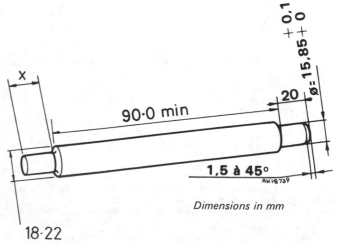

Dimensions in mm

18·22

Fig. 5.4 Check centralising tool and dimensions (Sec 7)

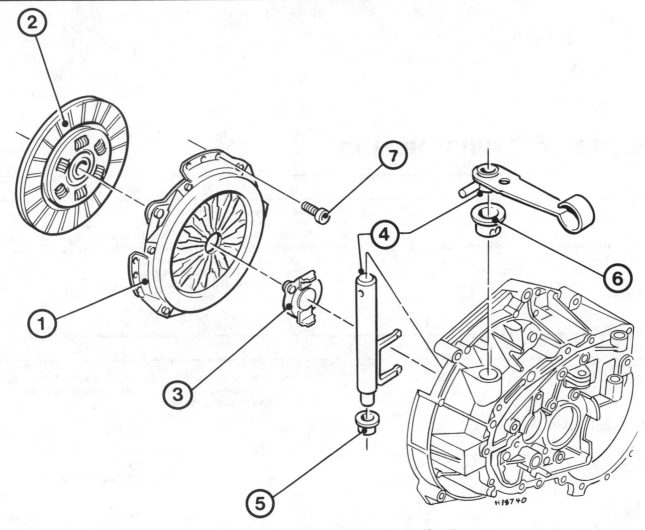

Fig. 5.5 Exploded view of the clutch assembly (Sec 8)

1 Clutch cover and diaphragm unit
2 Clutch driven plate
3 Release bearing
4 Release shaft
5 Release shaft bush
6 Release lever bush
7 Bolt

9 Fault diagnosis – clutch

Symptom	Reason(s)
Judder when taking up drive	Loose engine/gearbox mountings Badly worn friction linings or contaminated with oil Worn splines on input shaft or driven plate hub
Clutch drag (failure to disengage so that gears cannot be meshed)	Incorrect cable adjustment Rust on splines (may occur after vehicle standing idle for long periods) Damaged or misaligned pressure plate assembly Cable stretched or broken
Clutch slip (increase in engine speed does not result in increase in vehicle road speed – particularly on gradients)	Incorrect cable adjustment Friction linings worn out or oil contaminated
Noise evident on depressing clutch pedal	Dry, worn or damaged release bearing Excessive play between drive plate hub splines and shaft splines
Noise evident as clutch pedal released	Distorted driven plate Broken or weak driven plate cushion coil springs Release bearing loose on retainer hub

Chapter 6 Transmission

Contents

Specifications

Type .... Four or five forward speeds, one reverse. Synchromesh fitted to all forward gears. Unit mounted transversely (in line with engine). Floor-mounted gearchange lever.

Gearbox application and type

	4-speed	5-speed
954 cc engine	2CA 02	–
1124 cc engine	2CA 01	2CA 04
1360 cc engine (except GT)	–	2CA 04
1360 cc engine (GT model)	–	2CA 09 or 2CA 28

Ratios:1

Transmission:

	1st	2nd	3rd	4th	5th	Reverse
2CA 02 and 2CA 01	3.41	1.80	1.12	0.81	–	3.58
2CA 04, 2CA 09 and 2CA 28	3.41	1.95	1.35	1.05	0.85	3.58

Final drive:

2CA 01	3.44 : 1
2CA 02	3.76 : 1
2CA 04	3.44 : 1
2CA 09	3.94 : 1
2CA 28	4.06 : 1

Lubrication

Lubricant type/specification .... Gear oil, viscosity 75W/80 (Duckhams Hypoid PT 75W/80)
Capacity .... 2 litres (3.5 pints)

Torque wrench settings

	Nm	lbf ft
Drain plug	25	19
Filler plug	25	19
Reversing light switch	25	19
Transmission-to-engine bolts	45	33
Pressed steel cover	18	13
Bearing half-rings	18	13
Intermediate plate-to-clutch/final drive housing	50	37
Output shaft nut (5-speed)	140	103
Clutch release bearing guide sleeve	6	4.5
Gear lever-to-floor mounting	6	4.5
Link rod-to-lever	10	7
Linkage-to-bulkhead	12	9
Linkage-to-transmission	10	7
Transmission mounting:		
Nuts	17	12
Bolt	50	37
Engine/transmission torque stay:		
Bulkhead-to-mounting	90	66
Engine-to-mounting	60	44

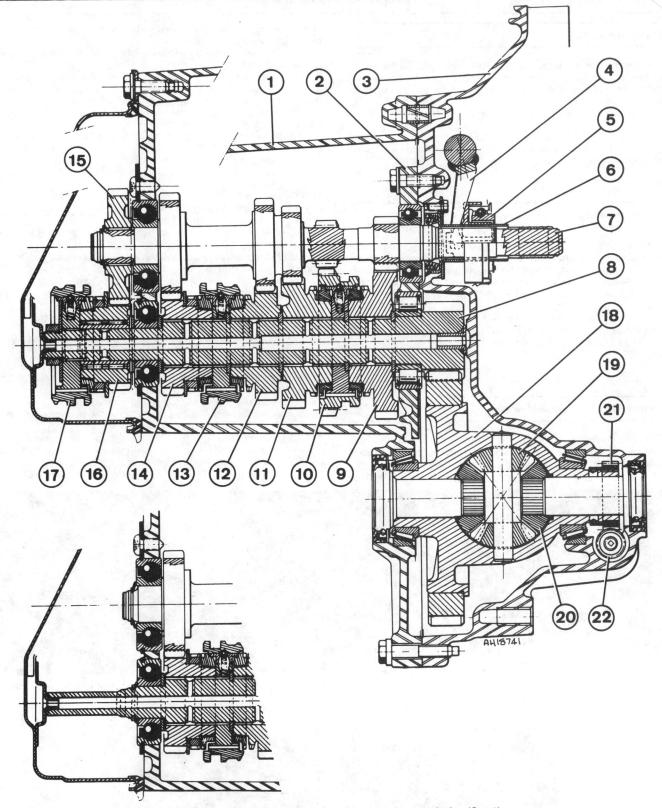

Fig. 6.1 Cross-Section of the five-speed transmission (Sec 1)

1 Gearbox housing
2 Intermediate plate
3 Clutch and final drive housing
4 Clutch fork (on shaft)
5 Release bearing
6 Release bearing guide
7 Input shaft

8 Output shaft
9 1st speed driven gear
10 1st/2nd speed synchroniser
  (and reverse driven gear)
11 2nd speed driven gear
12 3rd speed driven gear

13 3rd/4th speed synchroniser
14 4th speed driven gear
15 5th speed drive gear
16 5th speed driven gear
17 5th speed synchroniser

18 Differential housing
19 Differential pinions
20 Differential gears
21 Speedometer drive worm
22 Speedometer drive pinion

Inset shows 4-speed gearbox

1 General description

The transmission unit is mounted on the left-hand side of the engine. It has four or five forward gears depending on the model, all with synchromesh, and one reverse gear. All of the synchromesh units are located on the output shaft.

The final drive differential unit is located in the main transmission housing.

When required, the transmission can be removed either separately or together with the engine. No special tools are required to remove/refit the transmission, or to dismantle and overhaul it.

2 Routine maintenance

The transmission is a sealed for life type and therefore no routine maintenance requirements are required apart from periodically checking driveshaft output seals and the casing joints for any signs of lubricant leakage. If leaks are found to be evident, check and if necessary, top up the transmission oil level through the filler/level plug (photos).

If required, the transmission oil can be drained through the drain plug shown (photo). When topping up or refilling the transmission oil level, use only the specified type and quantity of oil.

3 Transmission – removal and refitting

1   The transmission can be removed and refitted on its own or as a unit with the engine. If the latter method is to be employed, refer to Chapter 1 for details for the removal and separation procedure.

2   If the transmission is being removed on its own, a suitable method of supporting the weight of the engine during the absence of the transmission will be required.

3   Start by draining the transmission oil into a suitable container with reference to Section 2.

4   Disconnect and remove the battery as described in Chapter 12.

5   Remove the air filter and the intake ducts as described in Chapter 3.

6   Remove the starter motor as described in Chapter 12.

7   Disconnect the clutch cable from the release lever and the support bracket on top of the transmission housing.

8   Disconnect the speedometer cable from the transmission as described in Chapter 12.

9   Disconnect the earth lead to the transmission.

10   Detach the lead from the reversing light switch on the transmission.

11   Ensure the handbrake is applied, then loosen off the front road-wheel bolts. Raise and support the car at the front end on axle stands. Allow a suitable working height underneath and sufficient clearance to lower and remove the transmission from under the vehicle. Remove the front roadwheels.

12   Undo the retaining bolts and detach the suspension arm balljoint from the steering stub axle each side with reference to Chapter 10.

13   Remove both driveshafts as described in Chapter 7.

14   Prise free and detach the three transmission selector links at the transmission end balljoint linkages (photo).

15   Undo the retaining bolts and remove the engine/transmission torque stay unit.

16   Support the weight of the engine using a jack, wooden blocks or a suitable engine hoist.

17   Support the weight of the transmission unit with a suitable trolley jack underneath, or a sling and hoist from above. If a trolley jack is used, an assistant will be required to help steady the transmission as it is detached from the engine and lowered from the car.

18   Unscrew the retaining nuts and remove the transmission mounting on the left-hand side (photo).

19   Undo and remove the four transmission-to-engine retaining bolts, then tilt the engine and transmission a little and carefully withdraw the transmission from the engine and lower it from the engine compartment. Withdraw the transmission from under the front of the car.

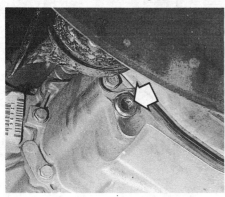

2.1A Transmission oil filler/level plug (arrowed)

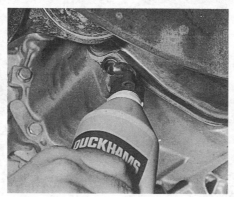

2.1B Topping up the transmission oil level

2.1C Transmission oil drain plug (arrowed)

3.14 Disconnect the selector links which are viewed from underneath

3.18 Transmission mounting retaining nuts and bolts (arrowed)

4.4A Unscrew the retaining bolt ...

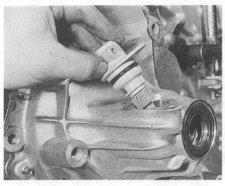

4.4B ... and remove the speedometer drive pinion

4.5A Unscrew the retaining bolts ...

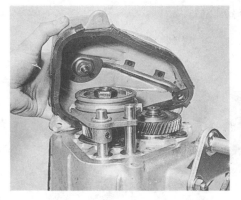

4.5B ... and remove the pressed-steel housing and gasket

4.8A Remove the 5th synchro nut ...

4.8B ... and lockwasher

4.9 Removing the 5th synchro unit and selector fork

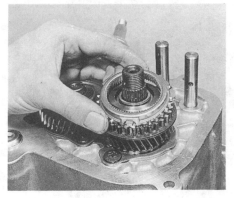

4.10A Remove the 5th synchro-ring ...

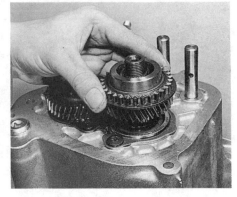

4.10B ... the 5th speed driven gear ...

20 Refitting is a reversal of removal, but note the following points:

  (a) It is recommended that the driveshaft oil seals and filler/drain plug washers are renewed
  (b) Tighten all nuts and bolts to the specified torque
  (c) Lubricate the input shaft splines, clutch release bearing sleeve and fork fingers with molybdenum disulphide grease
  (d) Refill the gearbox with the correct grade and quantity of oil
  (e) Adjust the clutch cable with reference to Chapter 5

4 Transmission – dismantling into major assemblies

1 With the unit removed from the car, clean all exterior surfaces and wipe dry.
2 Pull the clutch release bearing from the guide sleeve, and release the spring clips from the fork ends.

3 Position the gearbox with the clutch end downwards.
4 Unbolt and remove the speedometer drive pinion (photos).
5 Unbolt the pressed-steel housing. Remove the rubber gasket (photos).

5-speed gearbox only
6 Drive the pin from the 5th speed selector fork.
7 Engage both reverse and 5th gears with reference to Fig. 6.2, then loosen the nut on the end of the output shaft. Return the gears to neutral.
8 Remove the nut and lockwasher (photos).
9 Remove the 5th synchro unit together with its selector fork, making sure that the sleeve remains central on the hub to avoid loss of the internal balls and springs (photo).
10 Remove from the output shaft the 5th synchro-ring, followed by the 5th speed driven gear, needle bearing, sleeve, and thrustwasher (photos).
11 Extract the circlip from the end of the input shaft, followed by the special washer, noting that the convex side is uppermost (photo).

4.10C ... the needle bearing ...

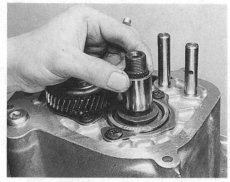

4.10D ... the sleeve ...

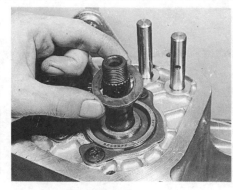

4.10E ... and thrustwasher

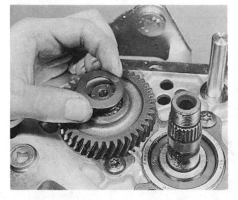

4.11 Remove the special washer from the input shaft ...

4.12 ... then the 5th speed drive gear

4.13A Remove the Torx retaining screws ...

4.13B ... and the bearing half-rings

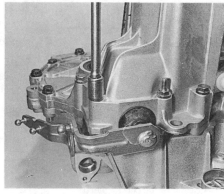

4.14 Unbolt the gearbox housing

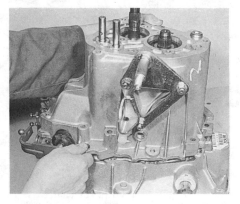

4.15 Lift the gearbox housing from the clutch/final drive housing

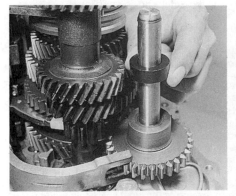

4.16A Remove the plastic ring ...

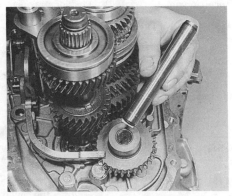

4.16B ... the reverse idler gear shaft ...

4.16C ... and the reverse idler gear

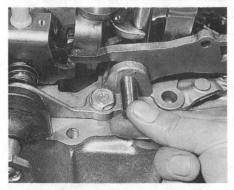

4.17A Removing the reverse selector shaft ...

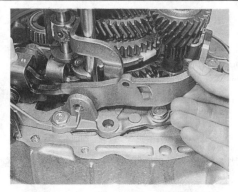

4.17B ... and arm

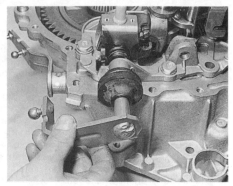

4.20 Remove the selector shaft

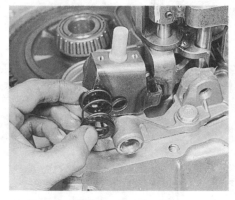

4.21 Remove the neutral return spring and plastic cups

4.22A Interlocking key and selector finger unit

4.22B Interlocking key and selector finger separated

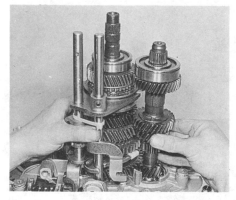

4.24 Lift and withdraw the input, output and selector shafts as a unit from the clutch/final drive housing

4.25 Intermediate plate removal

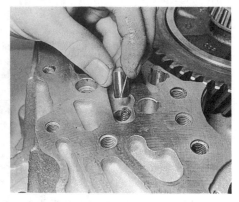

4.26A Remove the reverse lock plunger ...

4.26B ... and spring

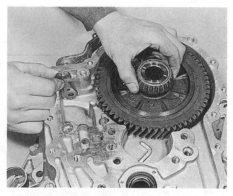

4.27 Remove the differential unit

12   Using a suitable puller if necessary, pull the 5th speed drive gear from the splines on the input shaft (photo).

4 and 5-speed gearboxes

13   Unscrew the Torx screws and extract the half-rings from the grooves in the shaft bearings, noting their locations (photos).
14   Unscrew the bolts securing the gearbox housing to the clutch/final drive housing, noting the location of the bolts (photo).
15   Lift the gearbox housing from the clutch/final drive housing (photo), at the same time guiding the selector fork shafts through the housing. Do not prise the housings apart with a screwdriver, but use a wooden or hide mallet to release them from the sealant.
16   Remove the plastic ring from the reverse idler gear shaft, then remove the shaft from the clutch/final drive housing and remove the idler gear (photos).
17   Press down on the reverse selector arm directly over the shaft, and at the same time extract the shaft from the intermediate plate. Remove the reverse selector arm (photos).
18   Lift the gate lever to the 1st/2nd position and support with a block of wood.
19   Using a suitable pin punch, drive out the pin securing the selector finger to the selector shaft. Recover the pin and return the gate lever to neutral.
20   Pull out the selector shaft and remove the rubber boot from it (photo).
21   Prise out the neutral return spring together with the two plastic cups (photo).
22   Lift the gate lever, and at the same time remove the interlocking key and selector finger (photos).
23   Tie the two selector fork shafts together using a plastic cable tie as an aid to reassembly.
24   Using both hands, lift the input and output shafts, together with the selector fork shafts, directly from the clutch/final drive housing (photo). Separate the input shaft from the output shaft, and disengage the selector forks from the synchro units on the output shaft.
25   Unscrew the bolts and remove the intermediate plate from the clutch/final drive housing (photo). Adhesive is used on assembly, so some difficulty may be experienced, however do not lever directly on the mating faces.
26   Remove the reverse locking plunger and spring, using a magnet if available (photos).
27   Lift out the differential unit (photo).
28   The gearbox is now dismantled into its major assemblies.

5   Transmission – examination and renovation

1   Clean all of the dismantled sub-assemblies and examine them thoroughly for wear or signs of damage. If major damage has occurred, the transmission is probably best exchanged for a replacement unit as the renewal of numerous internal components will prove more expensive.
2   Circlips, locking pins, gaskets and oil seals must all be renewed as a matter of course.
3   Read through the reassembly instructions to list the necessary replacements and items required.

6   Clutch/final drive housing – overhaul

1   Using a suitable punch, drive out the locking pin and remove the gate lever from the shaft (photo).
2   Withdraw the shaft and prise the oil seal from the housing.
3   Prise out the driveshaft and input shaft oil seals (photos).
4   If necessary drive out the location dowels.
5   If necessary drive out the right-hand final drive bearing outer track, using a punch through the cut-outs provided (photo).
6   Unbolt the clutch release bearing guide sleeve (photo).
7   Clean all the components.
8   Commence reassembly by refitting the clutch release bearing guide sleeve, together with a new input shaft seal. Apply jointing compound

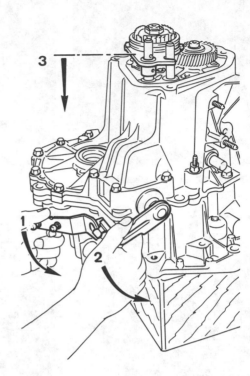

Fig. 6.2 Sequence for selecting reverse and 5th gear simultaneously (Sec 4)

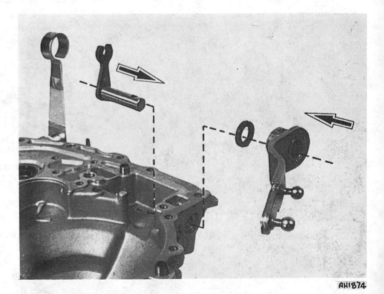

Fig. 6.3 Gate lever shaft reassembly (Sec 6)

to the threads, then insert and tighten the bolts. Smear a little oil on the seal.
9   Using a metal tube or drift, drive the right-hand final drive bearing outer track fully into the housing.
10   Drive in the location dowels.
11   Oil the new driveshaft oil seal, and drive it into the housing using a block of wood.
12   Oil the new gate lever shaft oil seal and drive it into the housing. Oil the shaft and refit it.
13   Locate the gate lever on the shaft towards the final drive, align the holes and drive in the new locking pin.

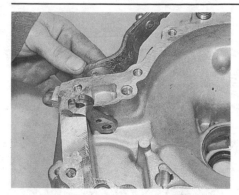

6.1 Remove the gate lever

6.3A Prising out the right-hand driveshaft oil seal ...

6.3B ... the left-hand driveshaft oil seal ...

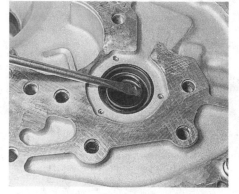

6.3C ... and the input shaft oil seal

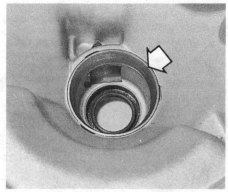

6.5 Right-hand final drive bearing outer-track (arrowed)

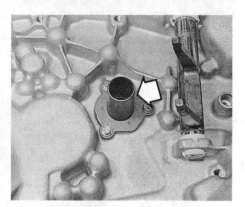

6.6 Clutch release bearing guide sleeve (arrowed)

7.2 Left-hand final drive bearing track

8.3 Input shaft and bearings

9.2 Output shaft bearing removal

7 Transmission housing – overhaul

1   Prise out the driveshaft oil seal.
2   If necessary, drive out the left-hand final drive bearing outer track using a punch through the cut-outs provided (photo).
3   Using a metal tube or drift, drive the new outer track fully into the housing.
4   Oil the new driveshaft oil seal and drive it into the housing using a block of wood.

8 Input shaft – dismantling and reassembly

1   On the 4-speed gearbox, extract the circlip with circlip pliers and remove the washer.
2   On 4 and 5-speed gearboxes, pull the bearing from the 4th speed end of the input shaft using a suitable puller. Similarly pull the bearing from the 1st speed end. Note that the re-use of removed bearings is not recommended.

3   To reassemble, drive the bearing on the 1st speed end of the shaft using a length of metal tube on the inner track. Similarly drive the bearing on the 4th speed end, but note that the groove in the outer track must be towards the end of the shaft (photo).
4   Locate the washer over the end of the shaft on the 4-speed gearbox. Rest the circlip on the tapered end of the shaft, and use a socket to drive it into the groove. Check that the circlip is seated correctly by squeezing it with pliers.

9 Output shaft – dismantling and reassembly

1   On the 4-speed gearbox, extract the circlip with circlip pliers and remove the washer.
2   On 4 and 5-speed gearboxes, pull the bearing from the shaft using a suitable puller if necessary (photo).
3   Remove the thrustwasher, followed by 4th gear, the 4th synchro-ring, the 3rd/4th synchro unit, and the 3rd synchro-ring (photos). Keep the synchro unit sleeve central on the hub.

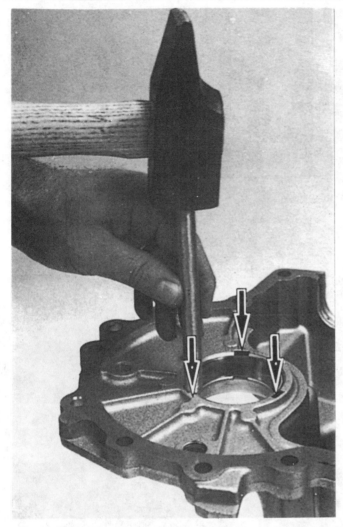

Fig. 6.4 Driving the new bearing into the left-hand transmission housing (Sec 7)

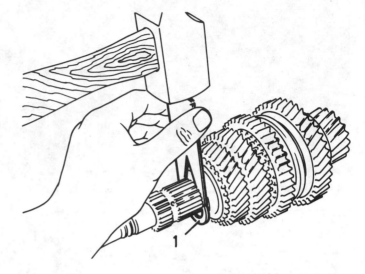

Fig. 6.5 Forked tool (Citroën No. 4508-TV) for removing C-clips (1) from the output shaft (Sec 9)

plastic lubrication disc.

8   Press the C-clip into its groove, followed by 1st gear and the next C-clip (photo).

9   Fit the 1st synchro-ring, then lower the 1st/2nd synchro unit onto the splines with the selector groove downwards, at the same time aligning the projections on the 1st synchro-ring with the rockers on the synchro unit.

10   Fit the 2nd synchro-ring, aligning the projections as described in paragraph 9.

11   Fit the 2nd gear, the C-clip, 3rd gear, and the C-clip.

12   Fit the 3rd synchro-ring, 3rd/4th synchro unit, and the 4th synchro-ring as described in paragraph 9.

13   Fit the 4th gear and thrustwasher.

14   Locate the bearing on the shaft, with the groove towards the end of the shaft. Drive the bearing onto the shaft using a length of metal tube on the inner track (photo). Do not support the shaft on the plastic lubrication disc.

15   On the 4-speed gearbox, locate the washer on the end of the shaft. Rest the circlip on the tapered end of the shaft, and use a socket to drive it into the groove. Check that the circlip is seated correctly by squeezing it with pliers.

4   Tap out the C-clip using a screwdriver or a forked tool made with reference to Fig. 6.5 (photo).

5   Remove the 3rd gear, the C-clip, the 2nd gear, 2nd synchro-ring, 1st/2nd synchro unit, 1st synchro-ring, the C-clip, 1st gear, and the final C-clip (photos). Keep the synchro unit sleeve central on the hub.

6   Remove the final bearing using a suitable puller, or by supporting the bearing in a vice and driving the output shaft through it. Note that the re-use of removed bearings is not recommended.

7   To reassemble, drive the bearing onto the output shaft using a length of metal tube on the inner track. Do not support the shaft on the

10 Differential bearings – removal

1   Lever off the speedometer drive worm (photo).

2   Pull the bearings from both sides of the differential unit using a suitable puller. Identify them for location if they are to be re-used.

9.3A Remove the thrustwasher ...

9.3B ... 4th gear ...

9.3C ... 4th synchro-ring ...

9.3D ... 3rd/4th synchro unit ...

9.3E ... and the 3rd gear synchro-ring

9.4 Remove the C-clip ...

9.5A ... 3rd gear ...

9.5B ... and C-clip ...

9.5C ... 2nd gear ...

9.5D ... 2nd gear synchro-ring ...

9.5E ... 1st/2nd synchro unit ...

9.5F ... 1st synchro-ring ...

9.5G ... C-clip ...

9.5H ... 1st gear ...

9.5I ... and the final C-clip (arrowed)

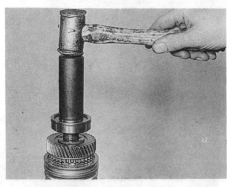

9.8 Inserting a c-clip   9.14 Driving the bearing onto the output shaft   10.1 Speedometer drive worm (arrowed)

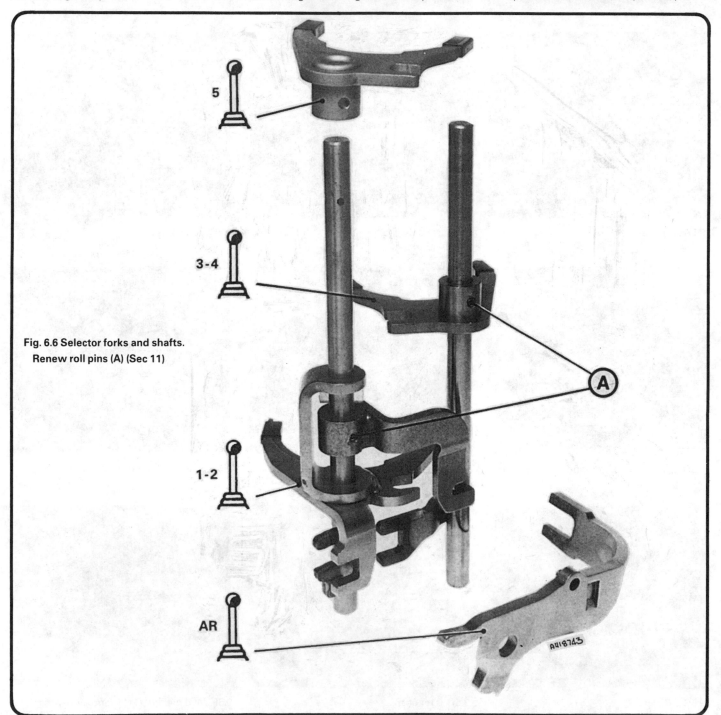

Fig. 6.6 Selector forks and shafts.
Renew roll pins (A) (Sec 11)

3 Drive the new bearings into position using a length of metal tube on their inner tracks.
4 Press the speedometer drive worm into position.

11 Selector fork shafts – dismantling and reassembly

1 Support the 3rd/4th selector fork shaft in a soft-jawed vice, then drive out the roll pin using a suitable punch. Slide off the selector fork, noting which way round it is fitted.
2 Similarly drive out the roll pin, and remove the 1st/2nd selector fork and the reverse control relay from the other shaft.
3 Reassembly is a reversal of dismantling, but use new roll pins.

12 Synchromesh units – dismantling and reassembly

1 Mark the hub and the outer sleeve in relation to each other to ensure correct reassembly.
2 Wrap the unit in a cloth, then slide the sleeve from the hub. Recover the three balls, three springs, and three rockers.
3 To reassemble the units, first insert the hub in the sleeve. The rocker slots in the hub and sleeve must be in alignment.
4 Pull out the hub until the rockers, springs and balls can be inserted, then press in the balls and push the hub fully into the sleeve. A large worm drive clip, piston ring compressor, or three narrow strips of metal may be used to press in the balls.

13 Transmission – reassembly

1 With the clutch/final drive housing on the bench, lower the differential unit into position.

2 Insert the reverse locking spring and plunger.
3 Apply Loctite Autoform 549 adhesive to the contact area on the intermediate plate, then lower the plate onto the clutch/final drive housing, at the same time guiding the gate lever through the hole provided (photos).
4 Apply locking fluid to the bolt threads. Insert the bolts and progressively tighten them to the specified torque (photos). Clean the excess adhesive from the bearing locations.
5 Tie the two selector fork shaft assemblies together (photo).
6 Engage the selector forks in the synchro unit grooves, and mesh the input and output shaft assemblies together. Using both hands, lower the complete assembly into the clutch/final drive housing (photo).
7 Locate the selector finger within the interlocking key, then lift the gate lever and insert the key assembly in the clutch/final drive housing. Make sure that the selector finger engages the fork gates, and that the gate lever engages the outer plate of the interlocking key.
8 Engage the plastic cups with the neutral return spring, and insert them between the interlocking key and intermediate plate (photos).
9 Fit the rubber boot on the selector shaft. Insert the shaft through the intermediate plate, interlocking key and selector finger, align the holes and drive in the locking pin (photos).
10 Insert the reverse selector arm in the intermediate plate, press down on it to depress the plunger, and insert the shaft. Make sure that the stud on the arm enters the cut-out on the control relay.
11 Engage the reverse idler gear with the selector arm, with the projecting shoulder uppermost, and insert the shaft, cut-out end downwards. Turn the shaft until the cut-out drops in the recess.
12 Fit the plastic ring on the shaft.
13 Apply a thin, even, coat of a silicone-based jointing compound to the mating face of the clutch/final drive housing (photo).
14 Lower the gearbox housing onto the clutch/final drive housing, at the same time guiding the input and output shaft bearings and selector fork shafts through their holes.
15 Insert the bolts in their previously-noted locations, and tighten them evenly to the specified torque.
16 Fit the retaining half-rings in the bearing grooves with the chamfers uppermost, then insert and tighten the bolts.

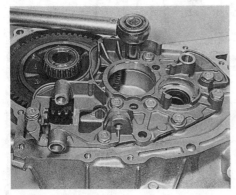

13.3A Applying adhesive to the intermediate plate

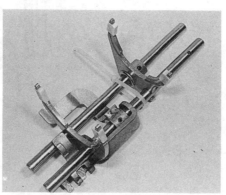

13.3B Guiding the gate lever through the intermediate plate

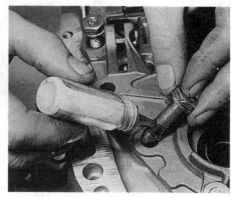

13.4A Apply locking fluid to the bolt threads ...

13.4B ... and tighten them to the specified torque

13.5 Selector forks and shafts tied together with a plastic strap

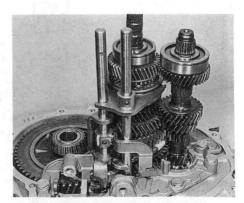

13.6 Shafts and selector forks assembled to the clutch/final drive housing

Fig. 6.7 Orientation and identification features of the synchromesh units (Sec 12)

Fig. 6.8 Exploded view of a synchro unit (Sec 12)

1 Sleeve
2 Hub
3 Ball
4 Spring
5 Rocker

Fig. 6.9 Locating the selector finger in the interlocking key (Sec 13)

13.8A Fitted neutral return spring and plastic cups (arrowed)

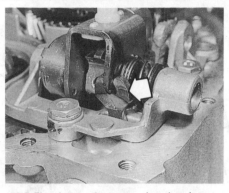

13.8B Fitted neutral return spring showing gate lever (arrowed) engaged with interlocking key

13.9A Insert the lock pin ...

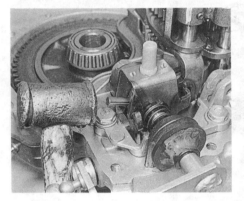

13.9B ... and drive it through the selector shaft

13.13 Apply jointing compound to the clutch/final drive housing

13.19 Squeezing the circlip into the groove in the input shaft

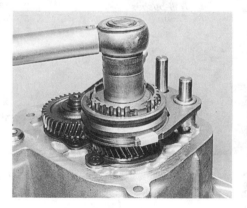

13.23 Tightening the 5th gear synchro nut

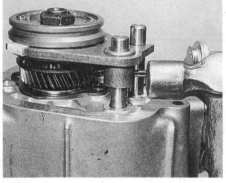

13.24 Driving in the 5th selector fork locking pin

5-speed gearbox only

17 Locate the 5th speed drive gear on the input shaft splines, support the opposite end of the shaft on a block of wood and fully drive the gear on the splines using a metal tube.

18 Fit the washer on the input shaft with its convex side uppermost.

19 Fit the circlip using a suitable socket and hammer. Check that it is fully entered in the groove by squeezing with pliers (photo).

20 Fit the thrustwasher to the output shaft (oil groove uppermost) followed by the sleeve, needle bearing, 5th speed driven gear and the 5th synchro-ring.

21 Engage the selector fork with the 5th synchro unit, then lower them onto the output shaft and selector fork shafts. Make sure that the projections on the synchro-ring are aligned with the rockers in the synchro unit.

22 Fit the special lockwasher and nut (finger-tight).

23 Engage both reverse and 5th speed gears with reference to Fig. 6.2. Tighten the nut to the specified torque, then return the gears to neutral (photo).

24 Align the holes in the 5th speed selector fork and shaft, and drive in the locking pin (photo).

4 and 5-speed gearboxes

25 Fit the dry rubber gasket to the pressed steel housing. Locate the housing on the gearbox housing, insert the bolts and tighten them to the specified torque.

26 Refit the speedometer drive pinion. Insert and tighten the bolt.

27 Apply a little grease to the guide sleeve, then refit the clutch release bearing and engage the spring clips with the fork ends.

---

14 Gear lever and selector rod – removal and refitting

---

1 Raise the car at the front end and support it on axle stands.

2 Improved access to the selector rod connections will be made by removing the exhaust system as described in Chapter 3.

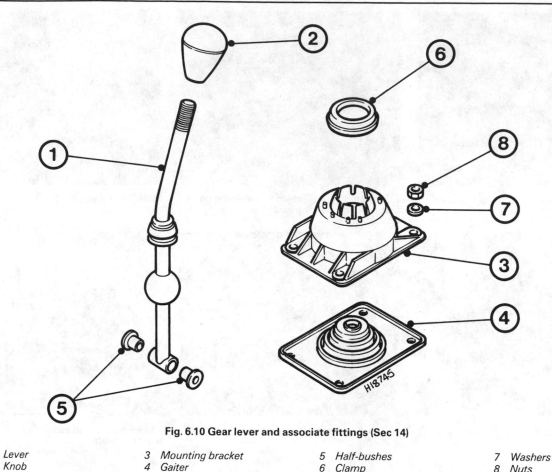

Fig. 6.10 Gear lever and associate fittings (Sec 14)

1 Lever   3 Mounting bracket   5 Half-bushes   7 Washers
2 Knob   4 Gaiter   6 Clamp   8 Nuts

PREVIOUS ASSEMBLY

MODIFIED ASSEMBLY

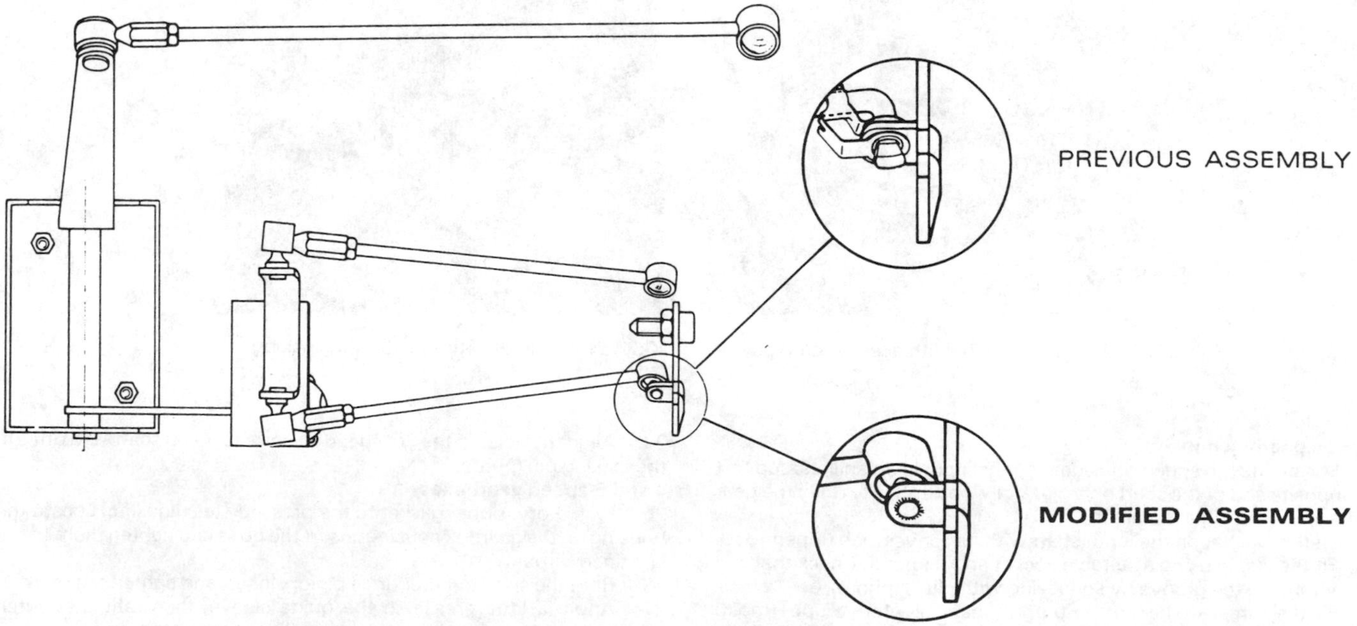

Fig. 6.11 Selector link rods and pivot unit. A balljoint replaces the original clip firing on the lower link rod on later models (as shown in the insets) (Sec 14)

Gear lever

3   Working under the car, unscrew the retaining bolt and nut and separate the gear lever from the selector rod. If they are excessively worn, renew the half-bushes in the lever eye (photo).

4   To remove the gear lever unit, first remove the floor console then unscrew the four retaining nuts and withdraw the lever upwards through the car (photo).

Selector rod

5   Detach the rod from the bottom end of the control lever as previously described.

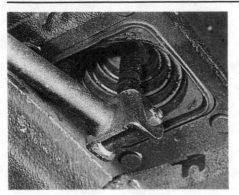

14.3 Gear lever to selector rod joint

14.4 Remove the four nuts to remove the gear lever unit

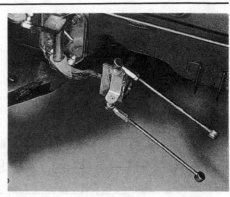

14.6 Selector rod and pivot mounting

6   Disconnect the three selector link rods from their balljoint connections at the selector rod pivot, then undo the nut and bolt securing the pivot to the crossmember and remove the main selector rod (photo).

Refitting

7   Refitting is a reversal of the removal procedure. Lubricate the joints with a medium multi-purpose grease. On completion check that all gears can be positively engaged.

15   Fault diagnosis – transmission

Symptom	Reason(s)
Weak or ineffective synchromesh	Synchromesh units worn, or damaged
Jumps out of gear	Gearchange mechanism worn Synchromesh units badly worn Selector fork badly worn
Excessive noise	Incorrect grade of oil or oil level too low Gear teeth excessively worn or damaged Worn bearings
Difficulty in engaging gears	Clutch pedal adjustment incorrect Worn selector components Worn synchromesh units

Chapter 7 Driveshafts

Contents

Specifications

Type .... Constant velocity joint, tripod type at gearbox end, ball pattern at outer end. Right and left driveshafts are of unequal length

Driveshaft CV joint lubricant
Type .... Special lubricant supplied in repair kit
Capacity.. 160 grams per joint

Torque wrench settings

	Nm	lbf ft
Hub nut	250	185
Suspension lower balljoint nut	28	21

1 General description

Drive to the front wheels is transmitted from the final drive unit to the front hubs by two driveshafts. The driveshafts incorporate inner and outer joints to accommodate suspension and steering angular movement.

The inner ends of the driveshafts are splined to the final drive/differential side gears, and the outer ends are splined to the front hubs.

2 Routine maintenance

Carry out the following procedures at the intervals given in *Routine maintenance* at the beginning of the manual.

1 Jack up the front of the car and support on axle stands. Apply the handbrake.
2 Thoroughly examine the rubber bellows at each end of the driveshafts for splitting, damage and grease leakage (photo). If evident renew the bellows.
3 If the driveshaft joints are excessively noisy, perhaps more noticeable when turning corners, renew the driveshaft or obtain an exchange unit.

3 Driveshaft – removal and refitting

1 Position a suitable container beneath the transmission drain plug, then unscrew the plug and drain the transmission oil. Clean the plug and refit it, tightening it to the specified torque wrench setting (see Specifications in Chapter 6).
2 Apply the handbrake, loosen off the front roadwheel bolts on the side concerned, then raise and support the car at the front end on axle stands. Remove the front roadwheel(s).

3 Using a suitable punch, relieve the staking of the locknut, then unscrew the nut using a 30 mm (1.18 in) socket. Prevent the hub from turning by screwing two of the wheel bolts into position and jamming them with a suitable bar. If it is available, use the special Citroën tool No 6310-T (Fig. 7.2). Remove the nut.
4 Unscrew and remove the suspension arm/hub carrier balljoint nut, extract the bolt (noting orientation of fitting), then carefully prise free the balljoint. Take particular care not to damage the balljoint gaiter when prising the suspension arm free.
5 Pull the hub carrier outwards and simultaneously extract the driveshaft from the hub. It may be necessary to detach the tie-rod end to allow the hub sufficient movement to disengage the driveshaft from the hub (refer to Chapter 10 for details).
6 Withdraw the driveshaft from the transmission (photo).
7 With the driveshaft removed, the opportunity should be taken to renew the oil seal in the gearbox. To do this, prise out the old seal and wipe clean the recess. Fill the space between the new oil seal lips with grease then use a suitable block of wood to tap it into the casing. When fully fitted it should be slightly recessed.
8 Refitting is a reversal of removal, but make sure that the hub carrier to suspension arm balljoint retaining bolt is correctly fitted (with the balljoint protector positioned correctly as well). The balljoint clamp nut and the hub nut must be renewed and tightened to the specified torque wrench settings. When the hub nut is tightened to its recommended setting, lock it by staking the shoulder into the grooves of the shaft (photo).
9 Refit the roadwheel(s) and refill the transmission oil level to complete.

4 Driveshaft joint bellows – renewal

Inboard joint
1 With the driveshaft removed from the car, prise back the lip of the cover and then tap the cover off to expose the tulip yoke.

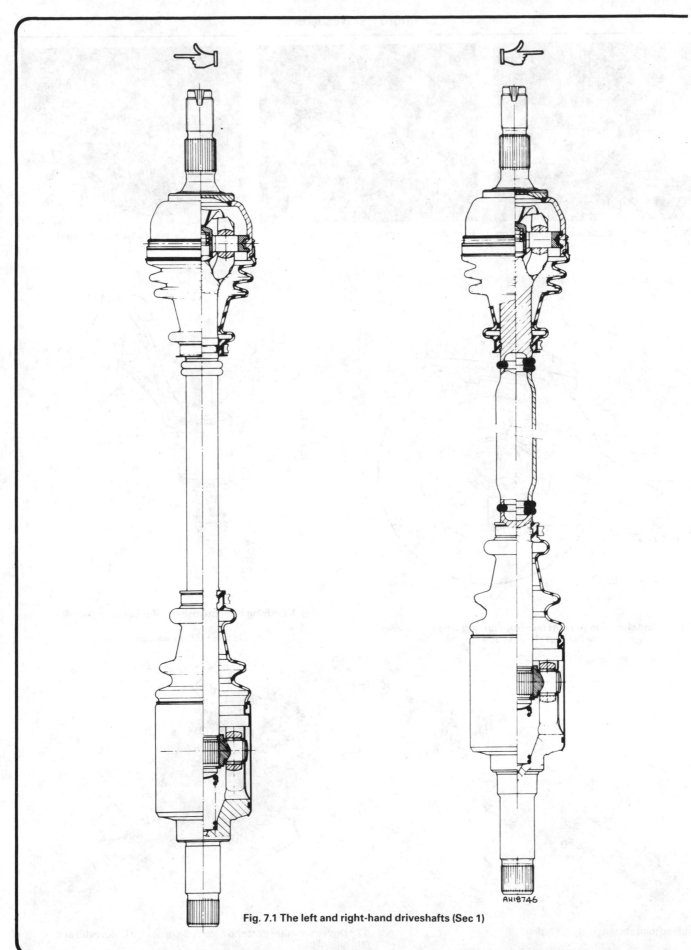

AH18746

Fig. 7.1 The left and right-hand driveshafts (Sec 1)

2.2 Check the driveshaft bellows and retaining clips for condition and security

3.6 Withdraw the driveshaft from the transmission

3.8 Tighten the hub nut to the specified torque setting

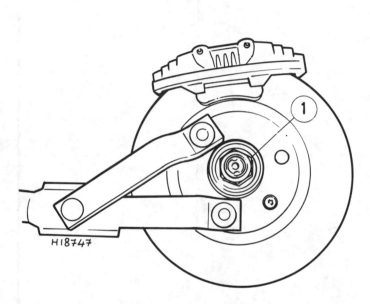

Fig. 7.2 Use tool shown to prevent hub from turning when removing the hub nut (1) (Sec 3)

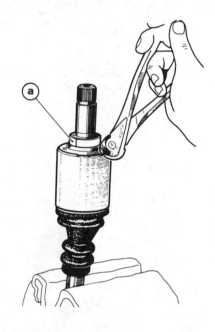

Fig. 7.3 Prising back driveshaft joint cover lip (Sec 4)

a   Oil seal rubbing surface

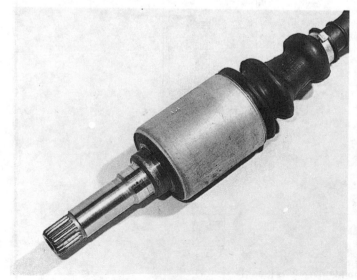

4.21 Inboard joint shown ready for fitting

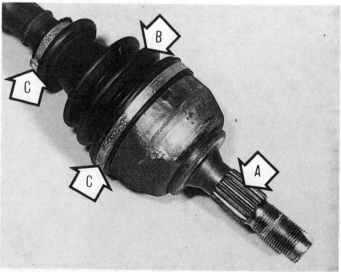

4.23 Driveshaft outer joint showing hub splines (A) bellows (B) and retaining clips (C)

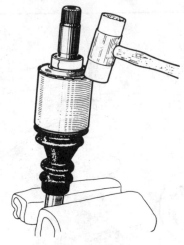

Fig. 7.4 Tapping off the driveshaft cover (Sec 4)

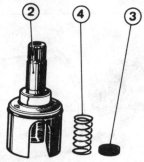

Fig. 7.5 Driveshaft inboard joint components (Sec 4)

2 Tulip   4 Spring
3 Thrust cap

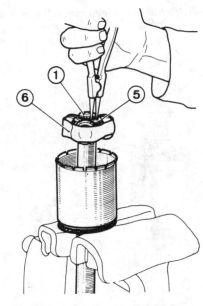

Fig. 7.7 Extracting spider circlip (Sec 4)

1 Shaft   6 Taped needle rollers
5 Needle roller cage

H145878

Fig. 7.6 Type of tool required for fitting the bellows (Sec 4)

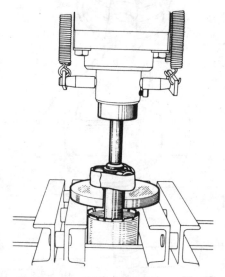

Fig. 7.8 Press the shaft through the spider (Sec 4)

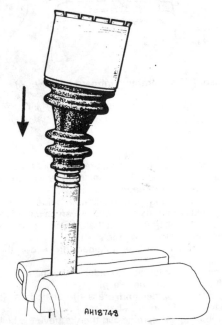

AH18748

Fig. 7.9 Fit the bellows and cover over the inboard end of the shaft (Sec 4)

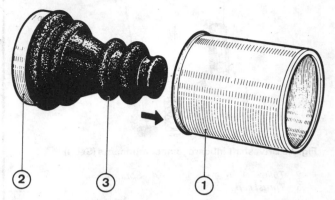

Fig. 7.10 Driveshaft inboard end joint cover (1) spacer (2) and bellows (3) (Sec 4)

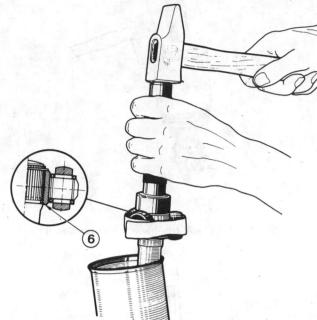

Fig. 7.11 Driving spider onto shaft (Sec 4)

6   Chamfered side

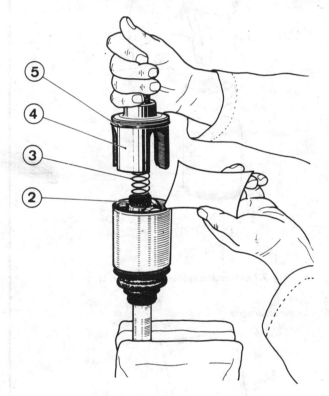

Fig. 7.12 Assembling inboard joint (Sec 4)

2	Thrust cap	4	Tulip
3	Spring	5	O-ring

2   Remove the tulip yoke, spring and thrust cup.
3   Wipe away as much of the original grease as possible.
4   If retaining circlips are not fitted, wind adhesive tape around the spider bearings to retain their needle rollers.
5   If it is now possible, borrow or make up a guide tool similar to the one shown (Fig. 7.6). The defective bellows can be cut off and the new ones slid up the tool (well greased) so that they will expand sufficiently to ride over the joint and locate on the shaft.
6   Where such a tool cannot be obtained, proceed in the following way.
7   Mark the relative position of the spider to the shaft.
8   Remove the spider retaining circlip.
9   Either support the spider and press the shaft from it, or use a suitable puller to draw it from the shaft.
10   Cut free the bellows securing clip then remove the bellows/cover from the shaft.
11   Commence reassembly by smearing the inside of the cover with

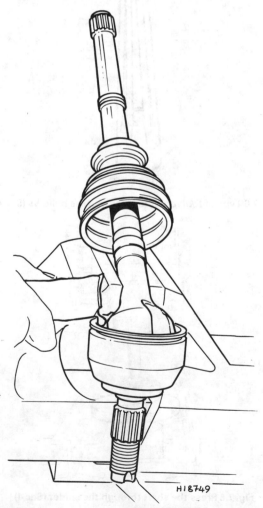

Fig. 7.13 Apply the specified amount of grease to the outer joint unit (Sec 4)

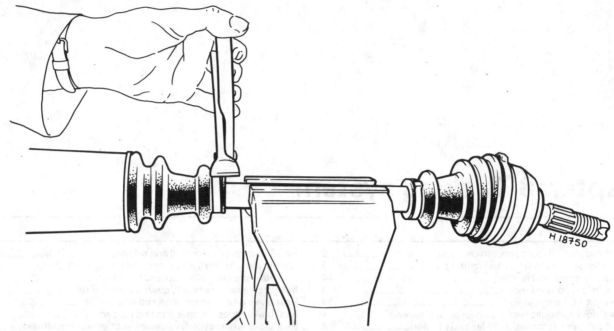

Fig. 7.14 Securing the new bellows retaining clips using suitable pincer pliers (Sec 4)

grease, fit the spacer to the new bellows which are supplied as a repair kit complete with grease sachet.

12   Insert the spacer/gaiter into the cover.

13   Slide the bellows and cover onto the shaft, but do not fit the new clip yet.

14   Using a piece of tubing as a drift, align the marks made before dismantling and drive the spider onto the shaft. Note that the chamfered side of the spider should go onto the shaft first.

15   Fit a new spider retaining circlip.

16   Remove the bearing retaining tape.

17   Draw the cover over the spider and apply grease from the sachet to all components. Refit the tulip yoke with spring and thrust cap. Use a new O-ring seal.

18   Peen the rim of the cover evenly all around the yoke.

19   Engage the retaining clip over the narrow end of the bellows. Secure the clip as shown in Fig. 7.14.

20   Carefully insert a thin rod under the narrow end of the bellows and release any trapped air.

21   When assembled, check that the bellows seat correctly without distortion or twisting (photo).

Outboard joint

22   If the guide tool mentioned in paragraph 5 is available, it is possible to cut the defective bellows from the shaft and fit the new bellows without dismantling the shaft. Where such a tool is not available, proceed in the following way.

23   With the driveshaft removed from the car and the inboard joint dismantled, as previously described, cut free the clip which retains the larger diameter end of the bellows (photo).

24   Cut free the clip from the smaller diameter end of the bellows and slide the bellows down the shaft.

25   Wipe away as much grease as possible from the joint and discard the defective bellows.

26   Apply the grease supplied with the repair kit evenly between the bellows and joint.

27   Locate the new bellows and retaining clips. Secure the clips as shown in Fig. 7.14.

28   Insert a thin rod under the narrow end of the bellows to release any trapped air.

29   Refit the inboard joint, as previously described.

---

5   Fault diagnosis – driveshafts

Symptom	Reason(s)
Knocking noise, particularly on full lock	Worn driveshaft joints
Clonk on taking up drive or on overrun	Worn driveshaft joints Worn shaft splines Loose driveshaft nut Loose roadwheel bolts

Chapter 8 Braking system

Contents

Specifications

Type ....

Front disc brakes, rear drum brakes. Servo-assistance on all models except AX 10 (up to 1987). Cable operated handbrake to rear wheels

Front disc brakes

Make	Teves
Disc diameter:	
All AX models except GT (1989 on)	238 mm (9.38 in)
GT (1989 on)	258 mm (10.2 in)
Disc thickness (new):	
All models except GT	8 mm (0.32 in)
GT	10 mm (0.39 in)
Disc thickness (minimum):	
All models except GT	6 mm (0.24 in)
GT	8 mm (0.32 in)
Maximum allowable run-out	0.1 mm (0.004 in)
Disc pad lining thickness:	
New	12 mm (0.47 in)
Minimum allowable	2 mm (0.08 in)

Rear drum brakes

Make	DBA
Drum diameter	
New	165 mm (6.5 in)
Maximum	166 mm (6.54 in)
Lining thickness:	
New	4.55 mm (0.18 in)
Minimum allowable	1.0 mm (0.04 in)
Rear wheel cylinder diameter	19 mm (0.75 in)

General

Master cylinder diameter	20.6 mm (0.81 in)
Master cylinder operating rod setting (rod front face-to-servo front face)	22.2 to 22.4 mm (0.87 to 0.88 in)
Servo unit diameter	187.5 mm (7.4 in)
Brake pedal pushrod setting (clevis pin centre-to-servo body rear face)	168.5 mm (6.6 in)
Stop light switch clearance	5.0 mm (0.2 in)
Brake fluid type/specification	Hydraulic fluid to DOT 4 (Duckhams Universal Brake and Clutch Fluid)
Fluid capacity	0.22 litre (0.39 pint)

Torque wrench settings

	Nm	lbf ft
Caliper Torx bolts:		
Upper	120	89
Lower	35	26
Rear hub nut	140	103
Master cylinder	14	10
Servo unit	14	10
Brake pedal hinge pin	25	18
Stop light switch locknut	10	7
Handbrake	14	10
Handbrake cable to brake unit	25	18

1   General description

The braking system is of hydraulic type with discs on the front and drums on the rear. The handbrake is cable-operated on the rear wheels.

The hydraulic circuit is of two independent diagonally opposed sections so that, in the event of the failure of one section, the remaining section is still functional.

A compensating valve (or valves) reduces the hydraulic pressure to the rear brakes under heavy applications of the brake pedal in order to prevent rear wheel lock-up.

A vacuum servo unit is fitted to all models except the AX 10 which had one fitted from 1987-on.

2   Routine maintenance

Carry out the following procedures at the intervals given in *Routine maintenance* at the beginning of the manual.

1   Check that the brake fluid level is near the top of the reservoir located on the master cylinder (photo). A slight fall in level is normal as the front disc pads wear, but a considerable drop will need investigating. If necessary top up the level after removing the filler cap.
2   Examine the hydraulic circuit lines and hoses for damage and deterioration, and for any signs of leakage. There is no need to retighten union nuts as this may distort the sealing faces.
3   Apply the handbrake and check that both rear wheels are locked.
4   Inspect the front brake disc pads, and renew them if necessary as described in Section 3.
5   Remove the inspection plate in the rear brake backplate and check the brake linings for excessive wear. Renew the linings as described in Section 6 if they are worn beyond the minimum specified thickness.
6   Renew the hydraulic fluid at the specified intervals. To renew the hydraulic fluid, remove the filler cap from the reservoir and use a syringe to remove the fluid from both compartments. Fill the reservoir with new hydraulic fluid and proceed to bleed the system, as described in Section 12. Allow 5 or 6 depressions of the brake pedal to clear old fluid.

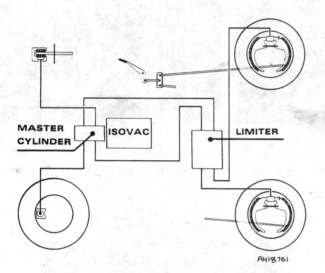

Fig. 8.1 Brake system layout with suspension mounted compensating valve unit (Sec 1)

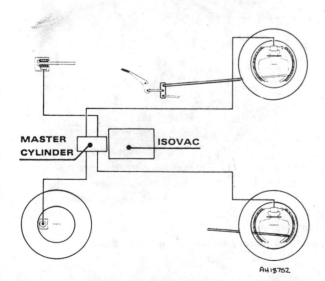

Fig. 8.2 Brake system layout with compensator units integral with the rear wheel cylinders (Sec 1)

3   Disc pads – inspection and renewal

1   Jack up the front of the car and support on axle stands. Apply the handbrake and remove the roadwheels.
2   If the friction material has worn down to 2.0 mm (0.079 in) then the pads must be renewed as an axle set.
3   Disconnect the brake pad wear warning lamp lead at the in-line connector near the calliper.
4   Withdraw the pad retainer pins by drifting them out with a punch.
5   Release and remove the retaining spring, then the pads. Note that the inboard pad has an engagement clip attached to its backing plate which has lugs that locate in the piston recesses (photo). If necessary, compress the inboard pad back against the piston to release and withdraw it, but watch for fluid spillage from the reservoir. Soak up any excess fluid with a clean cloth to prevent spillage.
6   Clean away all dust and dirt from the calliper. **Do not** inhale the dust, as it may be injurious to health. Check for brake fluid leakage around the piston dust seal and, if evident, overhaul the calliper, as described later in the Chapter. Check the brake disc for wear and also check that the rubber bellows on the cylinder sliding rods are in good condition.
7   Clean the backs of the disc pads and apply a little anti-squeal brake grease but take care not to get any grease onto the pad linings. Note the anti-rattle plate modification shown in Fig. 8.3.
8   Refit the brake pads in the reverse order of removal as shown in the accompanying photos. On completion, refit the front roadwheels and lower the car to the ground. Check and if necessary, top up the brake fluid level in the hydraulic reservoir.
9   Check for satisfactory operation of the brakes, but avoid excessive braking, unless in an emergency, during the initial miles so that the pads can wear in.

2.1 Topping up the hydraulic fluid level in the reservoir

3.5 Inboard brake pad showing engagement clip

3.8A Insert the brake pads...

3.8B ... locate the retaining spring...

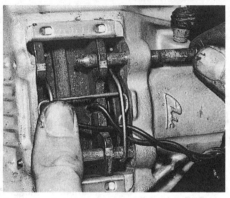

3.8C ... and pins

3.8D Brake pads and retainers reassembled

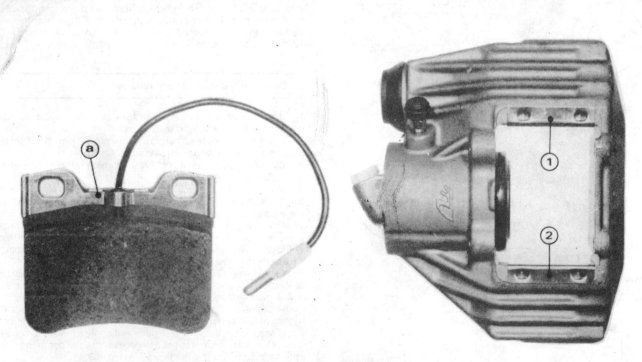

Fig. 8.3 Brake pad and calliper.
If fitting late style pads with anti-rattle plate (a) to earlier type calliper, remove stainless plates 1 and 2 (Sec 3)

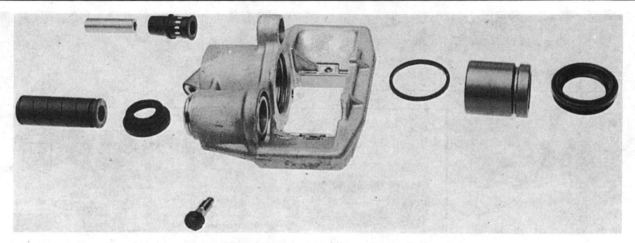

Fig. 8.4 Exploded view of the brake calliper unit (Sec 4)

4 Front brake calliper – removal, overhaul and refitting

1 Remove the front brake disc pads as described in the previous Section.

2 Fit a brake hose clamp to the flexible hose connected to the calliper. Alternatively remove the brake fluid reservoir filler cap and tighten it down onto a piece of polythene sheeting to reduce the loss of fluid when disconnecting the calliper.

3 Loosen the flexible hose union connection at the calliper.

4 Unscrew the two Torx type mounting bolts (one is covered by a rubber protector cup which pulls free), then withdraw the calliper from the disc and unscrew the calliper from the flexible hose. Plug the hose to prevent loss of fluid.

5 Clean the exterior of the calliper.

6 Prise the dust cover and ring from the end of the piston (photo).

7 Withdraw the piston from the cylinder. If necessary use air pressure from a foot pump in the fluid inlet to force the piston out.

8 Prise the seal from inside the cylinder, taking care not to damage the cylinder wall.

9 If required the sliding guide sleeves and their rubber dust covers can be removed, but keep them identified for location and note their orientation. Once removed, they should be renewed.

10 Clean all the components using methylated spirit or clean brake fluid then examine them for wear and damage. Check the piston and cylinder surfaces for scoring, excessive wear and corrosion, and if evident renew the complete calliper assembly. Similarly check the sliding guides. If the components are in good condition obtain a repair kit which will contain all the necessary rubber seals and other renewable items.

11 Dip the new seal in fresh brake fluid then locate it in the cylinder groove using the fingers only to manipulate it.

12 Dip the piston in brake fluid and insert it in the cylinder, twisting it as necessary to locate it in the seal.

13 Fit the dust cover and ring over the end of the piston and cylinder.

14 Lubricate the sliding guides with the grease supplied and refit them, together with the new dust covers.

15 To refit the calliper, first screw it onto the flexible hose and locate it over the brake disc so that the hose is not twisted.

16 Clean the mounting bolt threads and apply locking fluid. Insert the mounting bolts and tighten them to the specified torque.

17 Tighten the flexible hose union on the calliper. Check that the hose is clear of the strut and surrounding components and, if necessary, loosen the rigid pipe union on the body bracket, reposition the hose and retighten the union.

18 Refit the disc pads, as described in Section 3.

19 Remove the brake hose clamp or polythene sheeting and bleed the hydraulic system, as described in Section 12.

5 Brake disc – inspection, removal and refitting

1 Remove the disc pads, as described in Section 3.

2 Using a dial gauge or feelers and a fixed block, check that the disc run-out is within the specified limit. Do not confuse wheel bearing endfloat with disc wear. Also check the condition of the disc for scoring. Light scoring is normal, but if excessive, either renew the disc or have it ground to within the specified limit.

3 To remove the disc, unscrew the cross-head screw and withdraw the disc at an angle from the calliper and hub (photo).

4 Refitting is a reversal of removal, but make sure that the disc-to-hub mating surfaces are clean and that the cross-head screw is tightened fully. Refer to Section 3 when refitting the disc pads.

6 Rear brake shoes – inspection and renewal

1 Jack up the rear of the car and support it on axle stands. Chock the front wheels and release the handbrake.

2 As a general guide, the lining thickness may be provisionally inspected without removing the brake drum/hub by prising free the

4.6 Front brake calliper showing piston and dust cover

5.3 Brake disc showing retaining screw (arrowed)

6.4 Removing the grease cap...

6.5A ... the hub nut...

6.5B ... and washer

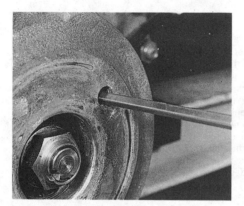

6.5C Releasing the brake adjustment

6.9 Rear brake assembly

6.10 Detaching the lower return spring

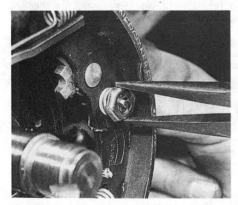

6.11 Releasing the brake shoe steady springs

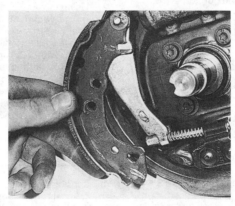

6.13 Handbrake cable attachment to shoe lever

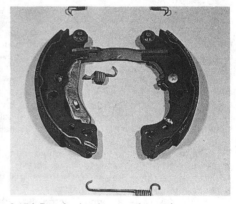

6.15A Rear brake shoes and associate components

rubber inspection plug from the backplate. Then, using a torch, check the lining thickness of the leading shoe through the inspection hole. If it is at, or near, the specified minimum thickness, remove the drum/hub and make a detailed inspection.

3   Remove the rear roadwheel each side.

4   Tap free the grease cap from the centre of the hub. It may well distort during removal, in which case it will need renewing (photo).

5   Wipe away any grease from the hub nut, then relieve the lock staking and unscrew the nut. Withdraw the nut, washer and the drum/hub (photos). If the drum is reluctant to be withdrawn, this will probably be due to, either the handbrake still applied, or the shoes wearing grooves in the drum. In this case, insert a screwdriver through one of the wheel bolt holes and depress the handbrake lever on the rear brake shoe so that it slides back behind the shoe (photo). This will retract the shoes and allow the hub/drum to be removed.

6   Brush the dust and dirt from the shoes, backplate and drum. **Do not** inhale it, as it may be injurious to health.

7   Repeat this procedure and remove the opposing rear brake drum.

8   Carefully inspect the rear brake linings on each side. If any are worn down to (or beyond) the specified minimum allowable thickness, renew the brake linings on both rear brakes.

9   Note the position of each shoe and the location of the return and steady springs (photo).

10   Unhook and remove the lower return spring (photo).

11   Remove the steady springs using pliers to depress the outer cups and turn them through 90° (photo). Remove the pins from the backplate.

12   Release the small return spring from the handbrake lever, then expanding the shoes at their lower end, detach them from the lower anchor, then from the wheel cylinder at the top end.

6.15B Leading shoe and associate fittings

6.15C Trailing shoe and associate fittings

6.18 Relocating the brake shoes

6.19 Refitting the handbrake lever return spring

6.24 Stake lock the nut ...

6.25 ... then fit the grease cap

13   As the shoe assemblies are removed, detach the handbrake cable from the actuating lever (photo).

14   If necessary, position a rubber band over the wheel cylinder to prevent the pistons coming out. Should there be evidence of brake fluid leakage from the wheel cylinder, renew it or overhaul it, as described in Section 7.

15   The rear hub nut must be renewed, also the stub axle seal. Do not allow oil, grease or hydraulic fluid to come into contact with the linings or friction surfaces during subsequent operations. Transfer the handbrake and automatic adjuster levers to the new shoes as required. Note that the levers and strut on each rear wheel are different, and that the leading and trailing shoes are fitted with different grade linings (photos).

16   Place the shoe assemblies on the bench in the order of fitting and locate the upper return spring.

17   Apply brake grease sparingly to the metal contact points of the shoes, then position them on the backplate and reconnect the handbrake cable. Engage the strut with the slots at the top of the shoes, making sure it is located correctly on the automatic adjuster lever. Engage the upper shoe ends on the wheel cylinder pistons.

18   Engage the lower ends of the shoes over the bottom anchor (photo).

19   Refit the handbrake lever return spring (photo).

20   Insert the steady spring pins in the backplate and through the shoe webs, then fit the springs and outer cups.

21   Move the serrated automatic adjuster lever quadrant against the spring tension to set the shoes at their minimum diameter.

22   Lubricate the new stub axle seal with grease then fit it into position.

23   Fit the hub/drum on the stub axle and retain with the washer and nut. (Always renew the nut).

24   Tighten the nut to the specified torque then lock it by staking the nut flange into the groove on the stub axle (photo).

25   Tap the grease cap into the hub/drum (photo).

26   Repeat all the operations on the opposite rear brake then refit the roadwheels and lower the car to the ground.

27   Apply the footbrake several times to set the shoes in their adjusted position.

28   Adjust the handbrake, as described in Section 15.

7   Rear brake wheel cylinder – removal, overhaul and refitting

1   Jack up the rear of the car and support on axle stands. Chock the front wheels and remove the relevant rear wheel.

2   Remove the hub/drum, as described in Section 6.

3   Note the location of the brake shoe upper return spring then unhook and remove it.

4   Disconnect the spring from the handbrake lever/trailing shoe, then prise free the shoes and locate a suitable spacer between them to keep them clear of the wheel cylinder.

5   Fit a brake hose clamp to the flexible hose supplying the rear brakes. Alternatively remove the brake fluid reservoir filler cap and tighten it down onto a piece of polythene sheeting to reduce the loss of fluid when disconnecting the wheel cylinder.

6   Unscrew the hydraulic pipe union nut from the rear of the wheel cylinder.

7   Unscrew the two mounting bolts and withdraw the wheel cylinder from the backplate (photo). Take care not to spill any brake fluid on the brake shoe linings.

8   Clean the exterior of the wheel cylinder. Note that on all three-door AX 10 and AX 11 models produced from September 1987, the rear wheel cylinder incorporates an integral pressure limiter, (instead of the limiter being fitted separately to the rear suspension). The rear wheel cylinders on these models must not be dismantled. If they are defective in any way, they must be renewed as a unit. On other models (with a suspension mounted limiter) proceed as follows.

9   Pull free the dust excluders, then extract the piston and seal assemblies, noting their orientation and fitting position.

10   Check the surfaces of the cylinder bore and pistons for scoring and corrosion and, if evident, renew the complete wheel cylinder. If the components are in good condition discard the seals and obtain a repair kit which will contain all the necessary renewable components.

11   Clean the pistons and cylinder with methylated spirit or clean brake fluid then dip each component in fresh brake fluid and reassemble in reverse order; making sure that the lips of the seals face into the cylinder. When completed, wipe clean the outer surfaces of the dust excluders.

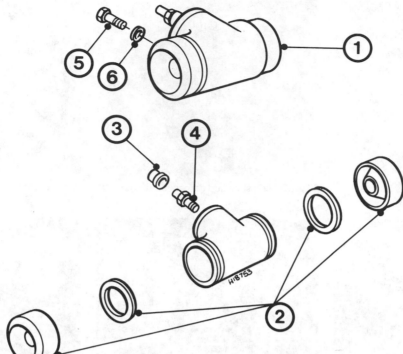

1   Cylinder body
2   Seals kit
3   Dust cap
4   Bleed nipple
5   Retaining bolt
6   Washer

Fig. 8.5 Exploded view of the rear wheel cylinder unit (non-compensator type) (Sec 7)

12   Clean the backplate and refit the wheel cylinder using a reversal of the removal procedure. Refer to Section 6 when refitting the hub/drum.
13   Make sure that the brake hose clamp or polythene sheeting is removed then bleed the hydraulic system, as described in Section 12.

8   Rear brake drum – inspection and renovation

1   Whenever the hub/brake drum is removed to check the linings, take the opportunity to inspect the interior of the drum.
2   If the drum is grooved, owing to failure to renew worn linings or after a very high mileage has been covered, then it may be possible to regrind it, provided the maximum internal diameter is not exceeded.
3   Even if only one drum is in need of grinding both drums must be reground to the same size in order to maintain even braking characteristics.
4   Judder or a springy pedal felt when the brakes are applied can be caused by a distorted (out-of-round) drum. Here again it may be possible to regrind the drums, otherwise a new drum will be required.

9   Brake compensator – description, removal and refitting

1   All models are fitted with a brake compensator. AX 10 and AX 11 three-door models produced from September 1987 are fitted with rear wheel cylinders which incorporate a compensator in each unit. All other three and five-door models have a separate compensator unit fitted, being located under the car floor just forward of the rear suspension. Its purpose is to maintain equal braking effect on the front and rear wheels and prevent the rear brakes from locking up.
2   If you find that, on applying the brakes, the effect is mainly on the front wheels and that it is impossible to lock the rear brakes without using the handbrake or, alternatively, if you find that the rear brakes invariably lock under heavy braking, it is likely that the compensator is defective.
3   A Citroën agent will have to test the component if its performance is in doubt as pressure test equipment is necessary. No attempt must be made to dismantle the unit.
4   Renewal of the separate type compensator unit is a straightforward removal and refitting procedure followed by bleeding of the hydraulic system. Ensure that the unit is correctly orientated when fitted.
5   Where the compensators are incorporated in the wheel cylinders the cylinder(s) will need replacing as a unit (Section 7).

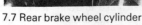

7.7 Rear brake wheel cylinder

11.4 Typical hydraulic flexible/rigid line connection and support bracket

12.2 Rear brake bleed nipple location (arrowed)

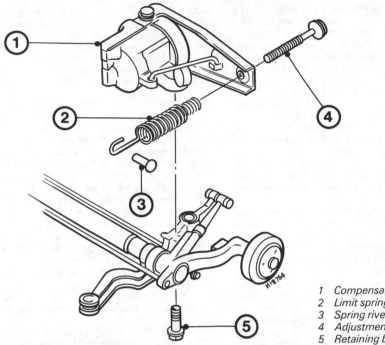

1 Compensator unit
2 Limit spring
3 Spring rivet
4 Adjustment screw (do not alter the setting)
5 Retaining bolt

Fig. 8.6 Brake compensator (suspension mounted type) (Sec 9)

10 Master cylinder – removal, overhaul and refitting

1   Detach the brake fluid low level warning lamp leads from the filler cap connectors, then release and remove the filler cap from the reservoir. Draw out the fluid from the reservoir using a syringe.
2   Prise the reservoir from the master cylinder and remove the seals.
3   Unscrew the union nuts securing the rigid brake lines to the master cylinder and pull out the lines. Cap the pipe ends to prevent loss of fluid.
4   Unscrew the mounting nuts and withdraw the master cylinder from the servo unit.
5   Using circlip pliers, extract the circlip from the mouth of the cylinder.
6   Remove the primary and secondary piston components noting their locations. If necessary tap the cylinder on a block of wood.
7   Clean all the components in methylated spirit. Check the surfaces of the cylinder bore and pistons for scoring and corrosion, and if evident renew the complete master cylinder. If the components are in good condition, note the orientation of the seals, then remove and discard them. Obtain a repair kit containing the necessary components for renewal.
8   Dip the new seals in fresh brake fluid and fit them to the pistons using the fingers only to manipulate them.
9   Reassemble the master cylinder in reverse order to dismantling and make sure that the circlip is fully engaged with the groove in the mouth of the cylinder.
10   Refit the master cylinder unit in the reverse order of removal. Tighten the retaining nuts to the specified torque wrench setting. Ensure that the connections are clean when reconnecting the hydraulic lines.
11   Top up the hydraulic fluid level in the reservoir and bleed the brake hydraulic system as described in Section 12.

11 Flexible and rigid hydraulic lines – inspection and renewal

1   Examine all the unions for signs of leaks. Then look at the flexible hoses for signs of fraying and chafing (as well as for leaks). This is only a preliminary inspection of the flexible hoses as exterior condition does not necessarily indicate interior condition which will be considered later.
2   The steel pipes must be examined equally carefully. They must be thoroughly cleaned and examined for signs of dents or other percussive damage, rust and corrosion. Rust and corrosion should be scraped off

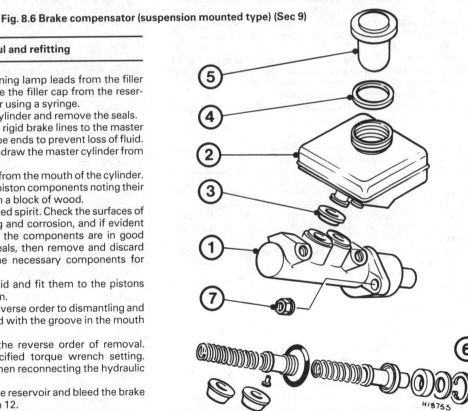

Fig. 8.7 Exploded view of the master cylinder unit (Sec 10)

1 Master cylinder   5 Cap
2 Reservoir   6 Seal/piston kit
3 Seal   (primary and Secondary)
4 Seal   7 Nut

and, if the depth of pitting in the pipes is significant, they will need renewal. This is most likely in those areas underneath the chassis and along the rear suspension arms where the pipes are exposed to the full force of road and weather conditions.
3   Rigid pipe removal is usually quite straightforward. The unions at

each end are undone and the pipe drawn out of the connection. The clips which may hold it to the car body are bend back and it is then removed. Underneath the car exposed unions can be particularly stubborn, defying the efforts of an open-ended spanner. As few people will have the special split ring spanner required, a self-grip wrench is the only answer. If the pipe is being renewed, new unions will be provided. If not then one will have to put up with the possibility of burring over the flats on the union and use a self-grip wrench for replacement also.

4   Flexible hoses are always fitted to a rigid support bracket where they join a rigid pipe, the bracket being fixed to the chassis or rear suspension arm (photo). The rigid pipe unions must first be removed from the flexible union, then the retaining plate must be pulled out and the flexible hose and fitting released from the bracket.

5   Depending upon the make of the particular calliper, the flexible hose may be connected simply by screwing it into its tapped hole or by using a hollow bolt with banjo end fitting. Use a new copper sealing washer on each side of the banjo union.

6   Once the flexible hose is removed examine the internal bore. If clear of fluid it should be possible to see through it. Any specks of rubber which come out, or signs of restriction in the bore, mean that the inner lining is breaking up and the hose must be renewed.

7   Rigid pipes which need replacement can usually be purchased at any local garage where they have the pipe, unions and special tools to make them up. They will need to know the pipe length required and the type of flare used at the ends of the pipe. These may be different at each end of the same pipe.

8   Installation of the pipes is a reversal of the removal procedure. The pipe profile must be pre-set before fitting. Any acute bends must be put in by the garage on a bending machine, otherwise there is the possibility of kinking them and restricting the fluid flow.

9   All hose and pipe threads and unions are to metric standards. Screw in new components by hand initially to ensure that the threads are compatible.

10   Remember that a metric hose end fitting seals at the tip of its threaded section and will leave a gap between the hexagon of the end fitting and the surface of the component. Do not attempt to overtighten the hose end fitting in order to eliminate the gap.

11   The hydraulic system must be bled on completion of hose or rigid pipe renewal with reference to Chapter 12.

12 Hydraulic system – draining and bleeding

1   If the hydraulic system is to be drained follow the procedure given in Section 2. If the master cylinder or connecting pipes have been removed, the complete hydraulic system must be bled, but if only a calliper or wheel cylinder has been removed then only that particular circuit need be bled.

2   If the complete system is being bled, the sequence of bleeding should be as follows:

Left-hand rear wheel
Right-hand front wheel
Right-hand rear wheel (photo)
Left-hand front wheel

3   Unless the pressure bleeding method is being used, do not forget to keep the level in the master cylinder reservoir topped up to prevent air from being drawn into the system which would make any work done worthless. Before commencing operations, check that all system hoses and pipes are in good condition with unions tight and free from leaks.

4   Take great care not to allow hydraulic fluid to come into contact with the vehicle paintwork as it is an effective paint stripper. Wash off any spilled fluid immediately with cold water.

5   On models with a vacuum servo destroy the vacuum by giving several applications of the brake pedal in quick succession.

Bleeding – two man method

6   Gather together a clean jar and a length of rubber or plastic tubing which will be a tight fit on the brake bleed screws.

7   Engage the help of an assistant.

8   Push one end of the bleed tube onto the first bleed screw and immerse the other end in the jar which should contain enough hydraulic fluid to cover the end of the tube.

9   Open the bleed screw one half a turn and have your assistant depress the brake pedal fully then slowly release it. Tighten the bleed screw at the end of each pedal downstroke to obviate any chance of air or fluid being drawn back into the system.

10   Repeat this operation until clean hydraulic fluid, free from air bubbles, can be seen coming through into the jar.

11   With the bleed screw tightened, remove the bleed tube and proceed to the next wheel.

Bleeding – using one-way valve kits

12   There are a number of one-man, one-way brake bleeding kits available from motor accessory shops. It is recommended that one of these kits is used wherever possible as it will greatly simplify the bleeding operation and also reduce the risk of air or fluid being drawn back into the system, quite apart from being able to do the work without the help of an assistant. To use the kit, connect the tube to the bleed screw and open the screw one half a turn.

13   Depress the brake pedal fully then slowly release it. The one-way valve in the kit will prevent expelled air from returning at the end of each pedal downstroke. Repeat the operation several times to be sure of ejecting all the air from the system. Some kits include a translucent container which can be positioned so that the air bubbles can actually be seen being ejected from the system.

14   Tighten the bleed screw, remove the tube and repeat the operations on the remaining brakes.

15   On completion, depress the brake pedal. If it still feels spongy, repeat the bleeding operations as air must still be trapped in the system.

Bleeding – using a pressure bleeding kit

16   These kits are available from motor accessory shops and are usually operated by air pressure from the spare tyre.

17   By connecting a pressurised container to the master cylinder fluid reservoir, bleeding is then carried out simply by opening each bleed screw in sequence and allowing the fluid to run out, rather like turning on a tap, until no air is visible in the expelled fluid.

18   By using this method, the large reserve of hydraulic fluid provides a safeguard against air being drawn into the master cylinder during bleeding which may occur if the fluid level in the reservoir is allowed to fall too low.

19   Pressure bleeding is particularly useful when bleeding the complete system at time of routine fluid renewal.

All methods

20   When bleeding is completed, check and top up the fluid level in the master cylinder reservoir.

21   Check the feel of the brake pedal. If it feels at all spongy, air must still be present in the system and the need for further bleeding is indicated. Failure to bleed satisfactorily after a reasonable repetition of the bleeding operations may be due to worn master cylinder seals.

22   Always discard brake fluid which has been bled from the system. It is almost certain to be contaminated with moisture, air and dirt, making it unsuitable for further use.

23   Clean fluid should always be stored in an airtight container as it absorbs moisture readily which lowers its boiling point and could affect braking performance under severe conditions.

13 Servo unit – removal and refitting

1   Remove the air cleaner unit and the intake ducting as described in Chapter 3.

2   Detach and remove the battery as described in Chapter 12.

3   Unscrew and remove the master cylinder retaining nuts, then carefully withdraw the master cylinder from the servo unit. As it is withdrawn, detach the brake pipes from the block retainers on the bulkhead, but take care not to distort the hydraulic pipes. Position the master cylinder so that it is clear of the servo unit, but leave the hydraulic pipes attached.

4   Disconnect the servo vacuum hose from the servo unit.

5   Working through the area vacated by the air cleaner unit, release the pushrod clevis pin retaining clip and withdraw the pin.

6   Unscrew the servo unit-to-mounting bracket retaining nuts. These are best accessible through the aperture in the left-hand wheel arch (photo).

7   As the servo unit is removed, collect any adjustment shims.

8   Refit in the reverse order of removal. Relocate any shims and

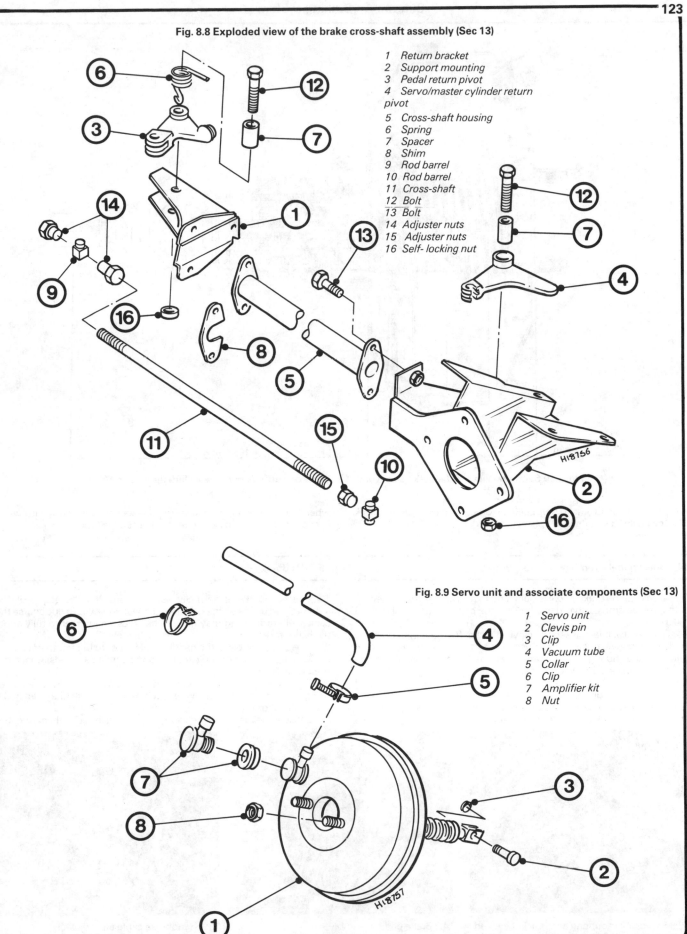

Fig. 8.8 Exploded view of the brake cross-shaft assembly (Sec 13)

1 Return bracket
2 Support mounting
3 Pedal return pivot
4 Servo/master cylinder return pivot
5 Cross-shaft housing
6 Spring
7 Spacer
8 Shim
9 Rod barrel
10 Rod barrel
11 Cross-shaft
12 Bolt
13 Bolt
14 Adjuster nuts
15 Adjuster nuts
16 Self- locking nut

H18756

Fig. 8.9 Servo unit and associate components (Sec 13)

1 Servo unit
2 Clevis pin
3 Clip
4 Vacuum tube
5 Collar
6 Clip
7 Amplifier kit
8 Nut

H18757

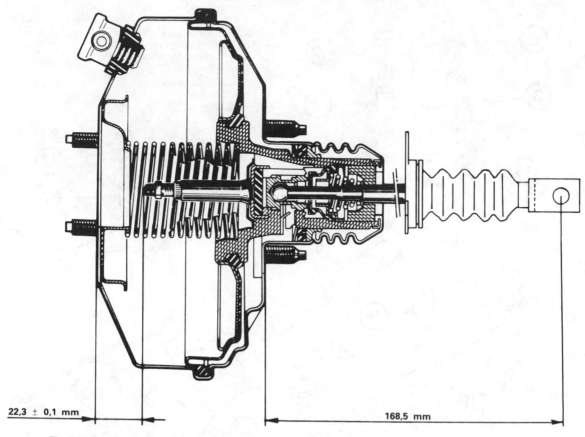

22,3 ± 0,1 mm   168,5 mm

Fig. 8.10 Sectional view of the brake servo unit. The pushrod settings must be as indicated (Sec 13)

tighten the retaining nuts to the specified torque wrench settings. Check that the pushrod setting is as specified.

14   Brake pedal – removal and refitting

1   Access to the brake pedal is poor, and to gain access the procedure is much the same as that described for the clutch pedal in Chapter 5 (Section 4).
2   Once accessible, release the clevis pin clip (from the inboard side). Undo the retaining nut and then push the pivot bolt through, release the return spring (noting its orientation), and remove the pedal (photo). Detach the brake light switch leads.
3   Refit in the reverse order of removal. Lubricate the pedal pivots and check for satisfactory operation of the pedal before refitting the items removed for access. Also check the operation of the brake light switch and if necessary, adjust the switch position to allow a nominal clearance

when the brake is released. Unscrew the locknut and screw the switch in or out as required to adjust, then retighten the locknut.

15   Handbrake – adjustment

1   The handbrake is normally kept adjusted by the action of the automatic adjusters on the rear brake shoes. However, in due course the cables will stretch and may have to be adjusted in order to fully apply the handbrake.
2   To adjust, first place the handbrake lever onto the fourth notch.
3   Jack up the rear of the car and support on axle stands. Chock the front wheels.
4   The cable to each rear brake unit is adjusted individually, an adjuster being fitted to each cable where it passes through the rear brake backplate (photo).
5   Loosen off the cable adjuster locknut each side, then turn the

13.6 Servo unit mounting and bracket viewed through the aperture in the left-hand wheel arch

14.2 Brake pedal assembly

15.4 Handbrake cable and adjuster

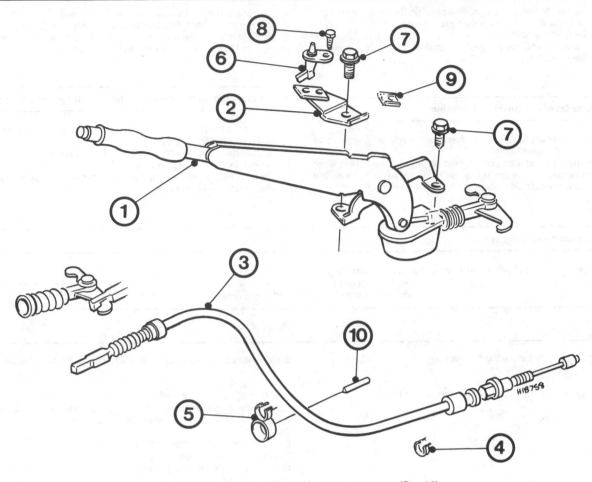

Fig. 8.11 Handbrake cable and lever components (Sec 16)

1 *Lever*	4 *Clip*	7 *Bolt*	9 *Captive nut*
2 *Bracket*	5 *Clip*	8 *Screw*	10 *Rivet*
3 *Cable*	6 *Warning switch*		

adjuster as required to set the handbrake adjustment. On the fourth notch position of the lever, the rear brake unit on each side should be felt to just start to bind and be fully locked when the lever is fully applied. Fully release the handbrake lever and check that the rear wheels spin freely without signs of binding, then tighten the adjuster locknuts to set the adjustment.

6   On completion, lower the car to the ground and remove the chocks from the front wheels.

16 Handbrake cables – removal and refitting

1   Remove the rear brake shoes as described in Section 6. When raising the car at the rear, support it on axle stands at a height suitable for working underneath the car.

2   Disconnect the right and left-hand cable from the backplate each side.

16.3A Handbrake cable connections to the rear brake and suspension arm (arrowed)

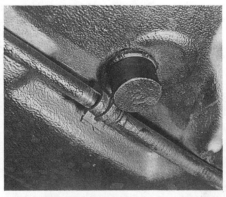

16.3B Handbrake cable to floor mounting clip

16.3C Handbrake cable equalizer unit

3   Release the cables from their retaining clips on the underside of the car and from the equalizer at the front end (photos).
4   Refit in the reverse order of removal, with reference to Section 6 where necessary. Finally, check and adjust the cable adjustment as described in Section 15.

17   Handbrake lever – removal and refitting

1   Move the front seats fully forward, remove the retaining screw and lift the cover from the handbrake lever.
2   Unscrew the lever retaining bolts, then disengage the cables from the equalizer underneath the car. It may be necessary to loosen off the adjusters to allow them to be detached (Section 15).

3   Separate the handbrake warning light switch and bracket, then detach the gaiter from the floorpan and withdraw the lever from the car.
4   Refit in the reverse order of removal. Adjust the cables as described in Section 15 and check for satisfactory operation.

18   Handbrake warning light switch – removal and refitting

1   Move the front seats fully forward, then remove the retaining screw and lift the cover from the handbrake lever.
2   Disconnect the switch lead, undo the retaining screw and remove the switch from the support bracket.
3   Refitting is a reversal of the removal procedure. Check for satisfactory operation on completion.

19   Fault diagnosis – braking system

Before diagnosing faults from the following chart, check that any braking irregularities are not caused by:

(a) Uneven and incorrect tyre pressures	*(c) Wear in the steering mechanism*
(b) Incorrect mix of radial and crossply tyres	*(d) Misalignment of the chassis geometry*

Symptom	Reason(s)
Pedal travels a long way before the brakes operate	Brake shoes set too far from the drums due to faulty self-adjusting mechanism
Stopping ability poor, even though pedal pressure is firm	Linings/pads and/or drums/disc badly worn or scored One or more wheel hydraulic cylinders or calliper pistons seized resulting in some brake shoes/pads not pressing against the drums/discs Brake linings/pads contaminated with oil Wrong type of linings/pads fitted (too hard) Brake shoes/pads wrongly assembled Faulty servo unit (where fitted)
Car veers to one side when the brakes are applied	Brake linings/pads on one side are contaminated with oil Hydraulic wheel cylinder/calliper on one side partially or fully seized A mixture of lining materials fitted between sides Unequal wear between sides caused by partially seized wheel cylinders/pistons
Pedal feels spongy	Air in the hydraulic system
Pedal feels springy when the brakes are applied	Brake linings/pads not bedded into the drums/discs (after fitting new ones) Master cylinder or brake backplate mounting bolts loose Out-of-round drums or discs with excessive run-out
Pedal travels right down with little or no resistance and brakes are virtually non-operative	Leak in hydraulic system resulting in lack of pressure for operating wheel cylinders/calliper pistons If no signs of leakage are apparent the master cylinder internal seals are failing to sustain pressure
Binding, juddering, overheating	One or a combination of causes given in the foregoing sections Handbrake over-adjusted Handbrake cable(s) seized
Lack of servo assistance	Vacuum hose leaking Non-return valve defective or leaking grommet Servo internal fault

Chapter 9 Suspension, hubs, wheels and tyres

Contents

Specifications

Front suspension

Type	Independent, MacPherson struts, coil springs. Anti-roll bar fitted to AX 14 and GT
Front suspension geometry	*Refer to Chapter 10*
Coil spring free length:	
AX 10 and AX 11 models...	339 mm (13.4 in) (colour code: green/red or green/green)
AX 14 models	387 mm (15.2 in) (colour code: yellow/red or yellow/green)
Hub bearings	Double-row ball-bearings
Hub bearing lubricant..	Multi-purpose lithium based grease (Duckhams LB10)
Torsion bar lubricant...	Special grease (Duckhams Admax B3)
Anti-roll bar diameter:	
AX 14 models	19 mm (0.75 in)
GT	21 mm (0.83 in)

Rear suspension

Type	Independent, cross tube with trailing arms, torsion bars, telescopic shock absorbers. Anti-roll bar fitted to GT
Anti-roll bar diameter (GT only)...	14 mm (0.55 in)
Torsion bar diameter/identification colour(s):	
AX 10 and AX 11 models:	
Left-hand bar	17.1 mm (0.67 in) 2 blue marks
Right-hand bar	17.1 mm (0.67 in) 1 blue mark
AX 14 models and GT:	
Left-hand bar	17.9 mm (0.71 in) 2 white marks
Right-hand bar	17.9 mm (0.71 in) 1 white mark
Hub bearing	Double-row ball-bearing (sealed)
Rear wheel toe setting (not adjustable):	
AX 10 and AX 11 models...	−2 ± 1 mm (0.08 ± 0.04 in) toe-out
AX 14 models and GT	−1 ± 1 mm (0.04 ± 0.04 in) toe-out

Suspension ride heights (± 10 mm/ 0.4 in):	Front	Rear
AX 10 and AX 11 models	214 mm (8.4 in)	418 mm (16.5 in)
AX 14 models	227 mm (8.9 in)	413 mm (16.3 in)
GT model	210 mm (8.3 in)	408 mm (16.1 in)
Torsion bar/anti-roll bar lubricant	Special grease (Duckhams Admax B3)	

Wheels

AX 10 and AX 11 models	4B. 13 (steel)
AX 11 models (option)	4.5B. 13 (steel)
Ax 11 TRE (option)	4.5J. 13 (alloy)
AX 14 models	4.5B. 13 (steel)
AX 14 models (option)	4.5J. 13 (alloy)
GT:	
To January 1989	5J. 13 (alloy)
From January 1989	5J. 14 (alloy)

Tyres

Sizes and pressure (cold) – lbf/in² (bar):	Front	Rear
AX 10:		
135/70 R13	29 (2.0)	29 (2.0)*
AX 11:		
135/70 R13	29 (2.0)	29 (2.0)
155/70 R13	28 (1.9)	28 (1.9)
AX 14:		
155/70 R13	28 (1.9)	28 (1.9)
GT:		
165/65 R13	28 (1.9)	29 (2.0)
155/65 R14	28 (1.9)	28 (1.9)
165/60 R14 (optional)	28 (1.9)	29 (2.0)

*Increase pressure by 3 lbf/in² (0.2 bar) for hard driving or maximum loading

Torque wrench settings

	Nm	lbf ft
Roadwheels		
Steel	90	66
Alloy	90	66
Front suspension		
Wheel hub nut	250	185
Suspension arm/hub carrier balljoint	28	21
Suspension arm pivot mounting nuts	55	41
Suspension arm pivot nuts	70	52
Strut upper mounting bracket nuts	18	13
Shock absorber retaining plug	140	103
Strut/shock absorber top retaining nut	45	33
Anti-roll bar mounting nuts	30	22
Rear suspension		
Wheel hub nut	140	103
Torsion bar Torx screws	20	15
Shock absorber: Brake backplate retaining screws	35	26
Upper mounting	90	66
Lower mounting	110	81
Trailing arm pivot	55	41
Axle unit mountings (to floor)	55	41
Anti-roll bar lever bolt	35	26

1 General description

The front suspension is of independent MacPherson strut type, incorporating coil springs and integral telescopic shock absorbers. The lateral and longitudinal movement of the struts is controlled by lower suspension arms. The arms have rubber inner mounting bushes and a balljoint at their outer end. An anti-roll bar is fitted to the front suspension on the AX 14 and GT models.

The front wheel hub carriers are attached to the struts, the hubs running on double row ball bearings.

The rear suspension is of trailing arm type with torsion bars and on the GT model, an anti-roll bar is fitted. The double-acting telescopic shock absorbers are fitted in a horizontally inclined position. The rear wheel stub axles and the rear wheel bearings are carried on the suspension arm each side, the bearings being of double-row ball-bearing type. Combined rear hub/brake drums are fitted each side at the rear.

2 Routine maintenance

Carry out the following procedures at the intervals given in *Routine maintenance* at the beginning of the manual.

1   Check and adjust the tyre pressures and make sure that the caps are securely fitted to the valves.
2   Thoroughly examine the tyres for wear, damage and deterioration. If necessary, use a trolley jack to raise each wheel clear of the ground so that a complete check can be made. Further information concerning tyres is given in Section 16.
3   Jack up each wheel in turn, then grip the top and bottom and attempt to rock the wheel. Any excessive play indicates wear in the hub bearings although, on the front wheels, check that the movement is not due to a worn lower suspension balljoint.
4   A very slight free play in the above mentioned check is normal but if free play felt is considerable, investigate further as follows.

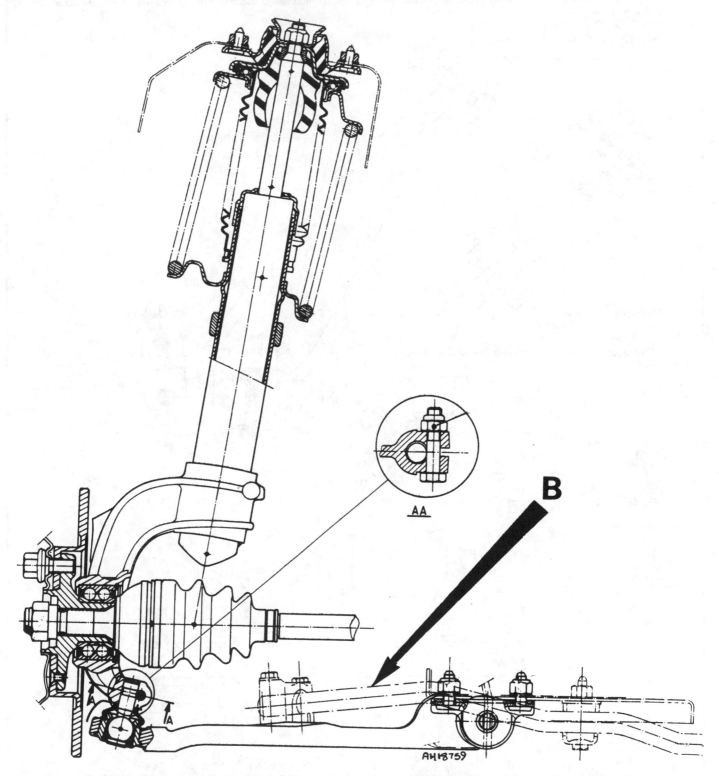

Fig. 9.1 Sectional view of a front suspension unit. Note that the anti-roll bar (B) is not fitted to all models (Sec 1)

5   Get an assistant to apply the footbrake, then rock the wheel as previously described. If the excessive play is reduced or eliminated, then the hub bearings are probably worn beyond a serviceable amount. If the free play is still excessive when the brakes are applied, the wear is in the suspension joints and/or mountings. Check each in turn and renew any that are found to be worn beyond an acceptable amount as described in the appropriate Section of this Chapter.

6   The hub bearings can be checked by gripping the wheel at the nine o'clock and three o'clock positions, and then rocking it as previously described. Excessive movement in this instance is most likely caused by wear in steering joints (refer to Chapter 10).

7   To check the shock absorbers for efficiency, the car should be free standing (on its wheels). Bounce the car at each corner in turn and check that when released the body returns to its normal position without continuing to rock up and down. If suspect, they must be further checked and if necessary renewed. Further check the shock absorbers by visually inspecting them for signs of fluid leakage (photo). Also check their upper and lower mountings for excessive wear and/or insecurity.

Fig. 9.2 Sectional view of the suspension arm showing its mountings and those of the anti-roll bar (where fitted) (Sec 1)

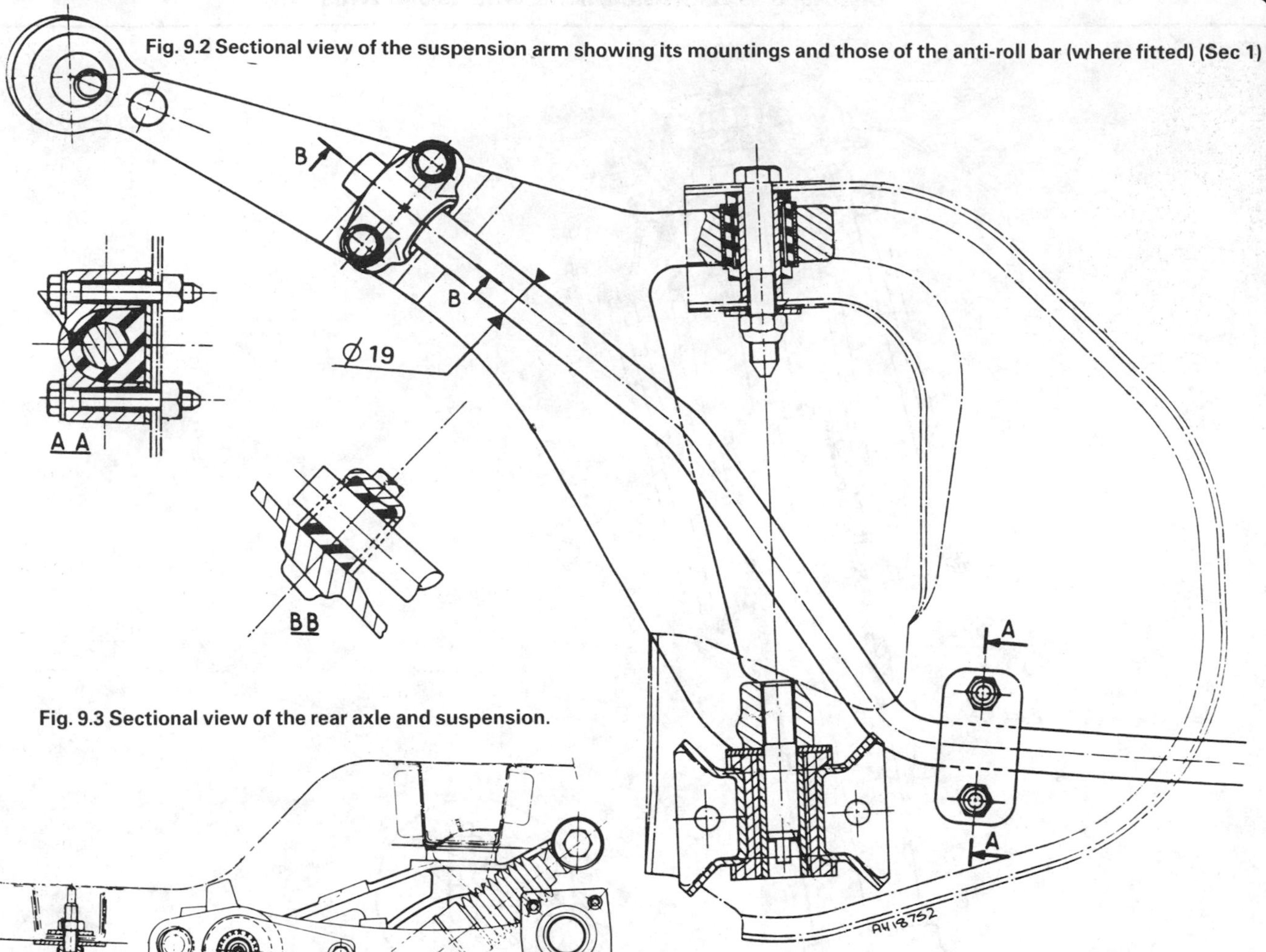
B
B
Ø19
A A
BB
A
A
A418752

Fig. 9.3 Sectional view of the rear axle and suspension.

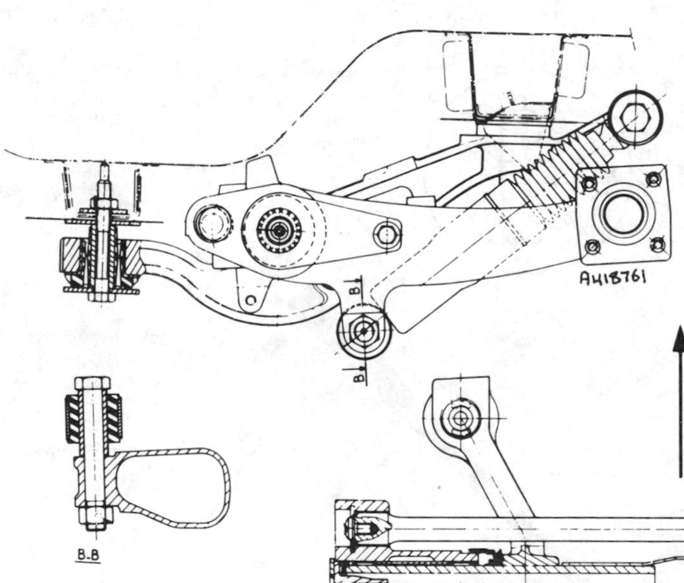
A418761
B
B
B-B

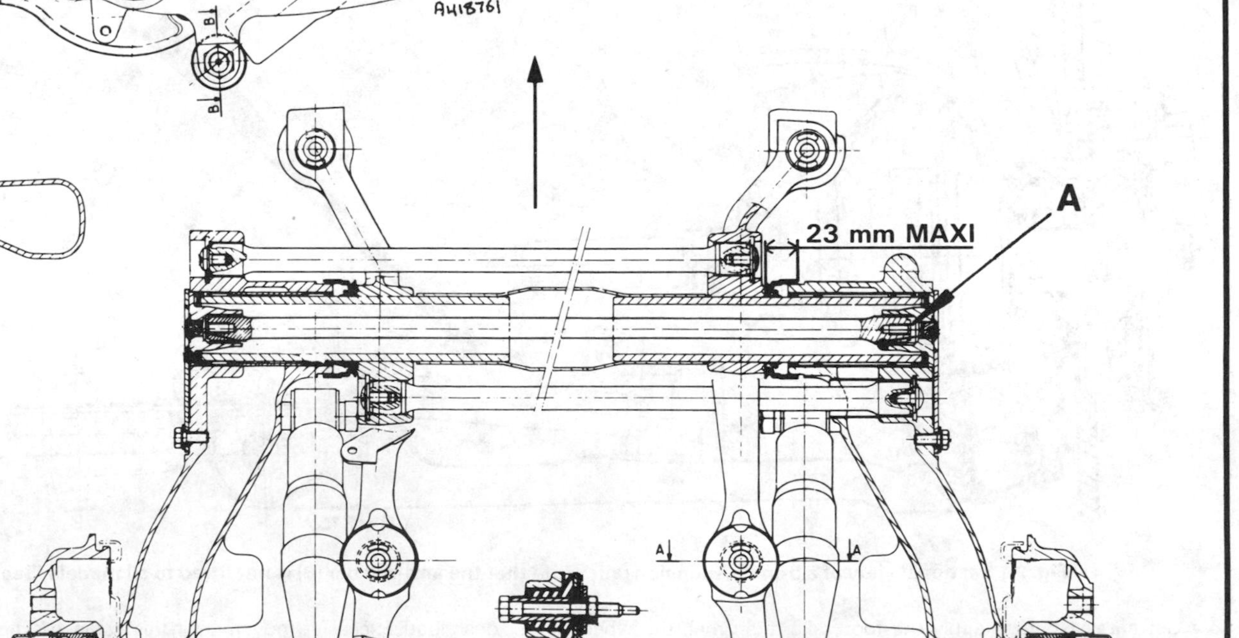
23 mm MAXI
A
A
A
A-A

Note that the anti-roll bar (A) is not fitted to all models (Sec 1)

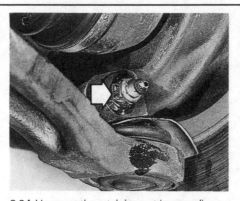

2.7 Front strut assembly. Check for signs of leakage from the shock absorber

3.2A Unscrew the retaining nut (arrowed)...

3.2B ... and withdraw the balljoint clamp bolt. Note the protector shield location (arrowed)

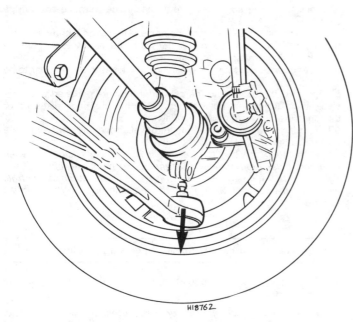

Fig. 9.4 Press suspension arm down to separate it from the balljoint clamp (Sec 3)

Renew if necessary as described in Section 5 (front) or Section 9 (rear).

8   Raise the car at the rear, support it on axle stands, then make a general visual inspection of the rear axle and suspension components for signs of wear and insecurity. Check the rear wheel hub bearings in the same manner as that described for the front bearings in paragraph 3. Renewal of the rear hub bearings is described in Section 8.

3 Front suspension arm – removal and refitting

1   Apply the handbrake, raise and support the car at the front end on axle stands.

2   Undo the retaining nut securing the suspension arm to the hub carrier balljoint. Remove the bolt (noting its direction of fitting) (photos).

3   Lever open the slot, then press down on the suspension arm to separate it from the hub carrier.

4   Working in the car on the side concerned, fold back the carpet from the front floorpan and lift up the flap panel in the insulation to gain access to the suspension arm rear mounting nuts. Unscrew and remove the nuts (photos).

5   Where fitted, detach the anti-roll bar from the suspension arm (Section 4).

6   Unscrew the retaining nut from the front inboard mounting pivot bolt, then supporting the weight of the arm, withdraw the bolt and lower the arm. As the arm is removed, withdraw the flexible bush (photo).

7   Check the inner pivot bushes for wear and deterioration. Check the lower balljoint on the outer end of the arm for excessive wear indicated

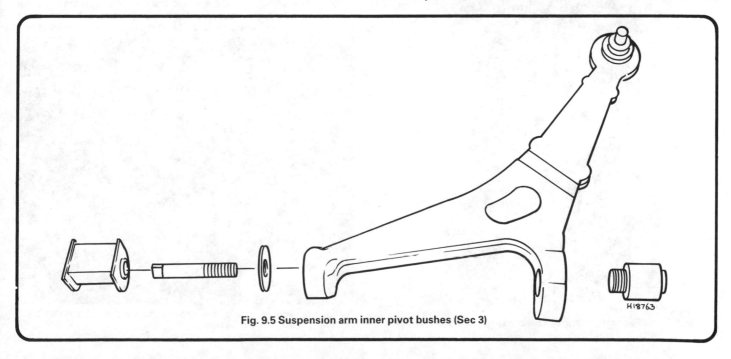

Fig. 9.5 Suspension arm inner pivot bushes (Sec 3)

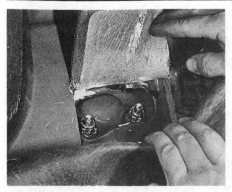

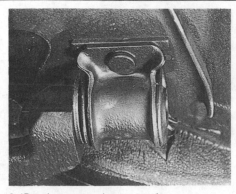

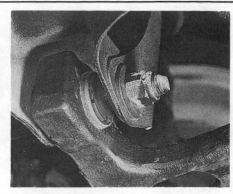

3.4A Fold back the carpet insulation for access to the nuts...

3.4B ... that secure the suspension arm rear mounting

3.6 Suspension arm front mounting (inboard)

by up and down movement of the ball in the socket. Check the arm for damage or deterioration. The bushes may be renewed using a simple puller consisting of a metal tube and washers, together with a long bolt and nut. When fitting the new bush to the spindle of the rear inboard mounting/pivot, ensure that its flat face is correctly orientated (parallel to the arm). Lubricate the spindle with a multi-purpose grease to ease assembly.

8   The balljoint can be renewed, but is a task best entrusted to a Citroën dealer. If a suitable press is available, the old joint can be pressed out and the new joint pressed in, but take care to support the arm with a suitable steel tube to prevent distorting the arm.

9   Refitting is a reversal of the removal procedure but when reconnecting the arm to the hub carrier, ensure that the protector shield is fitted correctly as shown in photo 3.2B. Tighten all fittings to their specified torque wrench settings.

---

4   Front anti-roll bar – removal and refitting

1   Loosen off the front roadwheel bolts, then raise the car at the front end and support it on axle stands. Remove the front roadwheels.

2   Unscrew and remove the anti-roll bar inboard mounting bolts each side from the suspension arm supports. Remove the bridge clamp and the spacer plate.

3   Unscrew and remove the outboard mounting bolts securing the

anti-roll bar to the suspension arms each side, remove the bridge clamps.

4   The anti-roll bar is now disconnected and free to be withdrawn from the car. If difficulty is encountered, it may be necessary to first detach the suspension arms at their inboard ends and to pivot them downwards to provide the required clearance to allow the anti-roll bar to be removed.

5   Examine the bushes on the bar and if they are perished or excessively worn they must be replaced. If the bar has been distorted or damaged in any way, it must be renewed.

6   Refitting is a reversal of the removal procedure, but note the following points.

When fitting the bar, ensure that it is centrally positioned when mounted. It is recommended that the clamp bolts are initially hand tightened, then fully tightened when the car is free standing, with its weight on the suspension. Tighten the retaining bolts to the specified torque wrench settings

---

5   Front shock absorber – removal, inspection and refitting

1   Before starting on this operation, note that the following special tools will be required:

(a)   *A coil spring compressor or, if applicable, the Citroën tool no. 4107-T*
(b)   *A suitable tool to extract the retaining plug (Citroën tool nos 4501-T. A1 and A2)*

It should also be noted that if a shock absorber or coil spring are to be renewed, it is strongly recommended that both units on that axle also are renewed at the same time to ensure even handling characteristics.

Fig. 9.6 The Facom type spring compressor fitted into position (Sec 5)

5.4 Earth lead connection on pressed nut. Also shown are the two top mounting bracket retaining nuts

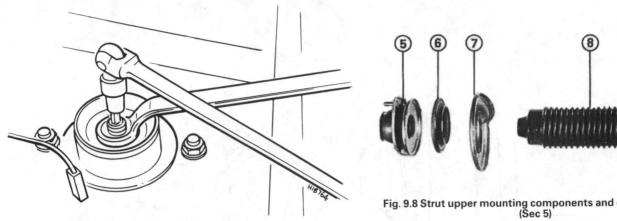

Fig. 9.7 Unscrewing the top retaining nut (3) with Torx key holding the spindle (Sec 5)

Fig. 9.8 Strut upper mounting components and order of fitting (Sec 5)

5   Bracket
6   Thrust bearing
7   Cup

8   Rubber gaiter
9   Bump stop

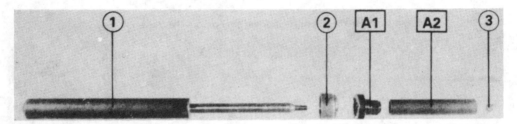

Fig. 9.9 Showing shock absorber cartridge (1) plug (2) and nut (3). A1 and A2 are Citroën plug removal tools (Sec 5)

2   Apply the handbrake, loosen off the front roadwheel bolts on the side concerned, then raise and support the car at the front end on axle stands. Unbolt and remove the front roadwheel(s).

3   Clean away the external dirt from the coil spring, then turn the steering to the full left-hand lock position and fit the coil spring compressor, positioning it so that it compresses five coils.

4   Working in the engine compartment, detach the earth lead from the terminal of the pressed nut on the top end of the strut spindle. Unscrew and remove the pressed nut (photo).

5   Check that the spring is securely compressed by the compression tool, then unscrew and remove the top retaining nut. As the nut is removed, prevent the spindle from turning by holding it with a suitable Torx key. Remove the nut.

6   Unscrew and remove the two top bracket retaining nuts.

7   Lower and detach the upper end of the strut from the wheel arch, then remove the items shown in Fig. 9.8. Withdraw them over the top of the spring and strut noting their orientation and order of fitting.

8   Compress the shock absorber, then lift the spring and compression tool clear and remove it.

9   Slowly release the compressor from the coil spring.

10   To remove the shock absorber cartridge from the strut, unscrew the retaining plug using either a three-pin tool or the Citroën special tool no. 4501-T (A1 and A2). Jam a piece of wood between the steering arm and the wheel arch to prevent the strut unit from turning. Unscrew the retaining plug, then withdraw the shock absorber from the strut. Remove the special tool.

11   Clean and examine the various components for wear or damage and renew as necessary.

12   Check the free length of the coil spring and compare it with the length quoted in the Specifications for the model concerned. Renew if necessary.

13   Pump the shock absorber piston up and down to assess its resistance. If it is weak, lumpy or there are signs of fluid leakage, renew it.

14   Clean all components and seatings prior to assembly.

15   Locate the retaining plug over the shock absorber, then assemble the tool used to remove it and secure it with its retaining nut. Locate this combined unit into position in the strut, then tighten the plug to the

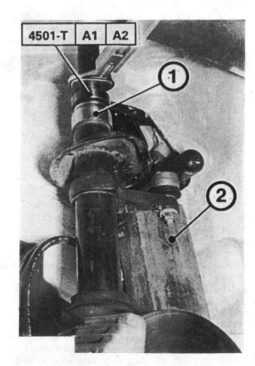

Fig. 9.10 Shock absorber cartridge retainer plug removal using special tools. Note position of wood block (Sec 5)

1   plug   2   wood block

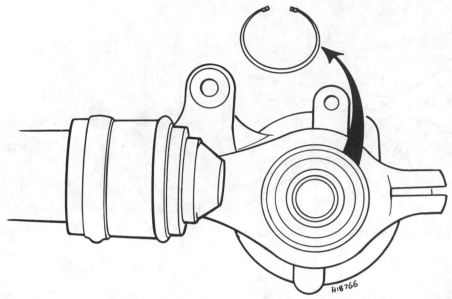

Fig. 9.11 Remove the bearing retaining circlip from the front hub (Sec 7)

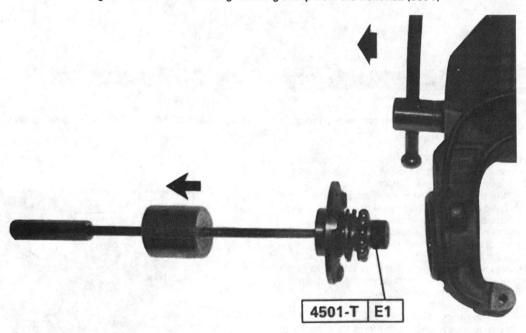

| 4501-T | E1 |

Fig. 9.12 Hub and bearing removal from carrier using a slide hammer (Citroën tool numbers given) (Sec 7)

specified torque wrench setting. Remove the special tool.

16   Relocate the compressor onto the coil spring and compress five coils as during removal.

17   Check that the steering is still set on the left-hand lock, refit the coil spring over the strut. Ensure that it is seated correctly then reassemble the bump stop, rubber gaiter, cup, ball thrust and the shock absorber top mounting bracket.

18   Refit and tighten the two top mounting nuts to the specified torque wrench setting.

19   Refit and tighten the top mounting nut onto the top end of the strut spindle. Tighten to the specified torque wrench setting. Prevent the spindle from turning by securing it with a Torx key (as during removal).

20   Relocate the pressed nut and connect the earth lead to it.

21   Carefully loosen off the spring compressor and remove it.

22   Refit the roadwheel and lower the car.

---

6   Front hub carrier and strut unit – removal and refitting

---

1   Apply the handbrake, loosen off the roadwheel bolts, then raise and

support the car at the front end on axle stands. Remove the front roadwheel(s).

2   Unscrew the tie rod balljoint nut, then using a balljoint separator, detach the tie rod from the steering arm (Chapter 10).

3   Refer to Chapter 7, Section 3 and disconnect the outer end of the driveshaft from the hub. Note that it is not necessary to drain the oil from the transmission.

4   Refer to Chapter 8 and unbolt the brake caliper unit from the hub carrier, and tie (or support) it up out of the way so that it is not stretching or distorting the brake hose.

5   Open and support the bonnet, then detach the earth lead from the pressed nut on the top of the strut spindle (photo 5.4).

6   Support the weight of the strut/hub carrier unit with a suitable jack, then unscrew and remove the two top mounting bracket retaining nuts.

7   Slowly lower the jack under the strut/hub carrier unit, and detach the strut and its upper mounting bracket from the wheel arch. Whilst it is removed, do not attempt to dismantle the strut and coil spring without first fitting a suitable coil spring compressor (see Section 5).

8   Refitting is a reversal of the removal procedure. The tie rod and driveshaft nuts must be renewed. Tighten all fittings to the specified

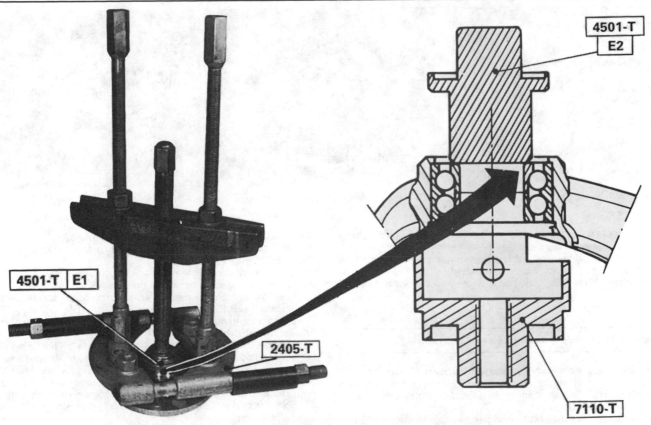

Fig. 9.13 Hub bearing removal using a separator tool (Citroën tool numbers given) (Sec 7)

torque wrench settings. Refer to Chapter 7 for details on refitting the driveshaft, Chapter 8 for details on refitting the brake unit, and Chapter 10 for details on refitting the tie rod.

7 Front hub unit – dismantling and reassembly

1 To remove the front wheel hub and bearings, the strut should first be removed from the car as described in Section 6. Removal of the strut allows the hub to be suitably supported during the hub and bearing removal/refitting procedures.

2 With the strut/hub unit removed, clean the hub externally, then extract the bearing retaining circlip from the inner side of the housing.

3 Support the strut/hub unit and using a suitable slide hammer or drift, withdraw the hub and bearing from the carrier (Fig. 9.12).

4 To remove the bearing from the hub, a suitable bearing separator will be necessary (Fig. 9.13). Once removed, a new bearing must always

be fitted.

5 To reassemble, first press the new bearing into the hub housing. If a tube is used to press the bearing into position, ensure that it bears against the bearing outer track. With the bearing fully fitted, insert a new circlip into the housing to secure the bearing.

6 Press or drive the hub through the bearing. When fitted, ensure that it rotates freely and without binding.

7 Refit the suspension strut/hub carrier unit with reference to Section 6.

8 Rear wheel hub and bearing – removal and refitting

1 The rear wheel hub is incorporated in the brake drum and therefore its removal and refitting details are described in Section 6 of Chapter 8. Once removed, the bearing can be renewed as follows.

2 Release and remove the retaining circlip using suitable circlip pliers.

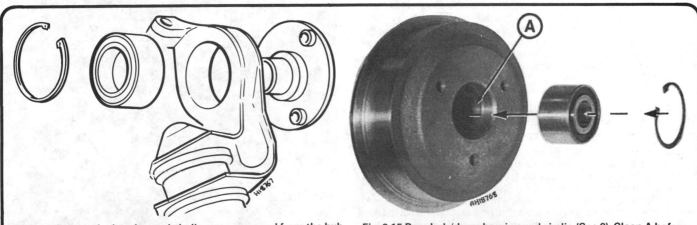

Fig. 9.14 Renew the bearing and circlip once removed from the hub unit (Sec 7)

Fig. 9.15 Rear hub/drum bearing and circlip (Sec 8). Clean A before inserting bearing (Sec 8)

8.2A Rear hub bearing and circlip (arrowed)

8.2B Press the rear hub bearing out in direction of arrow

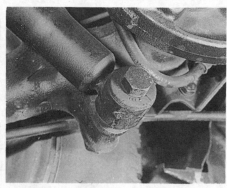

9.4 Rear shock absorber lower mounting bolt

Press or drift out the bearing from the inside outwards using a steel tube of suitable diameter (photos).

3   Fit the new bearing in the reverse order of removal. Ensure that the circlip is fully engaged in its groove when fitted.

4   The bearing is a fully sealed type and as such does not require lubrication.

9 Rear shock absorber – testing, removal and refitting

1   The efficiency of a rear shock absorber can be checked by depressing the rear corner of the car then releasing it quickly. If the body rises then stabilises, the shock absorber is good, but if there are several oscillations it should be renewed.

2   A visual check of the shock absorber can also be made. If a rear shock absorber shows signs of leakage, it must be renewed, (repair is not possible). It is advisable to renew both shock absorbers at the rear, even though one may appear quite serviceable, as this will ensure even suspension characteristics. To renew a rear shock absorber, proceed as follows.

3   Position the car on ramps or alternatively put the car in gear, chock the front wheels, jack it up and support it beneath the rear roadwheels. Remove the spare wheel for improved access.

4   Unscrew the shock absorber bottom mounting nut and tap the bolt through to disengage it from the axle arm/shock absorber (photo).

5   Unscrew the shock absorber upper mounting bolt, withdraw the bolt and lower the shock absorber unit (photo).

6   A more thorough check of the shock absorber may now be made by gripping the bottom mounting in a vice and attempting to extend and retract it. If the resistance is not firm and even in both directions, or if there are signs of leakage or damage, the shock absorber must be renewed.

7   Refitting is a reversal of removal, but ensure that the shock absorber unit is correctly orientated. Before tightening the retaining nuts to their specified torque wrench settings, set the distance between the mounting bolt centres at 260 mm (10.2 in). The Citroën tools 4028-T and 4502-TE normally used to set this distance may not be readily available and in this instance, load the rear of the car by trial and error to set the distance. If using the Citroën tool, take care not to damage the brake pipe attached to the rear axle crossmember.

8   On completion, lower the car and remove the chocks from the front wheels. Refit the spare wheel.

10 Rear torsion bar – removal and refitting

1   Jack up the rear of the car and support on axle stands under the body. Chock the front wheels and remove the rear wheels.

2   Remove the shock absorber on the side being worked on, with reference to Section 9.

3   In order to retain the suspension ride height it is necessary to hold the trailing arm stationary with the torsion bar relaxed. Note that the arm itself must be slightly raised to eliminate the effect of its own weight. If available use Citroën tool 4502-TA fitted in place of the shock absorber, otherwise firmly support the trailing arm and record the distance

between the shock absorber mounting bolt centres.

4   Undo the brake pipe retaining screw and detach the brake pipe from the axle.

5   Unscrew and remove the Torx screw retaining the torsion bar at the inboard end to the suspension mounting bar (Fig. 9.18).

6   Unscrew and remove the Torx screw retaining the torsion bar to the trailing arm (Fig. 9.19). Remove the washer.

7   Using a centre punch, mark the torsion bar and trailing arm in relation to each other.

8   Support the trailing arm then extract the torsion bar using a slide hammer and adaptor screwed into the end of the bar. As the torsion bar is withdrawn, support the arm to prevent it moving with the bar.

9   Before refitting the torsion bar, lubricate the splines with the specified grease. Note that the right and left-hand torsion bars are different – the right one is identified by one painted ring whereas the left one has two painted rings.

10   If the original torsion bar is being refitted and the ride height is correct, check that the dimension recorded in paragraph 3 is still correct. If the ride height is being adjusted refer to Section 15 and set the dimension accordingly. If a new torsion bar is being fitted, set the dimension by raising or lowering the trailing arm to the following table:

Model	Setting
AX 10 and AX 11	317 mm (12.5 in)
AX 14 and GT	312 mm (12.3 in)

Insert the small end through the arm and engage it with the splines on the suspension tube bracket. It will be necessary to try the bar in several positions if the original is not being refitted, and the bar will initially only enter by approximately 10.0 mm (0.4 in) as the splines at each end are

9.5 Rear shock absorber upper mounting bolt

not in the same plane. When the correct splines are engaged, drive the bar fully into position using the slide hammer and adaptor or a suitable drift.

11   When fitted, the arm seal should be in contact with the cup, if not move the seal up to the cup using a suitable screwdriver.

12   Fit the outboard end washer and insert the outboard and inboard end Torx screws and tighten them to the specified torque wrench setting.

13   Refit the brake pipe retaining screw.

14   Remove the trailing arm support (or Citroën tool 4502-TA) and refit the shock absorber (Section 9).

15   When the vehicle is lowered to the ground, check the rear height settings as described in Section 15.

11   Rear suspension trailing arm and bearings – removal and refitting

1   Raise the car at the rear and support it on axle stands. Chock the front wheels and remove the rear wheel on the side concerned.

2   Referring to Chapter 8 for details, disconnect/remove the following items:

   (a) *Disconnect the brake hydraulic line from the wheel cylinder*
   (b) *Remove the rear brake drum/hub unit*
   (c) *Detach the handbrake cable from the rear brake backplate on the side concerned*

3   Unscrew and remove the four Torx screws securing the brake backplate unit to the suspension arm, withdraw the backplate/brake unit.

4   Remove the rear shock absorber (Section 9) on the side concerned and locate Citroën spacer tool 4502-TA in its place to maintain the position of the axle arm (for refitting). If this tool is not available, a substitute spacer will need to be fabricated and fitted (see Section 10).

5   Where applicable, remove the anti-roll bar (Section 12).

6   Remove the Torx screw and washer securing the torsion bar and lever to the trailing arm.

7   Undo the bolt securing the spacer tool and then remove the suspension arm. Do not alter the set distance of the spacer tool.

8   Remove the cup and seal noting orientation.

9   An extractor is required to remove the inner and outer needle roller bearing units from the suspension arm, and if available use Citroën tools 1671-T and 2070-T assembled as shown in Fig. 9.25 to withdraw the bearings. A draw bolt and suitable washers may also suffice, but take care not to damage the bearing housing in the arm. Once removed the bearings must be renewed. Note the orientation of the bearings as they are withdrawn. The arm and bearings on the GT model differ from other models, but the fitting and removal procedures are the same.

10   Withdraw the inner bearing and spacer tube from the inboard side of the arm then press or drift out the outer bearing, and extract it from the outboard side of the arm.

11   Clean out the bearing housing in the arm, then insert the spacer tube and inner bearing, with its seal end facing as shown in Fig. 9.26. Carefully drive or press the two items into position in the housing using a tube of suitable diameter or preferably Citroën tool 4502-T.C1. When fitted the bearing must be flush with the rim of the housing.

12   Press the outer bearing into position with its recessed shoulder facing towards the outboard side of the arm and flush with the outer face when fitted. Lubricate the needle roller bearings before refitting the arm.

13   Ensure that the steel cup and the axle arm bearing surfaces are thoroughly clean. Lubricate the seal lips of the new oil seal with grease, then refit the cup and seal into position on the axle crossmember. Lubricate the torsion bar splines with the specified grease.

14   Fit the trailing arm over the axle tube, aligning it with the torsion bar and then refit the flat washer and retaining screw into the end face of the torsion bar. The screw must be tightened in a progressive manner

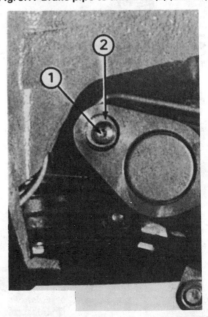

Fig. 9.17 Brake pipe to axle bolt (3) (Sec 10)

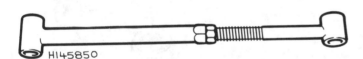

Fig. 9.16 Citroën tool 4502-TA for use as a dummy rear shock absorber (Sec 10)

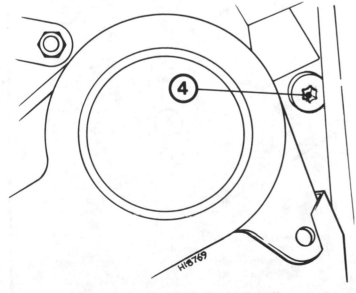

Fig. 9.18 Torx screw location (4) (Sec 10)

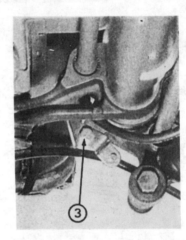

Fig. 9.19 Torsion bar Torx screw (1) and washer (2) (Sec 10)

Fig. 9.20 Mark a and b – relative positions of torsion bar and trailing arm (Sec 10)

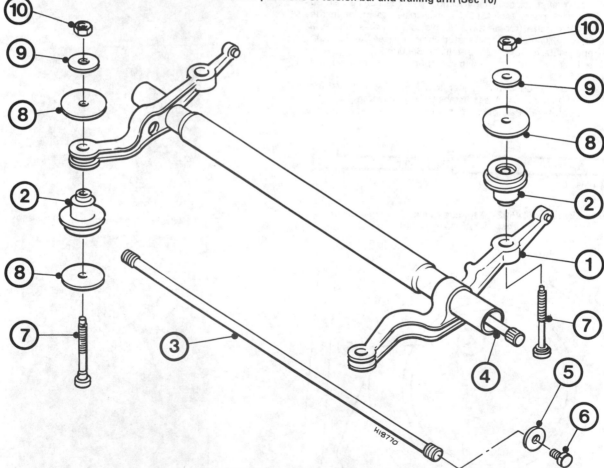

Fig. 9.21 Rear axle and associate components (Sec 10)

1 Axle	4 Anti-roll bar (where applicable)	7 Mounting bolt	9 Washer (small)
2 Support	5 Retainer	8 Washer (large)	10 Nut
3 Torsion bar	6 Capscrew		

Fig. 9.22 Torsion bar removal using Citroën slide hammer (Sec 10)

up to the specified torque wrench setting so that oil seal and suspension arm engagement is correctly made. When the assembly is complete, check that the seal is no more than 23 mm (0.9 in) from the cup, if it isn't, prise it closer using a suitable screwdriver.

15   Refit the rear brake backplate and tighten the four retaining screws to the specified torque wrench setting.

16   Reconnect the rear brake hose and the handbrake cable, then top up and bleed the brake hydraulic system as described in Chapter 8.

17   Refit the shock absorber (Section 9) and the roadwheel(s). Lower the car to the ground before fully tightening the shock absorber retaining bolts.

18   Check and if necessary, adjust the handbrake as described in Chapter 8.

12   Rear anti-roll bar – removal and refitting

1   Jack up the car at the rear and support it on axle stands. Chock the front wheels and remove the rear wheels.

2   Working on the left-hand side, unscrew and remove the anti- roll bar lever bolt.

3   Unscrew the plug from the end of the anti-roll bar then insert a well oiled bolt into the lever and tighten it until the lever is forced off. If available use Citroën tool 4514-TF. Remove the oil seal.

4   Working on the right-hand side, undo the anti-roll bar lever bolt and the plastic plug from the end of the bar on that side.

5   Withdraw the anti-roll bar to the left.

6   Mount the anti-roll bar in a vice with the lever uppermost then remove the lever using the procedure described in paragraph 3.

7   Before refitting the anti-roll bar, clean the splines both on the bar and levers and coat them with the specified grease. New oil seals must be fitted to the levers each side.

8   Assemble the left-hand lever onto the anti-roll bar, aligning the lever slotted hole with the index mark of the bar as shown in Fig. 9.32.

9   Screw a 100 mm (3.9 in) x 1.25 threaded rod into the end of the anti-roll bar, fit a flat washer and a nut onto the rod and tighten the nut to draw the lever onto the bar. When positioned correctly, remove the rod, washer and nut.

10   Insert the anti-roll bar and lever into position in the left- hand side of the suspension tube, screw in the retaining plug (to the bar), refit the anti-roll bar lever bolt and tighten it to the specified torque wrench setting.

11   Locate the right-hand lever onto the bar aligning the lever bolt hole with the threaded hole in the end of the suspension arm. Draw the lever onto the bar using the threaded rod method previously employed on the opposite side. When in position, remove the rod and nut.

12   Fit the retaining plug to the bar and the lever bolt to secure. Tighten the retaining bolt to the specified torque wrench setting.

13   Refit the roadwheels, lower the car, and remove the chocks from the front wheels.

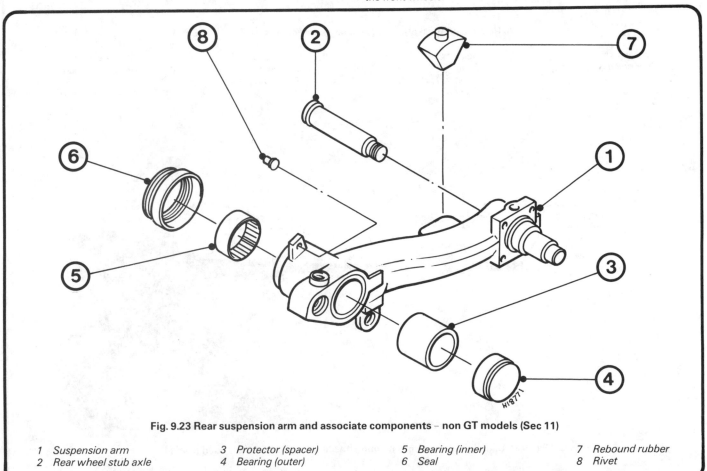

Fig. 9.23 Rear suspension arm and associate components – non GT models (Sec 11)

| 1 | Suspension arm | 3 | Protector (spacer) | 5 | Bearing (inner) | 7 | Rebound rubber |
| 2 | Rear wheel stub axle | 4 | Bearing (outer) | 6 | Seal | 8 | Rivet |

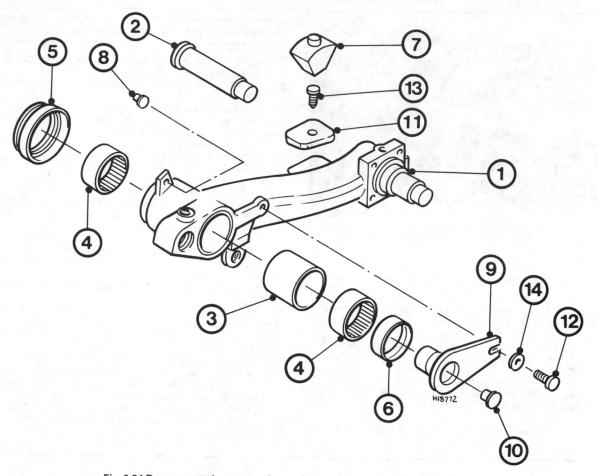

Fig. 9.24 Rear suspension arm and associate components – GT model (Sec 11)

1 Suspension arm
2 Rear wheel stub axle
3 Protector (spacer)
4 Bearing
5 Seal
6 Seal
7 Rebound rubber
8 Rivet
9 Bar lever
10 Plug
11 Arm stop
12 Lever screw
13 Capscrew
14 Spring washer

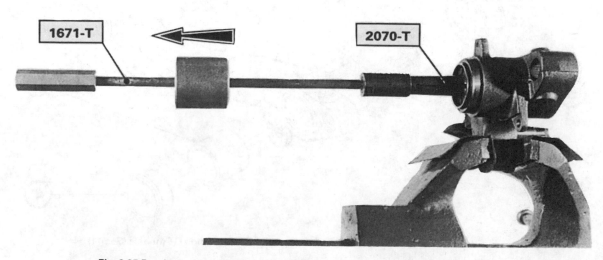

Fig. 9.25 Bearing removal from trailing arm showing Citroën tools used (Sec 11)

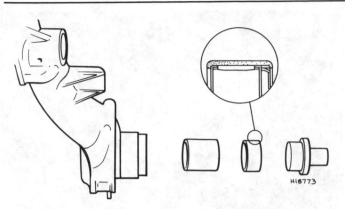

Fig. 9.26 Spacer and inboard bearing refitting. Inset shows fitting direction for bearing (Sec 11)

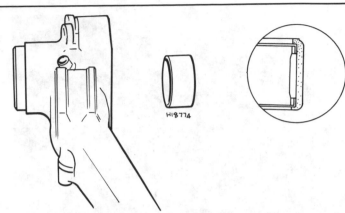

Fig. 9.27 Fitting direction for the outboard bearing. Inset shows the GT type (Sec 11)

13 Rear axle (suspension) unit – removal and refitting

1 Remove the rear seat unit, then raise and support the car at the rear on axle stands to a height of 600 mm (23.5 in) from bumper-to-ground. Leave the rear roadwheels in position.

2 As applicable, disconnect the hydraulic supply lines from the brake compensator unit or at the in-line connections to the rear brakes as described in Chapter 8.

3 Detach and remove the exhaust system as described in Chapter 3.

4 Disconnect the handbrake cables from the clips on the underside of the car and at the equalizer unit at the front end. The adjustment will need to be loosened off as described in Chapter 8.

5 Locate a suitable jack (trolley type if available) under the centre of the suspension/axle crossmember, and raise it so that it just takes the weight of the axle unit.

6 Unscrew and remove the four axle unit-to-body retaining nuts from the mounting studs. These are accessible through the apertures in the floor pan under the rear seat. Peel back the tape for access (photo).

7 Check that all attachments to the axle unit are clear, (brake lines and cables etc), then slowly and carefully lower the jack supporting the axle unit, to the point where it is self supporting on the rear roadwheels each side, and the jack in the centre. It can then be withdrawn rearwards from under the car.

8 Refitting is a reversal of the removal procedure. When aligning and refitting the unit, ensure that the thrustwashers are located each side of the mountings as shown in Fig. 9.37. Tighten the retaining nuts to the specified torque wrench setting.

9 Reconnect the brake lines and cables, bleed the brake hydraulic circuits and adjust the handbrake as described in Chapter 8.

10 Reconnect the exhaust system with reference to Chapter 3.

11 On completion, check the vehicle height setting as described in Section 15 of this Chapter.

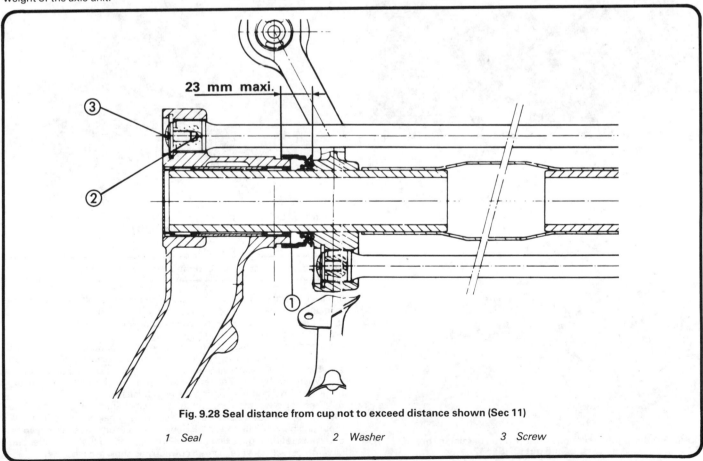

Fig. 9.28 Seal distance from cup not to exceed distance shown (Sec 11)

| 1 Seal | 2 Washer | 3 Screw |

Fig. 9.29 Showing anti-roll bar plastic plug (1) and lever bolt (2)
(Sec 12)

Fig. 9.30 Anti-roll bar lever removal method using Citroën tool
(Sec 12)

Fig. 9.31 Remove the oil seal (3) for renewal (Sec 12)

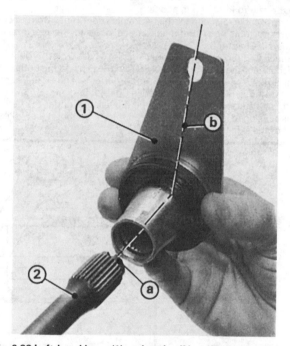

Fig. 9.32 Left-hand lever (1) and anti-roll bar (2) showing fitting
alignment A to align with B (Sec 12)

Fig. 9.33 Drawing the lever onto the anti-roll bar using threaded bar,
washer and nut (C) (Sec 12)

14   Rear axle (suspension) unit mountings – renewal

1   To inspect and renew the rear axle/suspension unit mountings, the axle unit must be removed from the car (Section 13).
2   If the bushes are to be renewed, replace them as a set on the right and left-hand side.
3   The old bushes can be extracted from the mounting arms using the Citroën tools shown in Fig. 9.38, or if these are not readily available, use a suitable draw bolt, tubes and washers of suitable diameter and a nut.
4   When the bushes are removed, clean out their housings in the mounting arms before inserting the new bushes.
5   Press or draw the new mounting bushes into position using the tools used to remove them. Align the cut-outs or paint marks of the new mounting bushes with the corresponding marks on the mounting arms.
6   When refitting the axle/suspension unit, ensure that the upper and lower thrustwashers are located correctly as shown in Fig. 9.37.

Fig. 9.34 Support points for the car and rear axle (Sec 13)

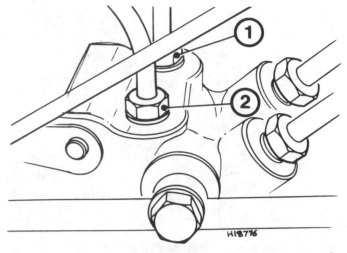

Fig. 9.35 Disconnect brake lines 1 and 2 from the compensator unit (where fitted) (Sec 13)

13.6 Rear axle unit retaining nut

15 Suspension ride height – checking and alignment

1   The suspension ride heights must be checked with the car unladen, on level ground, with the specified tyre pressures and ideally there should be 5 litres (1.1 gal) of fuel in the petrol tank.
2   It is recommended that the car is bounced before taking a measurement, and that the average of three successive measurements be taken as the final reading which should be as given in the Specifications at the start of this Chapter.
3   The ride heights are measured from the following points:

Front – *Between the ground and the suspension arm mounting face.*
Rear – *Between the ground and the underside of the floor pan cross-member adjacent to the axle unit mounting (photo).*

The maximum allowable height difference left-to-right is 7.5 mm (0.3 in).
4   The suspension ride height is only adjustable at the rear, and it should be noted that adjustment on one side will slightly alter the ride height on the opposite side.

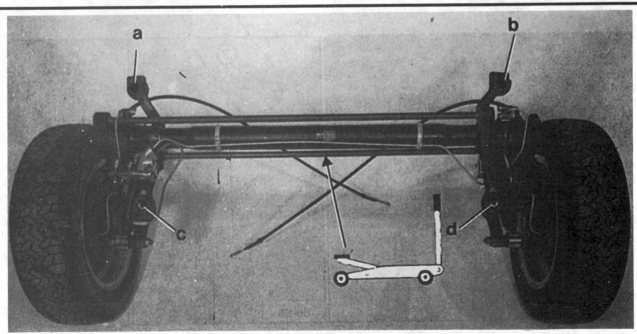

Fig. 9.36 Rear axle unit showing mounting points (Sec 13)

a   Front left   b   Front right   c   Rear left   d   Rear right

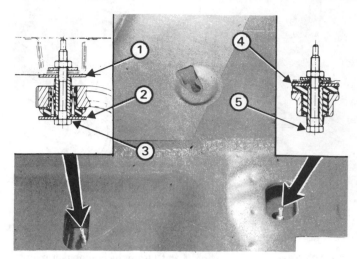

Fig. 9.37 Sectional views of the rear axle mountings (Sec 13)

1   Thrustwasher   4   Thrustwasher
2   Thrustwasher   5   Through bolt
3   Through bolts

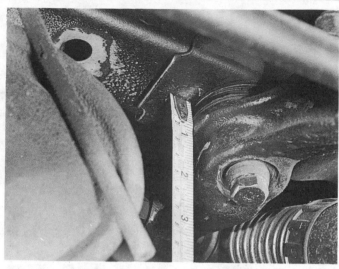

15.3 Rear suspension ride height measuring point

4502-T.D 2

4502-T.D 3

4502-T.D 5

Fig. 9.38 Showing Citroën tools used to withdraw the mounting bush from the rear axle (Sec 14)

Fig. 9.39 Bush with cutaway to be aligned as shown (Sec 14)

6   A change in the dimension between the shock absorber mounting bolt centres of 1.0 mm (0.04 in) is equivalent to a change in ride height of 3.0 mm (0.12 in). Therefore it is essential to record the existing shock absorber and ride height dimensions before making an adjustment. The torsion bar removal and refitting procedure is given in Section 10.

5   To adjust the ride height, the torsion bar(s) must be removed and repositioned after resetting the trailing arm. To increase the ride height, turn the left-hand torsion bar clockwise, the right-hand torsion bar anti-clockwise.

16   Wheels and tyres – general care and maintenance

Wheels and tyres should give no problems in use provided that a close eye is kept on them with regard to excessive wear or damage. To this end, the following points should be noted.

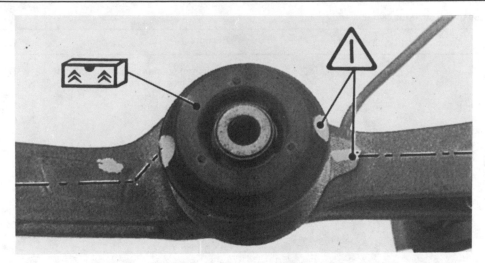

Fig. 9.40 Bush with paint marks to be aligned as shown (Sec 14)

Ensure that the tyre pressures are checked regularly and maintained correctly. Checking should be carried out with the tyres cold and not immediately after the vehicle has been in use. If the pressures are checked with the tyres hot, an apparently high reading will be obtained owing to heat expansion. Under no circumstances should an attempt be made to reduce the pressures to the quoted cold reading in this instance, or effective underinflation will result.

Underinflation will cause overheating of the tyre owing to excessive flexing of the casing, and the tread will not sit correctly on the road surface. This will cause a consequent loss of adhesion and excessive wear, not to mention the danger of sudden tyre failure due to heat build-up.

Overinflation will cause rapid wear of the centre part of the tyre tread coupled with reduced adhesion, harsher ride, and the danger of shock damage occurring in the tyre casing.

Regularly check the tyres for damage in the form of cuts or bulges, especially in the sidewalls. Remove any nails or stones embedded in the tread before they penetrate the tyre to cause deflation. If removal of a nail *does* reveal that the tyre has been punctured, refit the nail so that its point of penetration is marked. Then immediately change the wheel and have the tyre repaired by a tyre dealer. Do *not* drive on a tyre in such a condition. In many cases a puncture can be simply repaired by the use of an inner tube of the correct size and type. If in any doubt as to the possible consequences of any damage found, consult your local tyre dealer for advice.

Periodically remove the wheels and clean any dirt or mud from the inside and outside surfaces. Examine the wheel rims for signs of rusting, corrosion or other damage. Light alloy wheels are easily damaged by 'kerbing' whilst parking, and similarly steel wheels may become dented or buckled. Renewal of the wheel is very often the only course of remedial action possible.

The balance of each wheel and tyre assembly should be maintained to avoid excessive wear, not only to the tyres but also to the steering and suspension components. Wheel imbalance is normally signified by vibration through the vehicle's bodyshell, although in many cases it is particularly noticeable through the steering wheel. Conversely, it should be noted that wear or damage in suspension or steering components may cause excessive tyre wear. Out-of-round or out-of true tyres, damaged wheels and wheel bearing wear/maladjustment also fall into this category. Balancing will not usually cure vibration caused by such wear.

Wheel balancing may be carried out with the wheel either on or off the vehicle. If balanced on the vehicle, ensure that the wheel-to-hub relationship is marked in some way prior to subsequent wheel removal so that it may be refitted in its original position.

General tyre wear is influenced to a large degree by driving style – harsh braking and acceleration or fast cornering will all produce more rapid tyre wear. Interchanging of tyres may result in more even wear, but this should only be carried out where there is no mix of tyre types on the vehicle However, it is worth bearing in mind that if this is completely effective, the added expense of replacing a complete set of tyres simultaneously is incurred, which may prove financially restrictive for many owners.

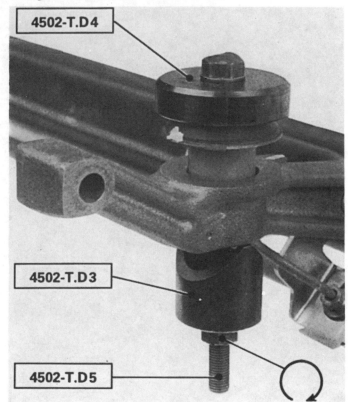

Fig. 9.41 Showing Citroen tools used to draw new mounting bush into the rear axle (Sec 14)

Front tyres may wear unevenly as a result of wheel misalignment. The front wheels should always be correctly aligned according to the settings specified by the vehicle manufacturer.

Legal restrictions apply to the mixing of tyre types on a vehicle. Basically this means that a vehicle must not have tyres of differing construction on the same axle. Although it is not recommended to mix tyre types between front axle and rear axle, the only legally permissible combination is crossply at the front and radial at the rear. When mixing radial ply tyres, textile braced radials must always go on the front axle, with steel braced radials at the rear. An obvious disadvantage of such mixing is the necessity to carry two spare tyres to avoid contravening the law in the event of a puncture.

In the UK, the Motor Vehicle Constructions and Use Regulations apply to may aspects of tyre fitting and usage. It is suggested that a copy of these regulations is obtained from your local police if in doubt as to the current legal requirements with regard to tyre condition, minimum tread depth, etc.

17   Fault diagnosis – suspension, hubs, wheels and tyres

Symptom	Reason(s)
Car pulls to one side	Worn front suspension lower balljoint Incorrect tyre pressures
Excessive pitching or rolling	Worn shock absorbers
Wheel wobble or vibration	Unbalanced wheels Damaged wheels Worn wheel bearings Worn shock absorbers
Excessive tyre wear	Incorrect tyre pressures Worn front suspension lower balljoint Unbalanced wheels

Chapter 10 Steering system

Contents

Specifications

General

Type	Rack and pinion steering gear unit. Steering column with universal joint
Ratio	18.8 : 1
Number of turns from lock-to-lock:	
AX 10 and AX 11 models	3.5
AX 14 models	3.2
Turning circle (between kerbs):	
AX 10 and AX 11 models	9.23 m (30 ft 3 in)
AX 14 and GT models	10.2 m (33 ft 6 in)
Lubricant type/specification	Multi-purpose lithium based grease (Duckhams LB 10)

Front wheel alignment

Toe setting	2 ± 1.5 mm (0.08 ± 0.06 in) toe-out
Camber angle (not adjustable)	0° 25′ 30′
Castor angle (not adjustable):	
AX 10, AX 11 and AX 14 models	9′30′
GT models	29′30′

Torque wrench settings

	Nm	lbf ft
Lower balljoint nut	28	21
Track rod end balljoint nut	35	26
Track rod-to-rack connector yoke	35	26
Track rod end locknuts	40	30
Steering gear unit mounting	18	13
Steering rack-to-connector yoke	24	18
Steering wheel nut	30	22
Steering column upper mounting	11	8
Steering column/pinion clamp bolt	18	13

---

1 General description

The steering gear is of rack and pinion type with track rods connected to the rack yoke bracket at their inboard ends. At their outer ends, the track rod balljoints are attached to the steering arms of the struts. The steering gear unit is attached to the bulkhead.

The steering column incorporates a single universal joint coupling located between the pinion and the column shaft. A padded, single spoke steering wheel is fitted to all models except for the GT model which has a padded three spoke steering wheel.

2 Routine maintenance

Carry out the following procedures at the intervals given in *Routine maintenance* at the beginning of the manual

1   Jack up the front of the car and support on axle stands. Apply the handbrake. Thoroughly examine the bellows at each end of the steering gear for splitting and deterioration and renew if necessary.

2   Check the track rod ends for excessive wear by attempting to move them up and down. If there is more than the very slightest movement the track rod end should be renewed. Similarly check the track rod inner

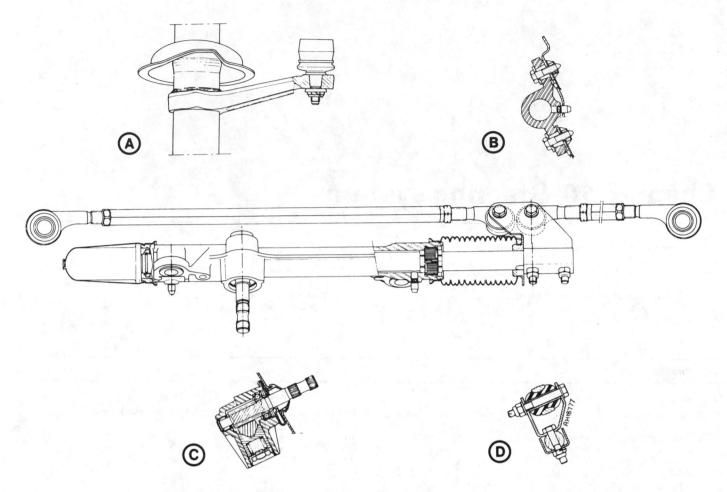

Fig. 10.1 Steering gear unit and track rods (left-hand drive type shown right-hand drive similar) (Sec 1)

A   *Steering arm and track rod   B   Steering gear mounting   C   Steering gear pinion   D   Steering yoke*
    end balljoint

joints by gripping the track rod through the bellows and attempting to move them up and down. Track rod ends should also be renewed if the rubber boots are split or damaged.

3   Steering wheel – removal and refitting

1   Set the front wheels at the straight-ahead position then lock the steering.
2   Prise free the centre pad from the steering wheel, then use a socket and extension bar to loosen off the retaining nut. Remove the nut and washer (photo).
3   Mark the hub in relation to the inner column then pull off the steering wheel. If it is tight a rocking action may release it from the splines.
4   Refitting is a reversal of removal, but check that the steering wheel is correctly centred with the front wheels straight-ahead. Tighten the nut to the specified torque while holding the steering wheel rim.

4   Steering column and lock – removal and refitting

Note: *If removal of the steering lock/ignition switch alone is required, refer to paragraphs 1, 2, 3 and 9 respectively*
1   Disconnect the battery earth lead.
2   Remove the steering wheel as described in the previous Section.
3   Undo the four retaining screws, and remove the upper and lower steering column shrouds (photo).
4   Detach and remove the parcel shelf under the facia on the drivers

side as described in Chapter 11.
5   Unclip and remove the insulation panel from the underside of the facia and steering column.
6   Mark the column lower universal joint in relation to the column shaft, then unscrew and remove the clamp bolt and nut (photo).
7   Unscrew and remove the column upper mounting nuts (photo), then lower the column from the mounting.
8   Detach the wiring connectors from the column switches, then pull the column upwards and disengage it from the universal joint coupling. Remove the column.
9   To remove the steering lock unit from the column, (disconnect the wiring if the column is not being removed) undo and remove the retaining screw, then with the ignition key positioned towards the 'A' location, depress the securing plunger in the housing and withdraw the lock unit (photo).
10   If the column is excessively worn or damaged it must be renewed.
11   Refit in the reverse order of removal. Tighten the retaining nuts and bolts to the specified torque wrench settings.
12   On completion, check the action of the steering and lock unit.
Note: *If a new column is being fitted, check that the steering gear unit is centralised (Section 5), and centralise the column before reconnecting at the universal joint coupling. With the front wheels in the straight-ahead position, the steering wheel spoke should be at the six o'clock position.*

5   Steering gear unit – removal and refitting

1   Fully apply the handbrake, then raise and support the car at the front end on axle stands. Remove the front roadwheels.

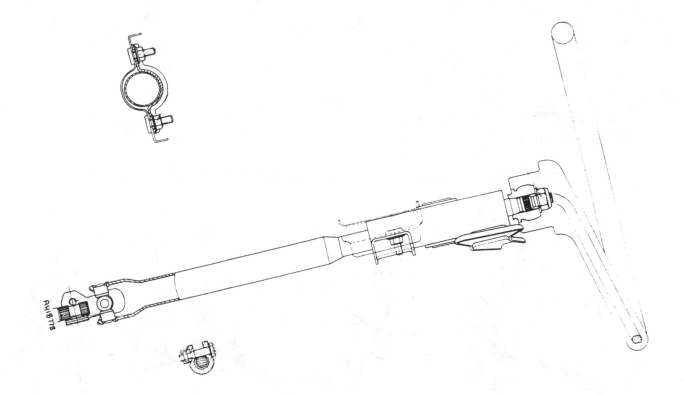

Fig. 10.2 Steering column unit (Sec 1)

3.2 Steering wheel nut and washer removal

4.3 Steering column shroud retaining screws

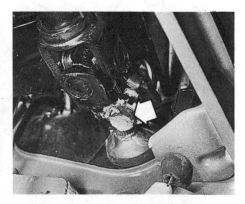

4.6 Steering column lower universal joint showing clamp bolt (arrowed)

4.7 Steering column upper mounting nuts (arrowed)

4.9A Steering lock screw (arrowed) ...

4.9B ... and retaining plunger (arrowed)

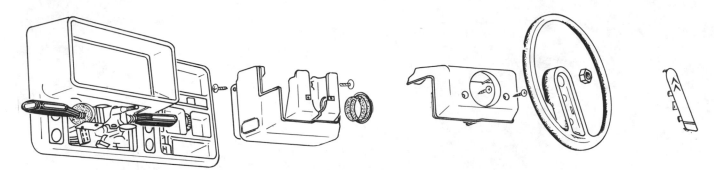

Fig. 10.3 Steering wheel, upper column and shrouds (left-hand drive shown right-hand drive similar) (Sec 4)

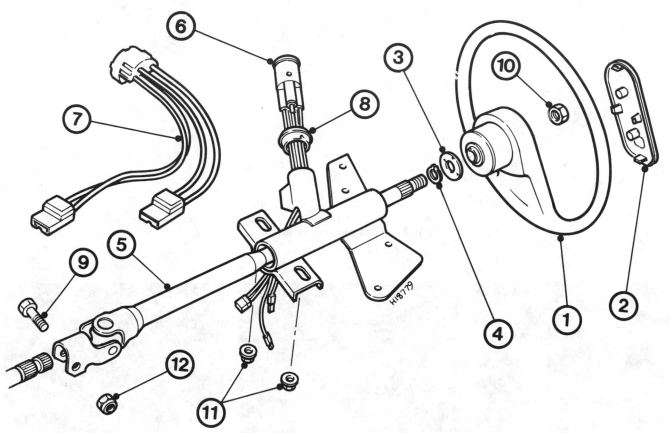

Fig. 10.4 Steering column and associate fittings (Sec 4)

1	Steering wheel	4	Stop ring	7	Wiring harness
2	Centre pad	5	Column	8	Gasket
3	Bowl washer	6	Steering lock/ignition switch unit	9	Bolt

10	Self-lock nut
11	Mounting nuts
12	Self-lock nut

2   Unclip and remove the side access panel(s) from under the front wheel arches for improved access. Also remove the air filter unit (Chapter 3) for the same reason.

3   Unscrew and remove the track rod end-to-steering arm nut each side and detach the track rod from the arms. A balljoint separator tool will probably be required to detach the joint (photo).

4   Working inside the car, remove the parcel shelf and the lower facia trim on the steering column side.

5   Mark the lower column in relation to the pinion on the steering gear.

6   Unscrew and remove the column-to-pinion clamp bolt.

7   Unscrew and remove the three mounting bolts and withdraw the steering gear from the bulkhead location dowels, then remove the unit from the side aperture under the right-hand wheel arch. The steering gear unit is removed complete with the track rods (photo).

8   Refitting is a reversal of the removal procedure. When assembling the unit to the bulkhead, engage it with the two dowels then insert the

three mounting bolts and tighten to secure. Tighten the retaining nuts and bolts to the specified torque wrench settings.

Note: *If a new steering gear unit is being fitted, centralise the rack before connecting the pinion to the column. To do this, move the rack fully from side-to-side and measure the full travel distance, then set the rack half-way between these points. Check that the steering column is set at the straight- ahead steering position (Section 4) before connecting the pinion and column shafts.*

6 Steering gear unit – overhaul

The steering gear has a very long life before any wear becomes evident; always provided that the bellows are kept in order to maintain adequate lubrication.

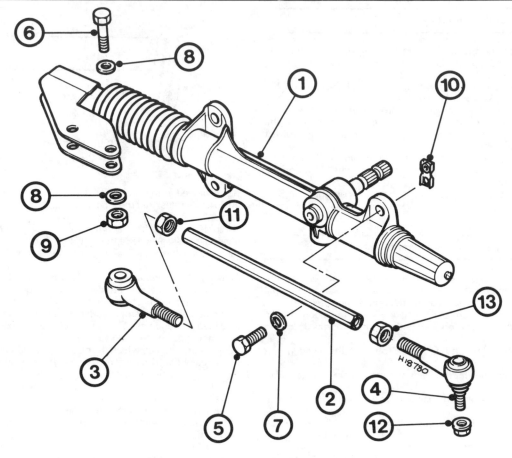

Fig. 10.5 Steering gear unit and associate fittings (Sec 5)

1	Steering gear unit	4	Balljoint	7	Washer	10 Caged nut
2	Track rod	5	Mounting bolt	8	Washer	11 Nut
3	End piece (inner)	6	Bolt	9	Self-lock nut	

In view of the special tools and gauges required to overhaul the steering gear it is recommended that, when the need for this arises, the assembly should be changed for a new or factory reconditioned one rather than dismantle the worn unit.

7 Track rod end – removal and refitting

1   Apply the handbrake, jack up the car and support it on axle stands and remove the relevant wheel.
2   Loosen the locknut on the track rod.
3   Unscrew the balljoint nut and use an extractor tool to separate the taper from the steering arm (photo 5.3). **Note:** *If difficulty is experienced in loosening or tightening a balljoint taper pin nut due to the taper pin turning in the eye, apply pressure with a jack or long lever to the balljoint socket to force the taper pin into its conical seat.*
4   Unscrew the track rod end from the track rod, noting the number of turns necessary to remove it.
5   Screw the new track rod end the same number of turns on the track rod.
6   Clean the taper surfaces then fit the balljoint to the hub carrier and tighten the nut to the specified torque.
7   Tighten the locknut on the track rod end.
8   Refit the roadwheel and lower the car to the ground.
9   Check and if necessary adjust the front wheel toe-out setting, as described in Section 10.

5.3 Track rod end balljoint and separator tool

5.7 General view of the steering gear unit and mounting points on the bulkhead

8.2 Track rod connections at their inner ends to the steering yoke

8 Track rod – removal and refitting

1   Disconnect the track rod end from the steering arm as described in paragraphs 1 and 3 of the previous Section. Unless the balljoint is being renewed, the locknut can be left tightened.
2   Unscrew the retaining nut, and withdraw the retaining bolt from the steering yoke (photo). Remove the track rod.
3   If required, the inner track rod end can be removed from the rod by loosening off the locknut and unscrewing the end piece. Count the number of turns required to remove the inner end to ensure correct positioning on reassembly.
4   Refit in the reverse order of removal. Ensure that the flat washers are positioned correctly, one each side of the yoke when inserting the bolt and fitting the nut.
5   On completion, check the steering alignment as described in Section 10.

9 Steering rack gaiter – removal and refitting

1   The right-hand end protector cap is a compression fit on the steering gear unit, and is readily accessible for removal and refitting if required through the access panel under the right-hand wheel arch.
2   To remove the gaiter from the left-hand side of the steering gear, remove the steering gear unit together with the track rods as described in Section 5.
3   Unbolt and detach the left-hand track rod from the steering rack yoke.
4   Unbolt and detach the steering bar yoke and buffer from the end of the rack.
5   Release the clips retaining the gaiter, then withdraw the gaiter and buffer.
6   Refit in the reverse order of removal. When in position, ensure that the gaiter is not twisted. Tighten the retaining nuts and bolts to the specified torque wrench settings.
7   On completion, check the steering alignment (Section 10) and the action of the steering for satisfactory lock-to-lock movement.

10 Steering angles and front wheel alignment

1   Accurate front wheel alignment is essential to provide good steering and roadholding characteristics and to ensure slow and even tyre wear. Before considering the steering angles, check that the tyres are correctly inflated, that the front wheels are not buckled, the hub bearings are not worn and that the steering linkage is in good order, without slackness or wear at the joints.
2   Wheel alignment consists of four factors:
Camber is the angle at which the roadwheels are set from the vertical

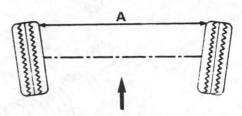

Fig. 10.6 Front wheel toe-out (Sec 10)

$A = 2 \pm 1.5$ mm

when viewed from the front or rear of the vehicle. Positive camber is the angle (in degrees) that the wheels are tilted outwards at the top from the vertical.
Castor is the angle between the steering axis and a vertical line when viewed from each side of the vehicle. Positive castor is indicated when the steering axis is inclined towards the rear of the vehicle at its upper end.
Steering axis inclination is the angle when viewed from the front or rear of the vehicle between vertical and an imaginary line drawn between the upper and lower strut mountings. Camber, castor and steering axis inclination are set during production of the car and any deviation from specified tolerance must therefore be due to gross wear in the suspension mountings or collision damage.
Toe is the amount by which the distance between the front inside edges of the roadwheel rims differs from that between the rear inside edges. If the distance between the front edges is less than that at the rear, the wheels are said to toe-in. If the distance between the front inside edges is greater than that at the rear, the wheels toe-out.
3   To check the front wheel alignment, first make sure that the lengths of both track-rods are equal when the steering is in the straight-ahead position.
4   Obtain a tracking gauge. These are available in various forms from accessory stores or one can be fabricated from a length of steel tubing suitably cranked to clear the sump and bellhousing and having a setscrew and locknut at one end.
5   With the gauge, measure the distance between the two wheel inner rims (at hub height) at the rear of the wheel. Push the vehicle forward to rotate the wheels through 180° (half a turn) and measure the distance between the wheel inner rims, again at hub height, at the front of the wheel. This last measurement should differ from the first by the appropriate toe-out according to specification (see Specifications Section).
6   Where the toe-out is found to be incorrect, release the track rod end locknuts and turn the track-rods equally. Only turn them a quarter of a turn at a time before rechecking the alignment, and release the bellows outer clips to prevent the bellows from twisting.
7   On completion tighten the track rod end locknuts.

11 Fault diagnosis – steering system

Symptom	Reason(s)
Stiff action	Lack of rack lubrication Seized track rod end balljoint Seized track rod inner balljoint
Excessive movement at steering wheel	Worn track rod end balljoints Worn rack and pinion
Tyre squeal when cornering and excessive tyre wear	Incorrect wheel alignment

Chapter 11 Bodywork and fittings

Contents

1 General description

The bodyshell is of unitary construction. The main body panels are steel but some body fittings such as the bumpers and the cowl between the windscreen and bonnet are manufactured in synthetic material. The lightweight high tensile and galvanised steel panels although of thin gauge, have increased strength and protection against corrosion.

The front wings are bolted to the main body, which in the event of accident damage, allows easy replacement. The bodywork is additionally given an extensive anti-corrosion treatment during manufacture.

2 Maintenance – bodywork and underframe

1 The general condition of a vehicle's bodywork is the one thing that significantly affects its value. Maintenance is easy but needs to be regular. Neglect, particularly after minor damage, can lead quickly to further deterioration and costly repair bills. It is important also to keep watch on those parts of the vehicle not immediately visible, for instance the underside, inside all the wheel arches and the lower part of the engine compartment.

2 The basic maintenance routine for the bodywork is washing – preferably with a lot of water, from a hose. This will remove all the loose solids which may have stuck to the vehicle. It is important to flush these off in such a way as to prevent grit from scratching the finish. The wheel arches and underframe need washing in the same way to remove any accumulated mud which will retain moisture and tend to encourage rust. Paradoxically enough, the best time to clean the underframe and wheel arches is in wet weather when the mud is thoroughly wet and soft. In very wet weather the underframe is usually cleaned of large accumulations automatically and this is a good time for inspection.

3 Periodically, except on vehicles with a wax-based underbody protective coating, it is a good idea to have the whole of the underframe of the vehicle steam cleaned, engine compartment included, so that a thorough inspection can be carried out to see what minor repairs and renovations are necessary. Steam cleaning is available at many garages and is necessary for removal of the accumulation of oily grime which sometimes is allowed to become thick in certain areas. If steam cleaning facilities are not available, there are one or two excellent grease solvents available which can be brush applied. The dirt can then be simply hosed off. Note that these methods should not be used on vehicles with wax-based underbody protective coating or the coating will be removed. Such vehicles should be inspected annually, preferably just prior to winter, when the underbody should be washed down and any damage to the wax coating repaired. Ideally, a completely fresh coat should be applied. It would also be worth considering the use of such wax-based protection for injection into door panels, sills, box sections, etc, as an additional safeguard against rust damage where such protection is not provided by the vehicle manufacturer.

4 After washing paintwork, wipe off with a chamois leather to give an unspotted clear finish. A coat of clear protective wax polish will give added protection against chemical pollutants in the air. If the paintwork sheen has dulled or oxidised, use a cleaner/polisher combination to restore the brilliance of the shine. This requires a little effort, but such dulling is usually caused because regular washing has been neglected. Care needs to be taken with metallic paintwork, as special non-abrasive cleaner/polisher is required to avoid damage to the finish. Always check that the door and ventilator opening drain holes and pipes are completely clear so that water can be drained out (photos). Bright work should be treated in the same way as paint work. Windscreens and windows can be kept clear of the smeary film which often appears by the use of a proprietary glass cleaner. Never use any form of wax or other body or chromium polish on glass.

5 Periodically lubricate the bonnet, tailgate and door hinges with oil. At the same time lubricate the bonnet release lock unit and the door locks (photo).

3 Maintenance – upholstery and carpets

Mats and carpets should be brushed or vacuum cleaned regularly to keep them free of grit. If they are badly stained remove them from the vehicle for scrubbing or sponging and make quite sure they are dry before refitting. Seats and interior trim panels can be kept clean by wiping with a damp cloth. If they do become stained (which can be more apparent on light coloured upholstery) use a little liquid detergent and a soft nail brush to scour the grime out of the grain of the material. Do not forget to keep the headlining clean in the same way as the upholstery. When using liquid cleaners inside the vehicle do not overwet the surfaces being cleaned. Excessive damp could get into the seams and padded interior causing stains, offensive odours or even rot. If the inside of the vehicle gets wet accidentally it is worthwhile taking

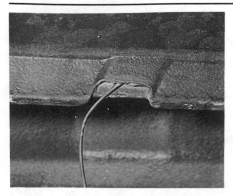

2.4A Clearing a body drain hole with a piece of rod

2.4B Where applicable, check the sunroof drain channels are clear of obstruction

2.5 Lubricating the bonnet lock

some trouble to dry it out properly, particularly where carpets are involved. *Do not leave oil or electric heaters inside the vehicle for this purpose.*

4 Minor body damage – repair to metal panels

The photographic sequences on pages 158 and 159 illustrate the operations detailed in the following sub-sections.

Note: *For more detailed information about bodywork repair, the Haynes Publishing Group publish a book by Lindsay Porter called The Car Bodywork Repair Manual. This incorporates information on such aspects as rust treatment, painting and glass fibre repairs, as well as details on more ambitious repairs involving welding and panel beating.*

Prior to undertaking such operations, it should be noted that some body panels have a galvanised coating treatment while others are of high-yield point type sheet metal (twice as strong, but 25% thinner gauge than conventional body panels). If welding and/or repair operations are being considered to accident damaged panels, the following points should be observed:

(a) *High yield point body panels should normally be renewed if they have suffered accident damage. If repaired, the yield point limit is reduced and satisfactory repairs are not possible. These panels must not be brazed or welded with oxyacetylene, or be heated to straighten*

(b) *If a galvanised panel is to be welded, it will first need to be cleaned by sanding or preferably by heating and then brushed with a wire brush. Avoid damaging the galvanised treatment in any other areas other than that being repaired. A conductive primer must be applied to the inner face of the steel panel prior to welding.*

Repair of minor scratches in bodywork

If the scratch is very superficial, and does not penetrate to the metal of the bodywork, repair is very simple. Lightly rub the area of the scratch with a paintwork renovator, or a very fine cutting paste, to remove loose paint from the scratch and to clear the surrounding bodywork of wax polish. Rinse the area with clean water.

Apply touch-up paint to the scratch using a fine paint brush; continue to apply fine layers of paint until the surface of the paint in the scratch is level with the surrounding paintwork. Allow the new paint at least two weeks to harden: then blend it into the surrounding paintwork by rubbing the scratch area with a paintwork renovator or a very fine cutting paste. Finally, apply wax polish.

Where the scratch has penetrated right through to the metal of the bodywork, causing the metal to rust, a different repair technique is required. Remove any loose rust from the bottom of the scratch with a penknife, then apply rust inhibiting paint to prevent the formation of rust in the future. Using a rubber or nylon applicator fill the scratch with bodystopper paste. If required, this paste can be mixed with cellulose thinners to provide a very thin paste which is ideal for filling narrow scratches. Before the stopper-paste in the scratch hardens, wrap a piece of smooth cotton rag around the top of a finger. Dip the finger in cellulose thinners and then quickly sweep it across the surface of the stopper-paste in the scratch; this will ensure that the surface of the stopper-paste is slightly hollowed. The scratch can now be painted over as described earlier in this Section.

Repair of dents in bodywork

When deep denting of the vehicle's bodywork has taken place, the first task is to pull the dent out, until the affected bodywork almost attains its original shape. There is little point in trying to restore the original shape completely, as the metal in the damaged area will have stretched on impact and cannot be reshaped fully to its original contour. It is better to bring the level of the dent up to a point which is about $\frac{1}{8}$ in (3 mm) below the level of the surrounding bodywork. In cases where the dent is very shallow anyway, it is not worth trying to pull it out at all. If the underside of the dent is accessible, it can be hammered out gently from behind, using a mallet with a wooden or plastic head. Whilst doing this, hold a suitable block of wood firmly against the outside of the panel to absorb the impact from the hammer blows and thus prevent a large area of the bodywork from being 'belled-out'.

Should the dent be in a section of the bodywork which has a double skin or some other factor making it inaccessible from behind, a different technique is called for. Drill several small holes through the metal inside the area – particularly in the deeper section. Then screw long self-tapping screws into the holes just sufficiently for them to gain a good purchase in the metal. Now the dent can be pulled out by pulling on the protruding heads of the screws with a pair of pliers.

The next stage of the repair is the removal of the paint from the damaged area, and from an inch or so of the surrounding 'sound' bodywork. This is accomplished most easily by using a wire brush or abrasive pad on a power drill, although it can be done just as effectively by hand using sheets of abrasive paper. To complete the preparation for filling, score the surface of the bare metal with a screwdriver or the tang of a file, or alternatively, drill small holes in the affected area. This will provide a really good 'key' for the filler paste.

To complete the repair see the Section on filling and re-spraying.

Repair of rust holes or gashes in bodywork

Remove all paint from the affected area and from an inch or so of the surrounding 'sound' bodywork, using an abrasive pad or a wire brush on a power drill. If these are not available a few sheets of abrasive paper will do the job just as effectively. With the paint removed you will be able to gauge the severity of the corrosion and therefore decide whether to renew the whole panel (if this is possible) or to repair the affected area. New body panels are not as expensive as most people think and it is often quicker and more satisfactory to fit a new panel than to attempt to repair large areas of corrosion.

Remove all fittings from the affected area except those which will act as a guide to the original shape of the damaged bodywork (eg headlamp shells etc). Then, using tin snips or a hacksaw blade, remove all loose metal and any other metal badly affected by corrosion. Hammer the edges of the hole inwards in order to create a slight depression for the filler paste.

Wire brush the affected area to remove the powdery rust from the surface of the remaining metal. Paint the affected area with rust inhibiting paint; if the back of the rusted area is accessible treat this also.

Before filling can take place it will be necessary to block the hole in some way. This can be achieved by the use of aluminium or plastic mesh, or aluminium tape.

Aluminium or plastic mesh is probably the best material to use for a large hole. Cut a piece to the approximate size and shape of the hole to be filled, then position it in the hole so that its edges are below the level of the surrounding bodywork. It can be retained in position by several blobs of filler paste around its periphery.

Aluminium tape should be used for small or very narrow holes. Pull a piece off the roll and trim it to the approximate size and shape required, then pull off the backing paper (if used) and stick the tape over the hole; it can be overlapped if the thickness of one piece is insufficient. Burnish down the edges of the tape with the handle of a screwdriver or similar, to ensure that the tape is securely attached to the metal underneath.

Bodywork repairs – filling and re-spraying

Before using this Section, see the Sections on dent, deep scratch, rust holes and gash repairs.

Many types of bodyfiller are available, but generally speaking those proprietary kits which contain a tin of filler paste and a tube of resin hardener are best for this type of repair. A wide, flexible plastic or nylon applicator will be found invaluable for imparting a smooth and well contoured finish to the surface of the filler.

Mix up a little filler on a clean piece of card or board – measure the hardener carefully (follow the maker's instructions on the pack) other-wise the filler will set too rapidly or too slowly. Using the applicator apply the filler paste to the prepared area; draw the applicator across the surface of the filler to achieve the correct contour and to level the filler surface. As soon as a contour that approximates to the correct one is achieved, stop working the paste – if you carry on too long the paste will become sticky and begin to 'pick up' on the applicator. Continue to add thin layers of filler paste at twenty-minute intervals until the level of the filler is just proud of the surrounding bodywork.

Once the filler has hardened, excess can be removed using a metal plane or file. From then on, progressively finer grades of abrasive paper should be used, starting with a 40 grade production paper and finishing with 400 grade wet-and-dry paper. Always wrap the abrasive paper around a flat rubber, cork, or wooden block – otherwise the surface of the filler will not be completely flat. During the smoothing of the filler surface the wet-and-dry paper should be periodically rinsed in water. This will ensure that a very smooth finish is imparted to the filler at the final stage.

At this stage the 'dent' should be surrounded by a ring of bare metal, which in turn should be encircled by the finely 'feathered' edge of the good paintwork. Rinse the repair area with clean water, until all of the dust produced by the rubbing-down operation has gone.

Spray the whole repair area with a light coat of primer – this will show up any imperfections in the surface of the filler. Repair these imperfections with fresh filler paste or bodystopper, and once more smooth the surface with abrasive paper. If bodystopper is used, it can be mixed with cellulose thinners to form a really thin paste which is ideal for filling small holes. Repeat this spray and repair procedure until you are satisfied that the surface of the filler, and the feathered edge of the paintwork are perfect. Clean the repair area with clean water and allow to dry fully.

The repair area is now ready for final spraying. Paint spraying must be carried out in a warm, dry, windless and dust free atmosphere. This condition can be created artificially if you have access to a large indoor working area, but if you are forced to work in the open, you will have to pick your day very carefully. If you are working indoors, dousing the floor in the work area with water will help to settle the dust which would otherwise be in the atmosphere. If the repair area is confined to one body panel, mask off the surrounding panels; this will help to minimise the effects of a slight mis-match in paint colours. Bodywork fittings (eg chrome strips, door handles etc) will also need to be masked off. Use genuine masking tape and several thicknesses of newspaper for the masking operations.

Before commencing to spray, agitate the aerosol can thoroughly, then spray a test area (an old tin, or similar) until the technique is mastered. Cover the repair area with a thick coat of primer; the thickness should be built up using several thin layers of paint rather than one thick one. Using 400 grade wet-and-dry paper, rub down the surface of the primer until it is really smooth. While doing this, the work area should be thoroughly doused with water, and the wet-and-dry paper periodically rinsed in water. Allow to dry before spraying on more paint.

Spray on the top coat, again building up the thickness by using several thin layers of paint. Start spraying in the centre of the repair area and then, using a circular motion, work outwards until the whole repair area and about 2 inches of the surrounding original paintwork is covered. Remove all masking material 10 to 15 minutes after spraying on the final coat of paint.

Allow the new paint at least two weeks to harden, then, using a paintwork renovator or a very fine cutting paste, blend the edges of the paint into the existing paintwork. Finally, apply wax polish.

5 Minor body damage – repair to plastic components

With the use of more and more plastic body components by the vehicle manufacturers (eg bumpers, spoilers, and in some cases major body panels), rectification of more serious damage to such items has become a matter of either entrusting repair work to a specialist in this field, or renewing complete components. Repair of such damage by the DIY owner is not really feasible owing to the cost of the equipment and materials required for effecting such repairs. The basic technique involves making a groove along the line of the crack in the plastic using a rotary burr in a power drill. The damaged part is then welded back together by using a hot air gun to heat up and fuse a plastic filler rod into the groove. Any excess plastic is then removed and the area rubbed down to a smooth finish. It is important that a filler rod of the correct plastic is used, as body components can be made of a variety of different types (eg polycarbonate, ABS, polypropylene).

Damage of a less serious nature (abrasions, minor cracks etc) can be repaired by the DIY owner using a two-part epoxy filler repair material. Once mixed in equal proportions, this is used in similar fashion to the bodywork filler used on metal panels. The filler is usually cured in twenty to thirty minutes, ready for sanding and painting.

If the owner is renewing a complete component himself, or if he has repaired it with epoxy filler, he will be left with the problem of finding a suitable paint for finishing which is compatible with the type of plastic used. At one time the use of a universal paint was not possible owing to the complex range of plastics encountered in body component applications. Standard paints, generally speaking, will not bond to plastic or rubber satisfactorily. However, it is now possible to obtain a plastic body parts finishing kit which consists of a pre-primer treatment, a primer and coloured top coat. Full instructions are normally supplied with a kit, but basically the method of use is to first apply the pre-primer to the component concerned and allow it to dry for up to 30 minutes. Then the primer is applied and left to dry for about an hour before finally applying the special coloured top coat. The result is a correctly coloured component where the paint will flex with the plastic or rubber, a property that standard paint does not normally possess.

6 Major body damage – repair

The construction of the body is such that great care must be taken when making cuts, or when renewing major members, to preserve the basic safety characteristics of the structure. In addition, the heating of certain areas is not advisable.

In view of the specialised knowledge necessary for this work, and the alignment jigs and special tools frequently required, the owner is advised to consult a specialist body repairer or Citroën dealer.

7 Bonnet – removal and refitting

1 Raise and support the bonnet. Detach the windscreen washer supply hose to the jet on the bonnet.
2 Use a felt tip pen or similar to make an outline marking around the periphery of the bonnet hinges. This will provide a guide to the adjustment position when refitting the bonnet.
3 Get an assistant to help support the bonnet, then unscrew the hinge bolts and lift the bonnet clear of the car (photos).
4 Refit in the reverse order of removal. Adjust the bonnet position to

7.3A Bonnet hinge bolts

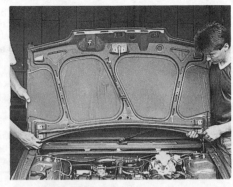

7.3B Bonnet removal

8.2 Bonnet lock and cable attachments

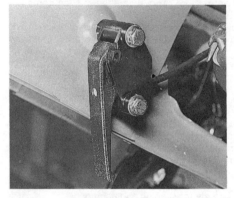

8.5 Bonnet release handle and retaining bolts

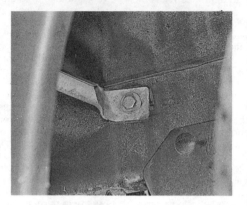

9.1 Front bumper stay bolt fixing

9.6 Adjust the rubber buffers to support the bonnet

provide an even clearance between its outer edge and the surrounding body panels. On completion, check for satisfactory operation of the bonnet lock and safety catch.

8   Bonnet lock and release cable – removal and refitting

1   Raise and support the bonnet. If the release cable has broken or seized, insert a suitable hooked rod through the front grille and actuate the lock to release the catch.

Lock unit
2   Unscrew the two retaining bolts and detach the bonnet lock and cable from the cross-panel. Disconnect the cable and remove the lock unit (photo).

Cable
3   Proceed as described in paragraphs 1 and 2 to detach the cable from the lock unit.
4   Release the cable from the retaining clips in the engine compartment.
5   Unbolt the release handle within the car, then pull the cable through the bulkhead and remove it (photo).
6   Refitting is a reversal of removal, but check that the striker enters the lock centrally and holds the front of the bonnet level with the front wings. If necessary loosen the lock bolts and move the lock within the elongated holes. Adjust the bonnet height by screwing the striker pin in or out. Adjust the rubber buffers to support the front corners of the bonnet (photo).

9   Bumpers – removal and refitting

Front
1   Unscrew and remove the bumper stay bolt from the side of the chassis member under the wheel arch each side (photo).
2   Firmly grip the bumper and pull it from the car, detaching it from the location points each side. As it is withdrawn, disconnect the headlight

washer hose and where applicable, the wiring to the auxiliary driving lamps.
3   Refit in the reverse order of removal.

Rear
4   Unscrew and remove the bumper retaining bolts from the under-panel and carefully withdraw the bumper rearwards from the car.
5   Refit in the reverse order of removal.

10   Front wing panel – removal and refitting

1   Disconnect the battery earth lead, then referring to Chapter 12, remove and detach the side indicator lamp from the wing panel on the side concerned.

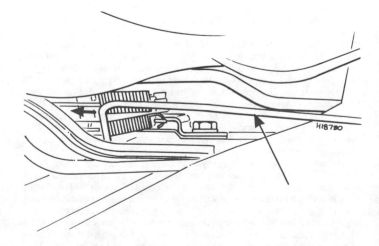

Fig. 11.1 Fabricated rod used to release the bonnet catch (Sec 8)

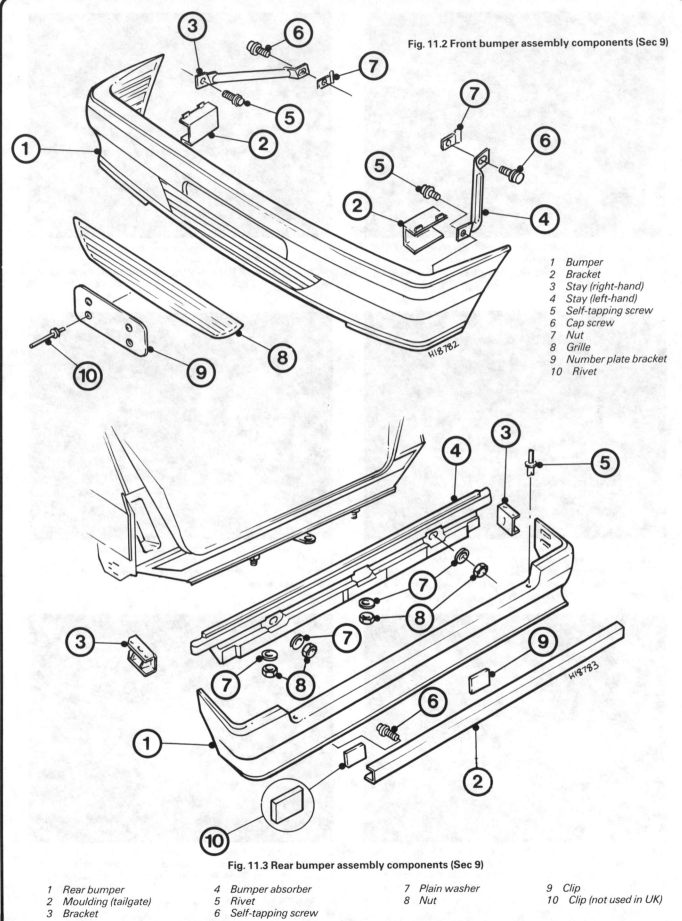

Fig. 11.2 Front bumper assembly components (Sec 9)

1 Bumper
2 Bracket
3 Stay (right-hand)
4 Stay (left-hand)
5 Self-tapping screw
6 Cap screw
7 Nut
8 Grille
9 Number plate bracket
10 Rivet

Fig. 11.3 Rear bumper assembly components (Sec 9)

1 Rear bumper
2 Moulding (tailgate)
3 Bracket
4 Bumper absorber
5 Rivet
6 Self-tapping screw
7 Plain washer
8 Nut
9 Clip
10 Clip (not used in UK)

This sequence of photographs deals with the repair of the dent and paintwork damage shown in this photo. The procedure will be similar for the repair of a hole. It should be noted that the procedures given here are simplified – more explicit instructions will be found in the text

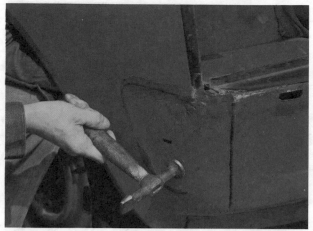

In the case of a dent the first job – after removing surrounding trim – is to hammer out the dent where access is possible. This will minimise filling. Here, the large dent having been hammered out, the damaged area is being made slightly concave

Now all paint must be removed from the damaged area, by rubbing with coarse abrasive paper. Alternatively, a wire brush or abrasive pad can be used in a power drill. Where the repair area meets good paintwork, the edge of the paintwork should be 'feathered', using a finer grade of abrasive paper

In the case of a hole caused by rusting, all damaged sheet-metal should be cut away before proceeding to this stage. Here, the damaged area is being treated with rust remover and inhibitor before being filled

Mix the body filler according to its manufacturer's instructions. In the case of corrosion damage, it will be necessary to block off any large holes before filling – this can be done with aluminium or plastic mesh, or aluminium tape. Make sure the area is absolutely clean before ...

... applying the filler. Filler should be applied with a flexible applicator, as shown, for best results; the wooden spatula being used for confined areas. Apply thin layers of filler at 20-minute intervals, until the surface of the filler is slightly proud of the surrounding bodywork

Initial shaping can be done with a Surform plane or Dreadnought file. Then, using progressively finer grades of wet-and-dry paper, wrapped around a sanding block, and copious amounts of clean water, rub down the filler until really smooth and flat. Again, feather the edges of adjoining paintwork

The whole repair area can now be sprayed or brush-painted with primer. If spraying, ensure adjoining areas are protected from over-spray. Note that at least one inch of the surrounding sound paintwork should be coated with primer. Primer has a 'thick' consistency, so will find small imperfections

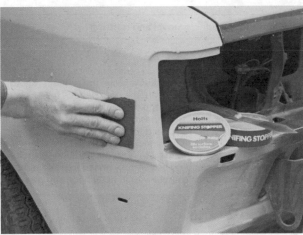

Again, using plenty of water, rub down the primer with a fine grade wet-and-dry paper (400 grade is probably best) until it is really smooth and well blended into the surrounding paintwork. Any remaining imperfections can now be filled by carefully applied knifing stopper paste

When the stopper has hardened, rub down the repair area again before applying the final coat of primer. Before rubbing down this last coat of primer, ensure the repair area is blemish-free — use more stopper if necessary. To ensure that the surface of the primer is really smooth use some finishing compound

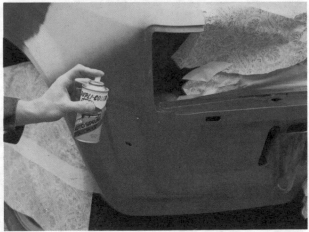

The top coat can now be applied. When working out of doors, pick a dry, warm and wind-free day. Ensure surrounding areas are protected from over-spray. Agitate the aerosol thoroughly, then spray the centre of the repair area, working outwards with a circular motion. Apply the paint as several thin coats

After a period of about two weeks, which the paint needs to harden fully, the surface of the repaired area can be 'cut' with a mild cutting compound prior to wax polishing. When carrying out bodywork repairs, remember that the quality of the finished job is proportional to the time and effort expended

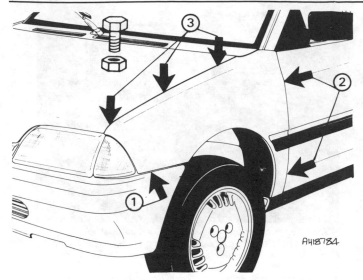

Fig. 11.4 Front wing panel fixing points (arrowed) (Sec 10)

2   Unbolt and detach the front bumper stay from the side member under the wheel arch.
3   Refer to Chapter 12 and remove the headlamp unit and the front indicator in the side concerned.
4   Unscrew the front wing panel retaining bolts from the locations indicated in Fig. 11.4. The bolts numbered 2 are accessible by opening the door.
5   Carefully detach and remove the front wing panel.
6   Clean and prepare the wing joint areas before refitting the wing. Refit the wing in the reverse order of removal. Check the panel for alignment before fully tightening the retaining bolts.
7   On completion, check the front headlights and indicators for satisfactory operation.

11   Doors – removal and refitting

1   The door hinges are welded to the door and body pillars. Before removing the door, first disconnect the battery earth lead.
2   Open the door and remove the courtesy lamp switch (Chapter 12).
3   If applicable, remove the trim panel and detach the wiring connections to the power window regulator motor and/or the door mounted speaker unit.
4   Using a suitable punch, drive out the roll pin from the door check strap (photo).
5   Support the door in the fully open position with blocks or a jack, but position a piece of rag between the base of the door and the jack to protect the paintwork.
6   Drive out the hinge pins and remove the door.
7   Refit in the reverse order of removal. When the hinge pins are refitted, close the door and check it for alignment and security in the closed position. To adjust the door for alignment, a special Citroën tool (No 8.1305) or a similar tool will be required. The tool is located over the hinge and the hinge levered in the required direction to suit.
8   Where necessary, the striker on the body pillar may be adjusted to ensure correct closure of the door.

12   Door trim panel – removal and refitting

Front door

1   Unscrew and remove the lower trim pocket screws (photo).
2   Undo the retaining screws and remove the armrest (photo).
3   Undo the retaining screw from the door panel. This screw is located just forwards of the window regulator (photo). To remove the manual regulator handle, note its fitted position with the window fully raised (or lowered) then pull it from its shaft (photo).
4   Prise free and remove the window seal from the door (photo).
5   Prise free the escutcheon plate from the door inner catch (photo).
6   The trim panels can now be carefully prised free and removed. If the main panel incorporates a speaker unit, detach its wiring as the panel is

11.4 Door hinge (A) check strap (B) and courtesy lamp switch (C)

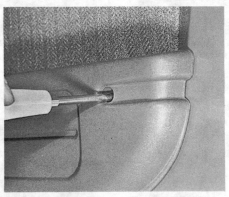

12.1 Door lower trim pocket screw removal

12.2 Door armrest retaining screw removal

12.3A Remove door forward trim screws ...

12.3B ... and the window regulator (manual) handle

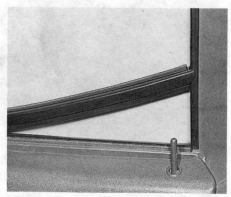

12.4 Removing the door window seal

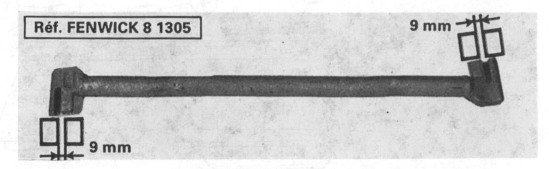

Fig. 11.5 Special tool used to align the doors (Sec 11)

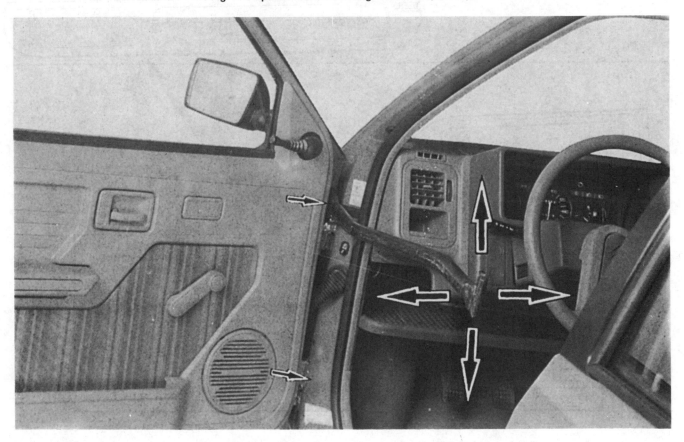

Fig. 11.6 Special tool in position to adjust the door (Sec 11)

12.5 Removing the escutcheon plate

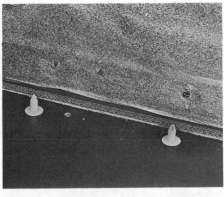

12.6 Door trim removal showing retaining clips

12.7 View of door with trim panel and insulation removed

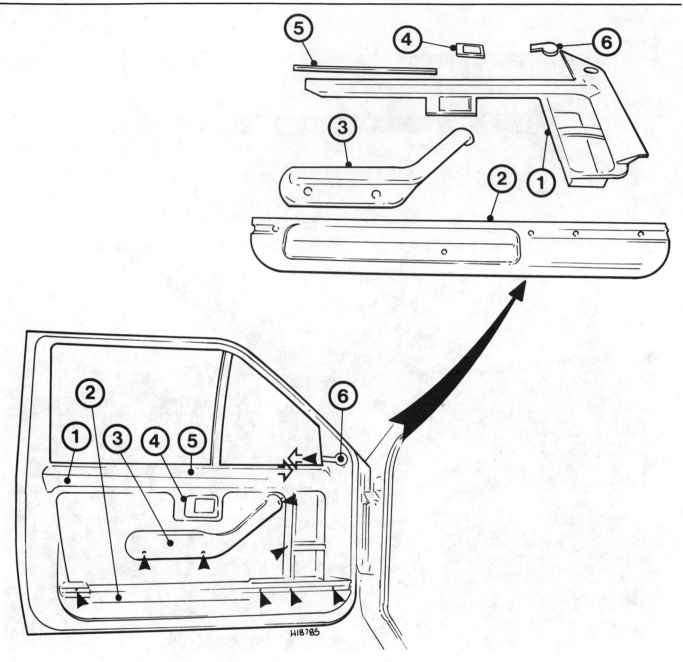

Fig. 11.7 Front door trim components and locations (Sec 12)

Arrows indicate screw Securing points

withdrawn. The speaker can be removed from the panel as described in Chapter 12.
7   Access to the inner door components can be made by carefully peeling free the insulation panel from the door (photo).
8   Refit in the reverse order of removal.

Rear door

9   The procedures closely follow those described for the front door. Refer to Fig. 11.8 for the relevant details of components.

13   Door – dismantling and reassembly

1   Remove the door trim panel as described in the previous Section.

Window regulator unit

2   To remove the manual type regulator unit, unscrew and remove the three regulator to door panel retaining nuts, then supporting the window, move it to a suitable access position and unscrew the two regulator-to-window support screws (photo).
3   The procedures for removing the electronic type regulator unit are similar but also detach the wiring at the block connector.
4   Support the window and withdraw the regulator unit through the door panel access aperture.

Door glass

5   To remove the door glass, first remove the window regulator then unbolt the glass side channels (photo), tilt the glass and withdraw it upwards.

Door Lock

6   To remove the manual type door lock and inner remote control handle, detach the link control rods as necessary, unscrew the link unit retaining screws and the outer release handle screw (photo). To remove

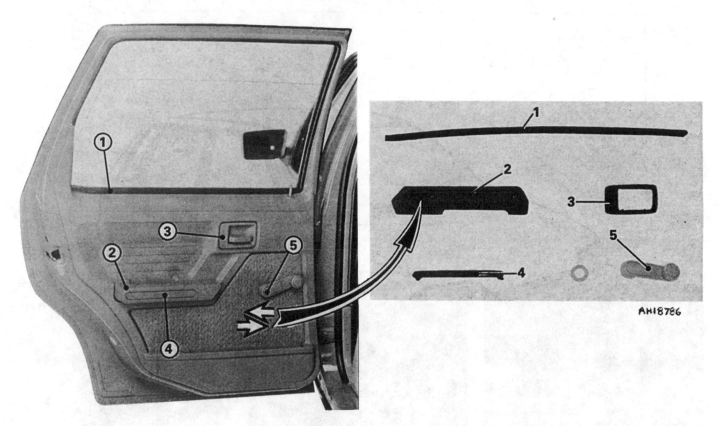

Fig. 11.8 Rear door trim components and locations (Sec 12)

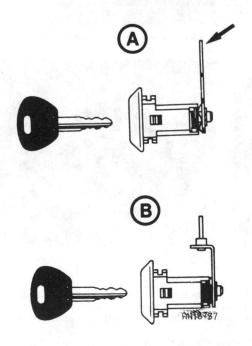

Fig. 11.9 Showing early (A) and late (B) type door lock barrel (Sec 13)

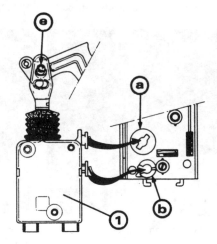

Fig. 11.10 Late type electric door lock (1) showing key slots (a) and (b), and the operating lever (e) (Sec 13)

the remote handle, slide it horizontally to disengage its retainers, then remove it with the connecting rod (photos).

7   The door lock barrel is secured by a flat spring clip which can be prised free to release the lock unit. Two types of lock unit have been fitted as shown in Fig. 11.9.

8   To remove the electric (central locking) type door lock, undo the retaining screws, disengage the actuating lever and detach the wiring. If fitting a later type of lock in place of an earlier type, fit a new lever to the barrel and on either early or late types, bend the inner operating rod at 'a' in Fig. 11.10 so that it is clear of peg 'b'.

9   If required, the operating lever can be transferred to the later type lock barrel if this is being renewed.

Exterior mirror

10   Remove the mirror inner trim panel, then undo the retaining bolts and remove the mirror (photo).

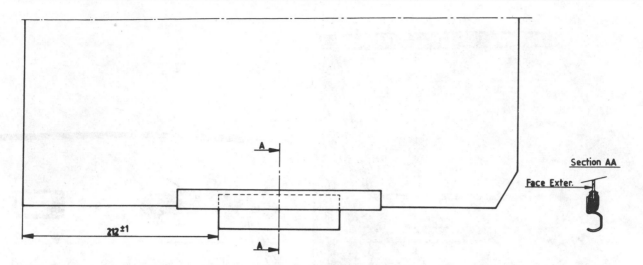

Fig. 11.11 Door glass support channel location (3-door model) (Sec 13)

13.2 Manual door window regulator retaining nuts

13.5 Door glass channel bolts

13.6A Removing the door lock release handle (outer)

13.6B Door lock retaining screws

13.6C Door lock inner release. Slide it forwards to detach it ...

13.6D ... and withdraw it from the door

Reassembly

11   Reassembly of the door is a reversal of the dismantling procedure. However, when refitting the door glass, adjust the position of the side channels so that the glass moves smoothly without excessive play. If the glass regulator/support channel is renewed, locate them as shown in Figs. 11.11, 11.12 and 11.13.

3   Disconnect the wiring for the heated rear window and if fitted, the tailgate wiper motor. Also detach the washer tube.
4   Drive out the hinge pins using a suitable drift and remove the tailgate.
5   Refit in the reverse order of removal. Check for satisfactory alignment. Also check the operation of the tailgate ancillary items.

14   Tailgate – removal and refitting

1   Open the tailgate and have an assistant support it.
2   Disconnect the struts from the body by prising out the clips and pulling off the sockets (photos).

15   Tailgate lock components – removal and refitting

1   Open the tailgate and prise free the trim panel for access to the lock components.
2   Remove the wiper motor cover, slide free the retaining clip, disconnect the connecting rod and remove the lock barrel unit (photo).

13.10 Door mirror retaining bolts

14.2A Prise free the retaining clip ...

14.2B ... and detach the stay from the ball socket

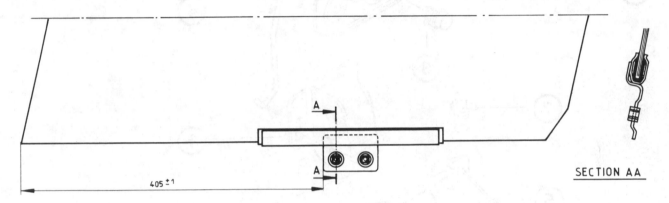

Fig. 11.12 Door glass support channel location (5-door model) (Sec 13)

405 ± 1

SECTION AA

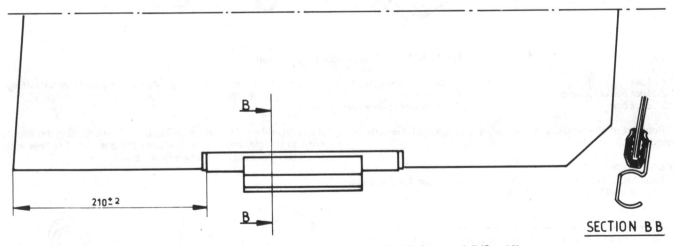

Fig. 11.13 Rear door glass support channel location (5-door model) (Sec 13)

210 ± 2

SECTION BB

3   To remove the latch, undo the retaining bolts, detach the connecting rod and remove the latch (photo). On central locking models, the actuator is removed in the same manner, but also disconnect the wiring from the actuator unit.

4   Refitting is a reversal of the removal procedure. Adjust the position of the striker plate, if required, to securely shut the tailgate.

16   Windscreen and tailgate glass – general

The renewal of both the windscreen and the tailgate glass are tasks which are best entrusted to a professional fitter. In each case some specialised tools and knowledge of the safe and successful fitting of these glass panels are essential. Unless they are correctly fitted, they may well leak and at worst prove dangerous, therefore entrust renewal to a specialist.

17   Rear quarter window – removal and refitting

3-door model

1   Open the window and get an assistant to support it.

2   Undo the retaining screws and remove the window.

3   If the surround seal is to be renewed, prise it free and clean the contact surfaces. Refit the seal using a length of cord inserted into its groove, then as the seal is fitted, pull the cord to engage the lips of the seal with the window frame.

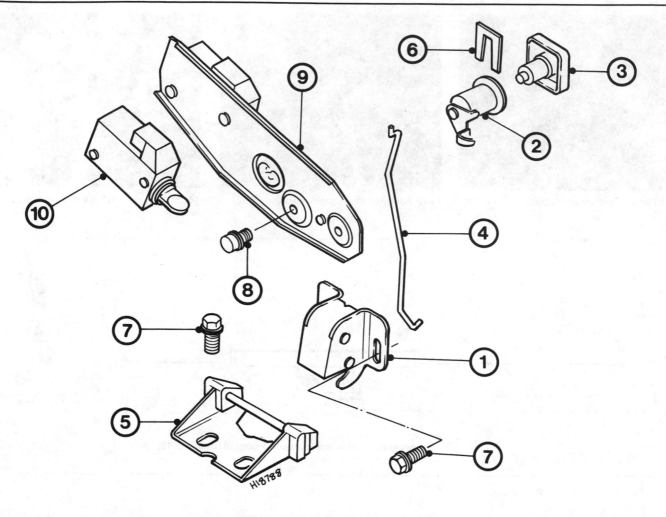

Fig. 11.14 Typical tailgate lock components (Sec 15)

1	Lock	4	Lock connecting rod	7	Bolt	9	Actuator support (central locking)
2	Lock barrel housing	5	Striker	8	Bolt	10	Actuator (central locking)
3	Lock barrel	6	Retainer clip (lock barrel)				

4   Refitting of the window is otherwise a reversal of the removal procedure.

5-door model

5   Renewal is best entrusted to a professional fitter for the same reasons outlined in the previous Section.

---

18   Rear side trim (3-door models) – removal and refitting

---

1   Remove the two screws retaining the armrest panel then pull the panel upwards to disengage it. The inner trim panel can now be detached and the speaker leads disconnected.
2   To remove the speaker unit, undo the four screws and detach it from the panel.
3   Refit in the reverse order of removal.

---

19   Air intake cowl – removal and refitting

---

1   Remove the windscreen wiper arm and blade as described in Chapter 12.
2   Unscrew the cowl retaining screws and nuts and then withdraw the cowl. Undo the three retaining screws and remove the deflector shield for access to the wiper motor (photos)

3   Refit in the reverse order of removal. When refitting the wiper arm onto its spindle, ensure that it is correctly positioned so that when in operation it has the correct sweep and parks correctly.

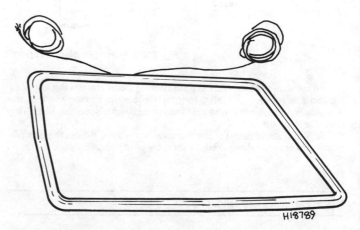

Fig. 11.15 Rear quarter window seal and fitting cord – 3-door model (Sec 17)

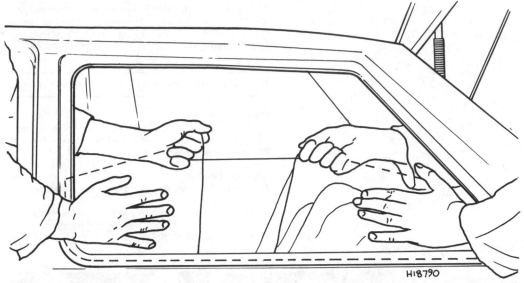

Fig. 11.16 Rear quarter window seal fitting method (Sec 17)

20 Seats – removal and refitting

Front

1   Unclip and detach the trim panel from the inboard side seat runner.
2   Move the seat fully to the rear then unscrew and remove the socket head runner retaining bolts at the front using a 5 mm Allen key.
3   Move the seat to the forward position then unscrew and remove the rear retaining bolts. Remove the seat (photos).
4   Refit in the reverse order of removal.

Rear seat

5   To remove the backrest, tilt it forwards about 45° and lift if from its pivot brackets as shown in Fig. 11.17

6   To remove the seat squab, lift it at the front edge and release it from its location.
7   Refit in the reverse order of removal.

21 Seat belts – general

1   The seat belts do not normally require any attention apart from periodically checking their condition and security.
2   If required, the belts can be cleaned using a mild soap and water solution, but for deep stains, try rubbing the affected area with methylated spirits or a lighter fuel.
3   Typical mounting points are shown in the accompanying photos.

15.2 Tailgate lock barrel and retaining clip

15.3 Tailgate latch

19.2A Cowl retaining screw (arrowed) ...

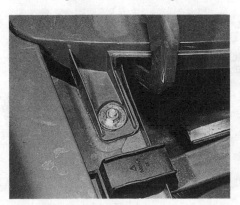

19.2B ... and nut/flat washer

19.2C Deflector shield

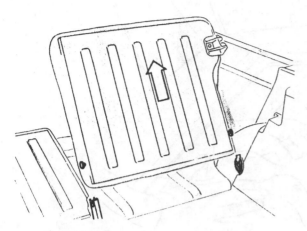

Fig. 11.17 Rear seat backrest removal (Sec 20)

Access to the mountings is obtainable after the removal of the appropriate trim panel (photos). Whenever the belt is removed and refitted, check it for satisfactory operation on completion by gripping the webbing and pulling it sharply. The inertia reel must lock.

22 Facia and associate trim components – removal and refitting

Parcel shelves
1   Prise free the two press clips securing the shelf on its outboard edge, then undo the two retaining screws from the inboard end. Withdraw the shelf (photo).

Centre console
2   Lift the oddment bin from the console, then unscrew the two upper retaining screws.
3   Release the gear lever gaiter from its floor mounting, and slide it up the lever to allow access to the console floor mounting screw. Undo the screw and remove the console, as it is withdrawn, detach wiring connectors from console mounted switches.

20.3A Front seat outboard rear mounting

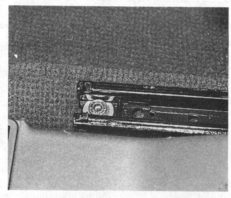

20.3B Front seat inboard rear mounting

21.3A Prise off the cap for access to the mounting bolt

21.3B Front seat belt inertia reel unit and mounting location (trim removed)

21.3C Rear seat belt inertia reel unit and mounting location (trim removed)

22.1 Parcel shelf retaining bolt

22.6 Removing a ventilation grille from the facia

22.10 Removing the switch panel trim

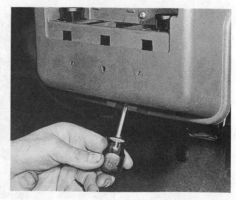

22.12 Removing the facia lower retaining screw

Facia unit

4   Disconnect the battery earth lead.

5   Remove the right and left-hand parcel shelves and the central console as previously described.

6   Remove the face level ventilation grilles by releasing the securing clip on the side of each and pulling them free. Do not lose the clips (photo).

7   Refer to Chapter 10 for details and remove the steering wheel and column.

8   Refer to Chapter 12 and remove the following:

    (a)   *Instrument panel*
    (b)   *Radio*
    (c)   *Windscreen wiper motor*
    (d)   *Fuse box*

9   Remove the heater control panel as described in Chapter 2.

10   Prise free and remove the centre switch panel (photo).

11   Disconnect the choke lead from the carburettor (Chapter 3).

12   Unscrew and remove the facia retaining screws, one on each side, and two to the heater unit (front and bottom) and two underneath the heater unit (photo).

13   Partial withdrawal of the facia unit is now possible, but for full removal, disconnect the wiring loom and connections. As they are disconnected, note their respective routings.

14   In all instances refitting is a reversal of the removal procedure. Ensure that all wiring connections are correctly and securely made. Route the looms as noted during removal.

15   Reconnect the choke cable as described in Chapter 3.

16   Refit the steering wheel and column as described in Chapter 10.

17   On completion, check for satisfactory operation of all components.

Chapter 12 Electrical system

Contents

Specifications

System type .... 12 volt, negative earth, alternator with integral regulator, pre-engaged starter motor

Battery
Type .... 12V-LC-150A or 12V-LV-175A (alternative for GT model)

Alternator
Make .... Paris-Rhone or Valeo 12V-50A
Reference number .... A13N 129 (Paris-Rhone) or YV 1925 (Valeo)
Drive tension (deflection) .... 6.0 mm (0.25 in) approximately

Starter motor
Make .... Ducellier
Reference number 534054

Bulbs

	Wattage
Main/dip	40/50 or 55/60
Long range driving lamps (GT models)	55
Indicators (front and rear)	21
Stop lamps	21
Reversing lamps	21
Tail lamps	5
Front sidelamps	4
Rear number plate lamps	4
Interior and luggage compartment lamps	5
Indicator, charge warning lamp, interior (spot) lamp	3
Instrument panel warning lamp	1.2
Speedometer illumination lamp	1.2
Cigar lighter lamp	1.2
Ashtray lamp	1.2
Interior heating control lamp	1.2
Switch warning lamps	1.2
Clock lamp	1.2

Fuses

Number	Circuit protected	Rating (amp)
1	Heated rear screen and warning lamp	10
2	Windscreen/rear window, wash/wipe, stoplamps interior spotlamp (GT model)	30
3	Instrument panel warning lamps, instrument lighting, fuel gauge, cigar light, heater control lighting and blower motor. Power window motor relay. Heated rear window relay. Direction indicator. Clock (+ ignition switch). Water level indicator	30
4	Long range driving lamps (GT model). Door locking (where applicable)	25
5	Engine cooling fan	30
6	Hazard warning lamp	10
7	Reversing lamps, oil level control unit, Duirnol lamps relay coil	10
8	Interior lamp, radio, clock, rear screen wiper park position feed, boot lamp and cigar lighter ..	20
9	Window regulator, carburettor heater..........	30
10	Horn..	20
11	Rear foglamp (and warning)...........................	5
12	Right or left-hand (according to model) side/tail lamps. Number plate light and dim-dip switches. Rear foglamps, hazard warning, rear screen wiper switch lighting	5
13	Left or right-hand (according to model) side/tail lamps. Number plate lamp. Sidelamp indicator lamp (on panel)...	5

1 General description

The electrical system is of the 12 volt negative earth type and the major components consist of a battery, of which the negative terminal is earthed, an alternator which is belt-driven from the crankshaft pulley, and a starter motor.

The battery supplies a steady amount of current for the ignition, lighting and other electrical circuits and provides a reserve of electricity when the current consumed by the electrical equipment exceeds that being produced by the alternator.

The alternator is controlled by a regulator which ensures a high output if the battery is in a low state of charge or the demand from the electrical equipment is high, and a low output if the battery is fully charged and there is little demand for the electrical equipment.

When fitting electrical accessories it is important, if they contain silicone diodes or transistors, that they are connected correctly, otherwise serious damage may result to the components concerned. Items such as radios, tape recorders, electronic tachometer, automatic dipping etc, should all be checked for correct polarity.

It is important that both battery leads are always disconnected if the battery is to be boost charged; also, if body repairs are to be carried out using electric arc welding, the alternator must be disconnected, otherwise serious damage can be caused to the more delicate instruments. Whenever the battery has to be disconnected it must always be reconnected with the negative terminal earthed.

2 Routine maintenance

Carry out the following procedures at the intervals given in *Routine maintenance* at the beginning of the manual.

1 Check the condition of the battery and its terminals, as described in Section 3.

2 Check the general condition of the alternator drivebelt. If it shows signs of excessive wear and/or cracking, it must be renewed. Check that the drivebelt tension is as specified. If not, adjust the tension of the drivebelt as described in Section 6.

3 Regularly top up the washer fluid reservoirs. The use of a good quality screen wash product is recommended. In winter add some methylated spirit to the fluid to prevent freezing. **Never** use cooling system anti-freeze as it will damage the paintwork.

3 Battery – maintenance and inspection

1 The battery fitted as original equipment is of low maintenance type; however if the battery has been replaced it may incorporate the standard cell covers for checking the electrolyte level. Under normal conditions it is not necessary to check the level, but if the battery is subject to severe conditions such as stop start driving or extreme temperatures, the level should be checked every 10 000 miles (15 000 km).

2 When topping-up is required use only distilled water and cover the battery plates to a depth of 10.0 mm (0.40 in).

3 Acid should never be required if the battery has been correctly filled from new, unless spillage has occurred.

4 Inspect the battery terminals and mounting tray for corrosion. This is the white fluffy deposit which grows at these areas. If evident remove the battery as described in Section 4, then clean the terminals and connectors of corrosion and treat with ammonia or baking soda. Apply petroleum jelly to the terminals and paint the battery tray with a suitable anti-corrosion preparation.

5 Keep the top surface of the battery casing dry.

6 An indication of the state of charge of a battery can be obtained by checking the electrolyte in each cell using a hydrometer. The specific gravity of the electrolyte for fully charged and fully discharged conditions at the electrolyte temperature indicated, is listed below.

Fully discharged	Electrolyte temperature	Fully charged
1.098	38°C (100°F)	1.268
1.102	32°C (90°F)	1.272
1.106	27°C (80°F)	1.276
1.110	21°C (70°F)	1.280
1.114	16°C (60°F)	1.284
1.118	10°C (50°F)	1.288
1.122	4°C (40°F)	1.292
1.126	-1.5°C (30°F)	1.296

7 There should be very little variation in the readings between the different cells, but if a difference is found in excess of 0.025 then it will probably be due to an internal fault indicating impending battery failure. This assumes that electrolyte has not been spilled at some time and the deficiency made up with water only.

8 If electrolyte is accidentally spilled at any time, mop up and neutralise the spillage at once. Electrolyte attacks and corrodes metal

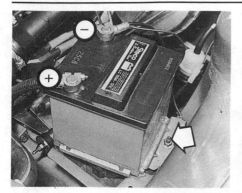

4.2A Battery showing earth (–) and positive (+) lead connections and the retaining clamp (arrowed)

4.2B Always detach the negative lead first (reconnect last)

6.4A Alternator mounting bolt (arrowed)

6.4B Alternator adjuster bolt (A) and lower mounting bolt (B)

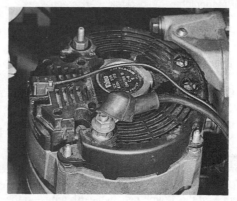

7.2 Disconnect the alternator wiring

rapidly; it will burn holes in clothing and skin. Leave the addition of acid to a battery cell to your dealer or service station as the mixing of acid with distilled water can be dangerous.

9   Never smoke or allow naked lights near the battery; the hydrogen gas which it gives off is explosive.

10   With normal motoring, the battery should be kept in a good state of charge by the alternator and never need charging from a mains charger.

11   However, if the daily mileage is low, with much use of starter and electrical accessories, it is possible for the battery to become discharged owing to the fact that the alternator is not in use long enough to replace the current consumed.

12   Also, as the battery ages, it may not be able to hold its charge and some supplementary charging may be needed. Before connecting the charger, disconnect the battery terminals or, better still, remove the battery from the vehicle as described in Section 4.

13   Specially rapid 'boost' charges which are claimed to restore the power of the battery in 1 to 2 hours are most dangerous as they can cause serious damage to the battery plates through overheating.

14   While charging the battery note that the temperature of the electrolyte should never exceed 38°C (100°F).

15   When charging a low maintenance battery **do not** remove the cell covers; however, on other types of battery, the cell covers should be removed.

4   Battery – removal and refitting

1   The battery is located in the front left-hand side of the engine compartment.

2   Disconnect the battery leads, negative lead first. If the battery is being disconnected rather then removed, detach the negative (earth) lead only. This is a useful facility when undertaking routine electrical jobs on the car (photos).

3   Release the battery clamp and lift the battery carefully from the engine compartment.

4   Refitting is a reversal of removal, but smear the terminals with petroleum jelly on completion. Ensure that the negative lead is reconnected last.

5   Alternator – general description and maintenance

1   All models covered by this manual are fitted with alternators. The alternator generates alternating current (AC) which is rectified by diodes into direct current (DC) which is the current needed for charging the battery.

2   The main advantage of the alternator lies in its ability to provide a high charge at low revolutions. Driving slowly in heavy traffic, even with the heater, wiper, lights and perhaps radio switched on, the alternator will ensure a charge reaches the battery.

3   The alternator is of the rotating field ventilated design and comprises principally a laminated stator, on which is wound the output winding, a rotor carrying the field winding and a diode rectifier.

4   The rotor is belt-driven from the engine through a pulley keyed to the rotor shaft. A fan adjacent to the pulley draws air through the unit. Rotation is clockwise when viewed from the drive end.

5   The voltage regulator is mounted externally on the rear cover of the alternator.

6   The equipment has been designed for the minimum amount of maintenance in service, the only items subject to wear being the brushes and bearings.

7   Brushes should be examined after about 80 000 miles (120 000 km) and renewed if necessary. The bearings are pre-packed with grease for life, and should not require further attention.

8   Regularly check the drivebelt tension, as described in Section 6.

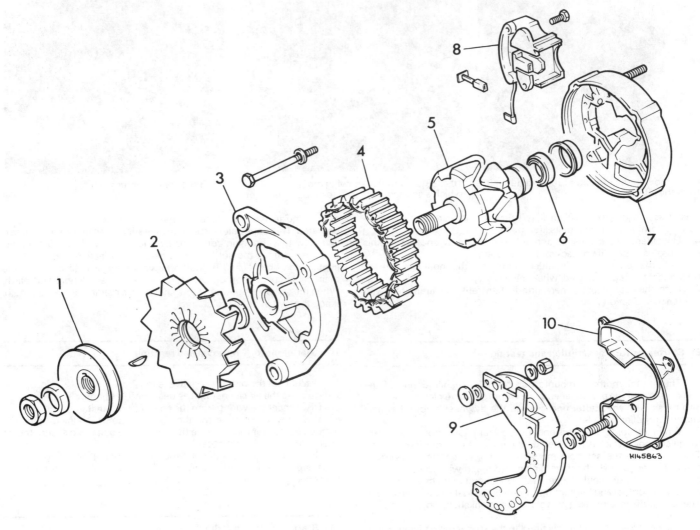

Fig. 12.1 Exploded view of a typical Paris-Rhone type alternator (Sec 8)

1 Pulley	4 Stator	7 Brush end housing	9 Diode plate
2 Fan	5 Rotor	8 Brush holder/regulator	10 Cover
3 Drive end housing	6 Bearing		

6 Alternator drivebelt – adjustment and renewal

1   Regularly inspect the condition and adjustment of the alternator drivebelt at the intervals given in the *Routine maintenance* Section at the start of the manual. If the drivebelt shows signs of excessive wear and is cracking, it must be renewed.

2   Check the tension of the drivebelt. When correctly tensioned, the alternator drivebelt will have a long and useful life. If the belt is loose, alternator performance will be affected and possibly the battery could be discharged. If the belt is too tight it will cause unnecessary alternator bearing wear. In either case the belt itself will suffer and its life will be shortened.

3   To check the tension of the drivebelt, depress it under firm thumb pressure at the midway point of the longest run between pulleys. The belt should deflect the specified amount, if not, adjust the tension as follows.

4   Loosen off the mounting bolts and then turn the tension adjuster in the required direction to adjust the tension. Retighten the mounting bolts when the tension is correctly set (photos).

5   If a new drivebelt is to be fitted, loosen off the mounting bolts and the tensioner bolt and remove the old drivebelt from the pulleys. Engage the new belt over the pulleys and reset the tension as described previously. After a new drivebelt has covered a nominal mileage, recheck and if necessary, adjust the tension.

7 Alternator – removal and refitting

1   Disconnect the battery negative (earth) lead.

2   Disconnect the wiring from the rear of the alternator (photo).

3   Loosen off the alternator mounting and tensioner bolts, release the tension on the drivebelt and then remove it from the alternator pulley.

4   Support the weight of the alternator, then undo the mounting bolts and remove it from the car.

5   Refitting is a reversal of the removal, but tension the drivebelt as described in Section 6.

8 Alternator – brush renewal

1   Remove the alternator (Section 7), then remove the rear shield (where fitted).

2   Remove the regulator/brush holder mounting screws and withdraw the assembly (photo). Disconnect the regulator lead (where necessary).

3   With the brush holder removed, check the condition of the slip rings. If they are blackened, clean them with a fuel- moistened rag. If they are

8.2 Removing the regulator/brush holder unit from the alternator

10.4A Starter motor showing mounting bolts which also secure the air filter support bracket

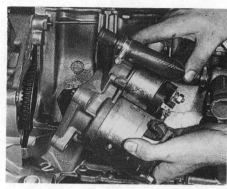

10.4B Starter motor removal

deeply scored or grooved then it will probably indicate that the alternator is coming to the end of its life.

4   Unsolder the old brushes and solder in the new ones. Have this done professionally if you lack skill in soldering.

5   Refit the regulator/brush holder and tighten the mounting screws. Reconnect the regulator lead, where necessary.

6   Refit the rear shield (where fitted) then refit the alternator, with reference to Section 7.

9   Starter motor – description and testing

1   The starter motor is mounted on the inlet manifold side of the engine and is of the pre-engaged type, where the drive pinion is brought into mesh with the starter ring gear on the flywheel before the main current is applied.

2   When the starter switch is operated, current flows from the battery to the solenoid which is mounted on the top of the starter motor body. The plunger in the solenoid moves inwards, so causing a centrally pivoted lever to push the drive pinion into mesh with the starter ring gear. When the solenoid plunger reaches the end of its travel, it closes an internal contact and full starting current flows to the starter field coils. The armature is then able to rotate the crankshaft, so starting the engine.

3   A special freewheel clutch is fitted to the starter drive pinion so that as soon as the engine fires and starts to operate on its own it does not drive the starter motor.

4   When the starter switch is released, the solenoid is de- energised and a spring moves the plunger back to its rest position. This operates the pivoted lever to withdraw the drive pinion from engagement with the starter ring.

5   If the starter motor fails to turn the engine when the switch is operated there are four possible reasons why:

(a)   The battery is discharged or faulty
(b)   The electrical connections between switch, solenoid, battery and starter motor are somewhere failing to pass the necessary current from the battery, through the starter to earth
(c)   The solenoid has an internal fault
(d)   The starter motor is electrically defective

6   To check the battery, switch on the headlights. If they go dim after a few seconds the battery is discharged. If the lamp glows brightly, next operate the ignition/starter switch and see what happens to the lights. If they do dim it is indicative that power is reaching the starter motor but failing to turn it. If the starter should turn very slowly go on to the next check.

7   If, when the ignition/starter switch is operated, the lights stay bright then the power is not reaching the starter motor. Check all connections from the battery to solenoid for cleanliness and tightness. With a good battery fitted this is the most usual cause of starter motor problems. Check that the earth cable between the engine and body is also intact and cleanly connected. This can sometimes be overlooked when the engine is taken out.

8   If no results have yet been achieved turn off the headlights, otherwise the battery will soon be discharged. It may be possible that a

clicking noise was heard each time the ignition/starter switch was operated. This is the solenoid switch operating but it does not necessarily follow that the main contact is closing properly. (If no clicking has been heard from the solenoid it is certainly defective.) The solenoid contact can be checked by putting a voltmeter or bulb between the main cable connection on the starter side of the solenoid and earth. When the switch is operated there should be a reading or a lighted bulb. If not, the switch has a fault.

10   Starter motor – removal and refitting

1   Disconnect the battery negative lead.

2   Remove the air cleaner unit as described in Chapter 3.

3   Disconnect the wiring from the starter motor unit.

4   Unscrew and remove the three starter motor retaining bolts and remove the starter motor. Note that two of the bolts also secure the air filter support bracket (photos).

5   Refit in the reverse order of removal. Ensure that all wiring connections are correctly and securely made. Refit the air filter unit as described in Chapter 3.

11   Starter motor – overhaul

1   Unscrew the nut and disconnect the starter motor cable from the solenoid (photo).

2   Unscrew the through-bolts and remove the solenoid from the drive end bracket, at the same time unhooking the solenoid core from the lever (photo).

3   Unscrew the bolt and remove the washers from the commutator end (photos).

4   Unscrew the nuts from the through-bolts and withdraw the end cover, at the same time extracting the field brush (photos).

5   Remove the thrustwashers from the armature (photo).

6   Mark the yoke and end bracket in relation to each other, then remove the yoke (photo).

7   Prise out the rubber bearing and withdraw the armature from the drive end bracket (photo).

8   Remove the rubber bearing from the lever (photo).

9   Remove the core and spring from the solenoid (photo).

10   Renew any defective or suspect components as necessary. The brushes are the most likely items requiring renewal. Wipe all components clean prior to reassembly.

11   Reassembly is a reversal of dismantling.

12   Fuses and relays – general

1   The fuse box unit is located in a recess directly in front of the instrument panel. Access to the fuses is made by removing the cover which is secured by two twist clips. Untwist each clip using a suitable coin and lift the cover clear (photo).

11.1 Starter motor cable from solenoid (arrowed)

11.2 Removing the solenoid from the drive end bracket

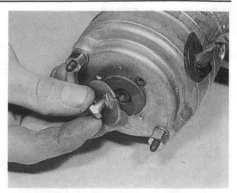

11.3A Unscrew the bolt ...

11.3B ... and remove the washers

11.4A Unscrew the through-bolt nuts (arrowed) ...

11.4B ... and withdraw the end cover

11.5 Removing the armature thrustwashers

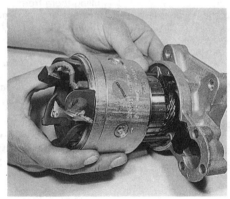

11.6 Removing the yoke

11.7 Withdrawing the armature from the drive end bracket

11.8 Armature and lever (rubber bearing removed)

11.9 Solenoid with core and spring

12.1 General view of the fuses with cover removed

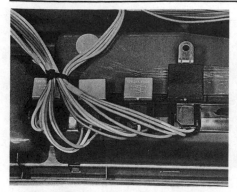

12.4 General view of the relay units (main block)

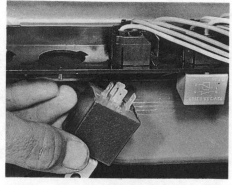

12.5 Removing a relay unit

12.6A Direction indicator relay unit (mounted on facia underside near the fusebox unit)

12.6B Rear window wiper relay unit (mounted on facia underside near the fuse box unit)

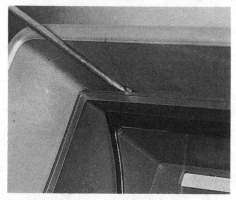

13.3 Instrument panel removal – releasing a retainer clip

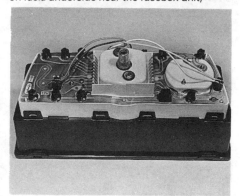

13.4 Instrument panel

2   The circuits protected by the fuses, together with their rating, are given in the Specifications at the start of this Chapter.
3   Always renew a fuse with one of similar rating and never renew it more than once without finding the source of trouble. If necessary, refer to the wiring diagrams at the end of this Chapter.
4   Relay units are located under the facia on the passenger side between the glovebox and the bulkhead (photo).

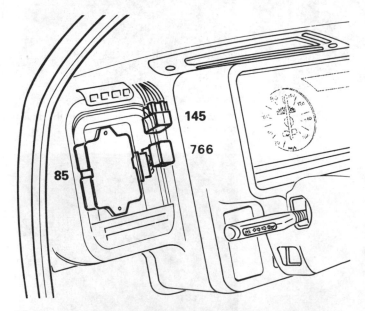

Fig. 12.2 View showing location of indicator/hazard warning flasher (145), coolant level indicator unit (85) and the rear screen wiper motor relay (766) (Sec 12)

(Left-hand drive shown, right-hand drive similar)

5   Relay units rarely give problems, but they can easily be renewed by pulling them from their location in the box. The relay units and their functions are also shown in the wiring diagrams at the end of this Chapter. Some relay units are connected in-line whilst some are separate (photo).
6   The direction indicator/hazard warning flasher unit is located under the facia, near the fuse board and controls both the direction indicator and hazard warning functions (photos).
7   In the event of either system not operating, or one lamp flashing very quickly, carry out the following checks before renewing the flasher unit itself.
8   Inspect the circuit fuse and renew it if it is blown.
9   Check the condition of all wiring and the security of the connections.
10   Check the lamp which is malfunctioning for a broken bulb.
11   Make sure that the lamp casing or bulb earth connection is making a good contact.
12   If required, the fuse box unit can be removed by sliding it towards the centre to release it then lifting it clear. The wiring connections can then be inspected and if necessary, detached. Refitting is a reversal of removal.

13   Instrument panel – removal and refitting

1   Disconnect the battery negative lead.
2   Remove the steering wheel as described in Chapter 10.
3   Release the four panel retaining clips using a suitable flat bladed tool or electricians screwdriver inserted between the edge of the panel and the facia surround. There are two clips along the top edge and two along the bottom edge. As the clips are released, simultaneously pull the instrument panel from the recess in the facia (photo).
4   Remove the fuse box inspection panel and then reach down through the aperture and detach the speedometer cable from the instrument panel on its rear face. Also disconnect the two wiring block connectors from the panel, then withdraw it (photo).
5   The instrument panel illumination bulbs can be removed for inspection and if required, renewal by untwisting the holder(s) and removing them (photo). Although an exploded diagram of the instrument panels are shown in Figs. 12.5 and 12.6, it is not recommended that they are

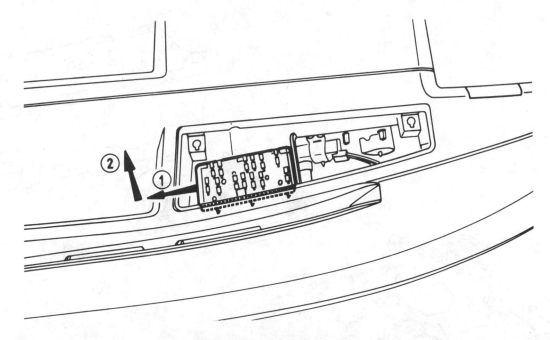

Fig. 12.3 Slide fuse box to side (1) then lift it out (2) (Sec 12)

(Left-hand drive tyre shown)

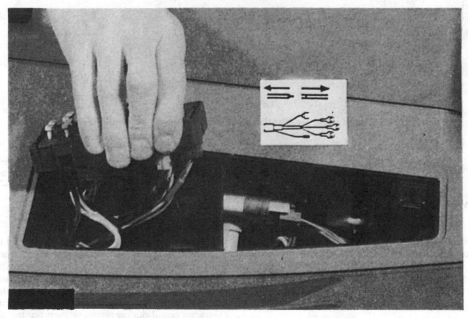

Fig. 12.4 Withdrawing the fuse box unit (Sec 12)

dismantled as the various components are fragile. It is therefore recommended that any testing or replacements be entrusted to a Citroën dealer.

6   Refit in the reverse order of removal. Ensure that all connections are securely made. Check the operation of the various instruments in the panel on completion.

14   Steering column switches – removal and refitting

1   Disconnect the battery earth lead.
2   Remove the steering wheel as described in Chapter 10.
3   Undo the two screws retaining the upper shroud.
4   Unscrew and remove the single screw each side and remove the lower shroud.
5   Undo the retaining screws on the under side of the switches,

withdraw the switches from the column, and detach the wiring block connectors (photo).

6   Refit in the reverse order of removal. Check for satisfactory operation of the various switch functions on completion.

7   For steering lock/ignition switch removal, refer to Chapter 10 Section 4.

15   Facia panel switches – removal and refitting

1   Prior to removing any of the facia mounted switches it is advisable to disconnect the battery negative lead.

Hazard warning switch and heated rear window switch

2   Reach up and under the central console panel and compress the

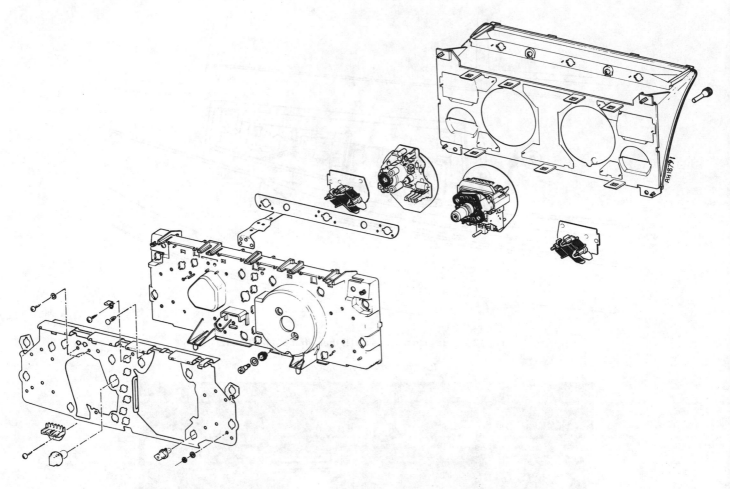

Fig. 12.5 Exploded view of the Jaeger instrument panel assembly (Sec 13)

switch clips and simultaneously push the switch out of its aperture in the panel. Detach the wiring connector.

Window regulator switch (electric)

3   Unclip and remove the lower facia panel for access to the switch(es). As the heater unit and possibly other adjacent fittings are likely to impair access, loosen off the two screws (one each side) and remove the console, undo the two screws to the heater, then raise the facia and pivot it upwards to allow the required access to the switch(es).
4   Release the switch from the panel and detach the wiring connectors.

Fan switch

5   Remove the knob, depress the clips at the front and remove the switch. Detach the wiring connectors.

Refitting

6   In all instances, the refitting details are the reverse of the removal procedures. Check for satisfactory operation on completion.

---

16   Door courtesy light switch – removal and refitting

1   Detach the battery negative lead.
2   Open the door, unscrew the retaining screw from the centre of the switch and withdraw it from the door (photo). Detach the wiring from the switch.
3   Refit in the reverse order of removal and check for satisfactory operation.

17   Brake warning light switches – removal and refitting

1   Disconnect the battery negative lead.

Stoplight switch

2   The footbrake stoplight switch is attached to a bracket on the foot pedal mountings. Remove the parcel shelf for access.
3   Detach the wire connector from the switch, note the clearance between the switch and the pedal, then unscrew the retaining nut and remove the switch from the support bracket (photo).
4   Refit in the reverse order of removal. Adjust the switch to pedal clearance noted during removal, then tighten the retaining nut. Check for satisfactory operation on completion.

Handbrake-on warning switch

5   Lift out the rear compartment ashtray from the handbrake trim console, then unscrew the retaining screws in the recess. Remove the console (photo).
6   Detach the lead from the switch. Undo the retaining screw and remove the switch from the support bracket (photo).
7   Refit in the reverse order of removal and check for satisfactory operation.

---

18   Cigar lighter – removal and refitting

1   Access to the cigar lighter unit for its removal is poor. Even with adjacent grille and the radio unit removed it is still difficult to reach and

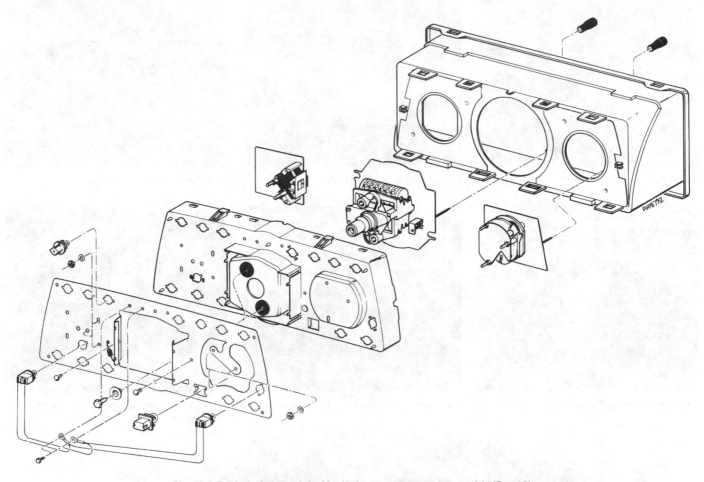

Fig. 12.6 Exploded view of the Veglia instrument panel assembly (Sec 13)

13.5 Instrument panel bulb and holder removed for inspection

14.5 Steering column and switch retaining screws

16.2 Door courtesy light switch retaining screw (arrowed)

release the retainer clips from the underside. It may well be found necessary to at least partially remove the facia unit as described in Section 15.

2   When suitable access is gained to the rear of the unit, disconnect the element wire and the illumination bulb wire, then compress the retaining clips and withdraw the cigar lighter unit (photo).

3   Refit in the reverse order of removal and check it for satisfactory operation.

19 Horn – removal and refitting

1   The horn is attached to the inner side of the front chassis member on the right-hand side. Access is best achieved from the underside of the car at the front end (photo).

2   Unscrew the mounting bracket retaining bolt, detach the earth lead wire and the horn feed wire. Remove the horn.

3   Refit in the reverse order of removal and check for satisfactory operation on completion.

20 Lights (exterior) – bulb renewal, unit removal and refitting

Headlight

1   The bulbs are renewed from the rear of the headlamp unit, access being from the engine compartment.

2   Pull free the wiring connector, release the bulb retaining clip and withdraw the bulb (photos).

17.3 Brake stoplamp switch

17.5 Handbrake trim rear retaining screw (arrowed)

17.6 Handbrake warning switch

18.2 Cigar lighter and wiring connectors

19.2 Horn location and wiring connections

20.2A Detach the wiring connector from the headlight ...

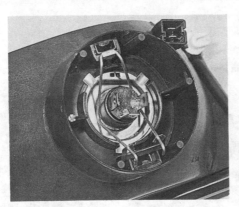

20.2B ... release the retaining clip ...

20.2C ... and extract the headlight bulb

3   Where halogen bulbs are fitted, do not touch the glass with your fingers or with a fluffy cloth and, if necessary, allow the bulb to cool before removing it. If the glass is inadvertently touched, clean it with methylated spirit.

4   Refitting is a reversal of the removal procedure. When inserting the bulb into position it must be correctly aligned with the location notches. Check the headlights for satisfactory operation and alignment on completion.

Removal

5   To remove a headlight unit, grip and pull the unit outwards from the front to disengage it from the two inboard adjusters, then pull it towards the centre to disengage it from the single outer adjuster. Detach the wiring connectors and remove the unit (photos).

Auxiliary (long-range) driving lamp

6   To remove the bulb, undo the two retaining screws and remove the rim and lens. Extract the bulb.

7   To remove the unit, undo the rim screws and withdraw the rim and lamp unit complete. Detach the wiring connector.

8   If when refitted the lamp unit requires adjustment, turn the screw

located beneath the inboard rim retaining screw in the required direction.

Sidelight

9   This bulb is located in the rear of the headlight unit. Pull free the bulbholder, complete with wiring connections, from the headlight unit then withdraw the bulb from its holder (photo).

Front indicator

10   Reach down within the front corner of the engine compartment on the side concerned, untwist the bulbholder and withdraw it from the light unit. Remove the bulb from the holder (photo).

11   Renew the bulb if necessary and refit in reverse order of removal.

Removal

12   Remove the headlight unit as described in paragraph 5.

13   Untwist the side retainer, press the retainer tab using a thin blade screwdriver on the other side and withdraw the unit (photos).

14   Detach the bulbholder.

20.5 Headlamp unit removal

20.9 Sidelight bulb and holder removal from headlamp

20.10 Front indicator bulb and holder removal

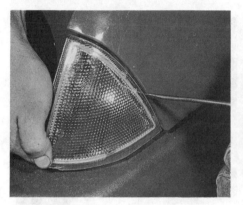

20.13A Front indicator light unit removal: Release the tab ...

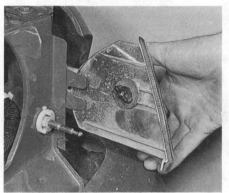

20.13B ... and withdraw the unit

20.13C Showing indicator location pegs and slots in wing

Side repeater light

15   Twist the light lens unit through 45° and withdraw it from the wing panel. Untwist the bulbholder from the lens for access to the bulb (photos).

Rear combination lamps

16   Open the tailgate, unscrew the two wing nuts and then withdraw the lamp unit and lens from the body. Detach the wiring connectors if the unit is to be removed completely (photo).
17   To remove the common bulbholder unit from the lens, release the retaining clip and separate the holder. Press and untwist the appropriate bulb from its holder (photos).

Rear number plate lamp

18   Open the tailgate, then remove the inner cover panel for access to the lamp unit. Prise open the black retainer clips and withdraw the bulbholder. To remove the unit, compress the inner lugs and press the unit out (photo).

Refitting

19   Refitting of all the units covered in this Section is a reversal of the removal procedure. Check for satisfactory operation on completion. Check for correct alignment in the case of the headlight and/or auxiliary driving lamp.

---

21   Headlight – beam adjustment

1   Accurate headlight beam alignment can only be made using optical beam measuring equipment and adjustment should therefore be entrusted to your local garage or Citroën dealer.
2   A temporary adjustment can be made however as each headlight unit has its own adjusters, but adjustment is only normally required after refitting a headlamp unit or if the car is carrying an abnormally heavy load.

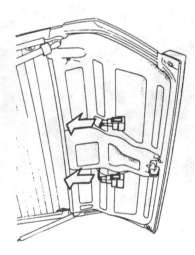

Fig. 12.7 Showing location of rear number plate lamp units and their withdrawal direction (arrowed) (Sec 20)

3   Access to the adjusters is made by raising and supporting the bonnet. Turn the individual adjusters as necessary to reset the beam alignment (photo).

---

22   Lights (interior) – bulb renewal

Interior roof lamp

1   Carefully prise free and withdraw the lamp unit. If a reading light is fitted, this can be removed in the same manner. Prise free the bayonet bulb from its holder to renew it. If required the lamp unit can be removed by detaching the wiring connectors (photo).

20.15A Remove the side repeater lamp from the body ...

20.15B ... and detach the lens from the bulbholder

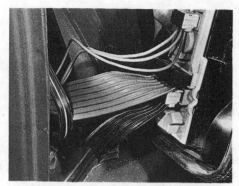

20.16 Rear combination lamp unit withdrawal showing wiring connectors

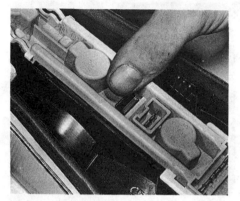

20.17A Release the retaining clip ...

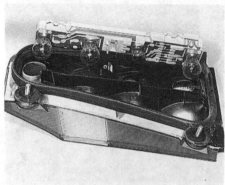

20.17B ... to detach the bulbholder from the combination lamp lens

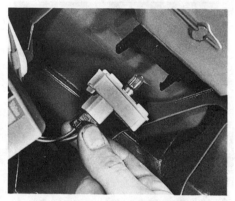

20.18 Rear number plate light bulbholder removal

21.3 Rear view of headlamp unit showing beam adjuster (arrowed)

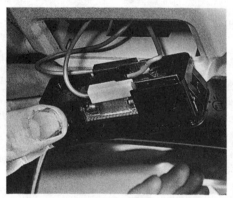

22.1 Interior roof lamp unit removal

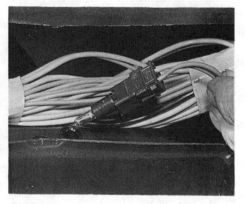

22.4 Bulb and holder removal from the facia panel

Luggage compartment lamp

2 Prise free the lens at one end to release and withdraw the lamp unit from the trim panel. Prise free the bayonet type bulb from its holder to renew it if required. To remove the lamp unit, disconnect the wires.

Instrument panel lamps

3 Refer to Section 13 for details.

Facia switch illumination lights

4 Remove the switch concerned as described in Section 15, then extract the bulb from its holder in the underside of the switch. The choke-on warning light and cigar lighter illumination light bulbs are renewed in the same manner, but to remove the choke cable, refer to Chapter 3 for details. In other instances withdraw the bulbholder from the panel then extract the bulb from it (photo).

Refitting

5 Refit in the reverse order of removal and check for satisfactory operation.

---

23 Electrically-operated front windows – general

1 Operation of the front door windows on some models is by electric motors controlled by two switches in the central facia.
2 Access to the motors is gained by dismantling the doors, as described in Chapter 11.
3 Before removing the regulator motor or a switch, first disconnect the battery earth lead.
4 The regulator motor is bolted in position and access to it is obtained

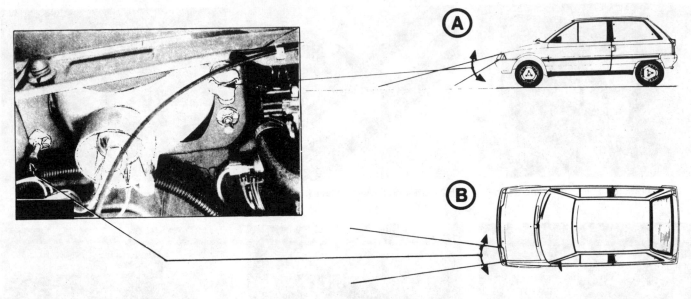

Fig. 12.8 Headlamp beam adjustment (Sec 21)

A   Vertical adjustment – turn inboard (upper) adjuster
B   Horizontal adjustment – turn outboard (lower) adjuster

through the inner door panel aperture in a similar manner described for the manual regulator type (Chapter 11).

5   To remove a window regulator switch, refer to Section 15 for details.

6   Refitting of the regulator motor and switch is a reversal of the removal procedure.

24   Central door locking system – general

1   On models fitted with the central locking system it is possible to lock all doors, including the tailgate, simply by locking a single door, or by pressing down the lock button in one of the front doors.

2   Electric actuators are used to operate the door/tailgate lock mechanisms. The actuators are accessible for inspection and if necessary removal after removing the door trim and/or the tailgate trim panel(s) (Chapter 11).

3   If removing an actuator unit, first disconnect the battery earth lead, then disconnect the lock connecting rod from the actuator unit, unbolt the unit and withdraw it. As it is being removed detach the wiring.

4   Refit in reverse order and check for satisfactory operation before refitting the trim panel.

25   Speedometer cable – removal and refitting

1   Disconnect the speedometer cable from the transmission by extracting the rubber cotter, and pulling the cable from the pinion housing.

2   To disconnect the speedometer cable at the instrument panel end remove the fuse box unit as described in Section 12, then working through the aperture in the top of the facia, detach the cable from the speedometer unit (photo).

3   Withdraw the cable through the bulkhead and remove it from the engine compartment side.

4   Refit in the reverse order of removal.

26   Wiper arms and blades – removal and refitting

1   Whenever the wiper blades fail to clean the screen (or rear window), the blades or their rubber inserts should be renewed.

2   To remove a blade, pull the arm from the glass, swivel the blade, pinch the two sides of the U-shaped block together and slide the assembly out of the hook of the arm (photo).

3   When refitting, note the pivot pin in the blade is offset to allow the blade to swivel fully against the glass. Make sure, therefore, that the blade is fitted the right way round so that the 'pip' on the plastic block locates in the cut-out in the hook of the wiper arm.

4   Before removing a wiper arm, note or mark its position on the windscreen using a felt tip pen so that its parked position on the windscreen can be restored when the arm is being refitted to the spindle splines.

5   Flip up the plastic cover, unscrew the nut and pull the arm from the spindle (photo).

6   Refitting is a reversal of removal.

27   Windscreen wiper motor and linkage – removal and refitting

1   Remove the wiper blades and arms, as described in Section 26.

2   Disconnect the battery negative lead.

3   Open the bonnet then remove the air intake cowl as described in Chapter 11.

4   Undo the three retaining screws and remove the water deflection panel from the outboard side of the wiper motor.

5   Detach the wiring connector from the wiper motor unit (photo).

6   Unscrew the two retaining screws and slide the wiper motor unit to the left and then remove it (photo).

7   To remove the motor from its support bracket, undo the nut securing the connector arm to the drive spindle, mark the relative positions of the arm and spindle then detach the arm (photo).

8   Undo the three retaining bolts and separate the motor from the support bracket.

9   Refit in the reverse order of removal. Ensure that the connector arm is correctly realigned.

10   Check for satisfactory operation on completion.

28   Tailgate wiper motor – removal and refitting

1   Disconnect the battery negative lead.

2   Remove the tailgate wiper arm and blade (Section 26).

3   Carefully prise free the trim cover clips and remove the cover.

25.2 Speedometer cable to instrument panel connection

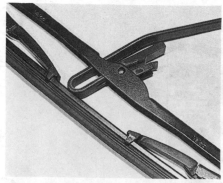

26.2 Removing the wiper blade from the arm

26.5 Wiper arm retaining nut

27.5 Windscreen wiper motor and wiring connector

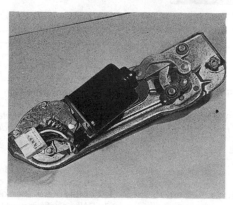

27.6 Windscreen wiper motor and support bracket unit

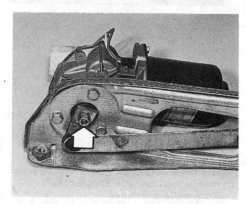

27.7 Windscreen wiper motor connector arm to spindle nut (arrowed)

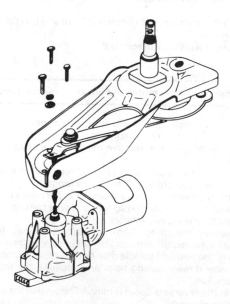

Fig. 12.9 Windscreen wiper motor and support bracket (Sec 27)

4   Disconnect the wiper motor lead connectors, then undo the two retaining bolts and remove the wiper motor from the tailgate (photo).
5   Refitting is a reversal of the removal procedure. Check that the wiper arm is correctly fitted on the shaft to provide the correct parked position.

29   Washer reservoir – removal and refitting

1   The reservoir is located under the right-hand front wing. Remove the front right-hand roadwheel for access.
2   Drain or syphon any remaining washer fluid from the reservoir.
3   To disconnect the pump units, detach the wiring connectors then supporting the reservoir, pull the pump units from it. To remove the pump units completely, also detach the washer hose to each unit (photo).
4   Disconnect the reservoir filler hose then remove the reservoir.
5   Refit in the reverse order of removal. If the washer fluid supply hoses were disconnected, it is likely that they will have hardened at their ends. This being the case, it is advisable to cut off approximately half an inch from the end. Then heat the end of the hose by immersing in hot water to make it more supple, and push it onto the nozzle of the pump unit. It should be a firm compression fit.
6   Top up the reservoir with washer fluid and check for satisfactory operation. If required, the washer jets can be adjusted by inserting a pin into their nozzles and moving them as necessary to provide the spray direction and pattern on the glass.

30   Heater/fresh air motor unit – removal and refitting

1   Disconnect the battery earth lead.
2   Detach and remove the parcel shelf on the right-hand side.
3   Unscrew and remove the two motor retaining nuts, withdraw the motor, detach the wiring and ducting.
4   Refit in the reverse order of removal.

31   Tailgate heated window – general

1   Take great care not to scratch the heater elements with carelessly stacked luggage or rings on the fingers.

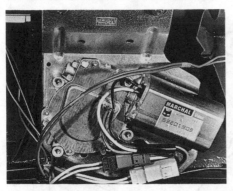

28.4 Tailgate wiper motor and mounting plate

29.3 Washer reservoir, pump units and connections

33.4 Speaker unit showing fixing screws

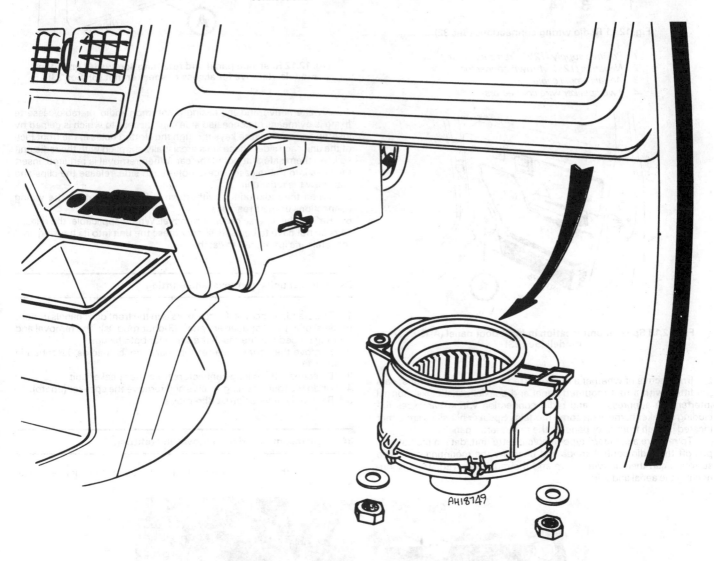

Fig. 12.10 Heater/fresh air blower motor removal (Sec 30)

2   Avoid sticking labels over the elements, and clean the glass interior surface with warm water and a little detergent, wiping in the same direction as the elements run.

3   Should an element be scratched, so that the current is interrupted, it can be repaired using one of the silver paint products now available for the purpose.

32 Radio – general

1   On some models a radio (or radio/cassette) is fitted as standard equipment, and is located in the central facia. On models where a radio is not fitted during production, an aperture is provided in the central facia, and is blanked off with a finisher panel.

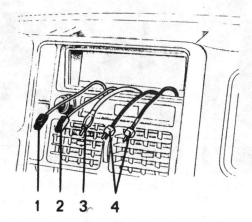

Fig. 12.11 Radio wiring connections (Sec 32)

1   *Positive supply (12V) – red connector*
2   *Negative (12V) – brown connector*
3   *Aerial coaxial cable*
4   *Two speaker wire connectors*

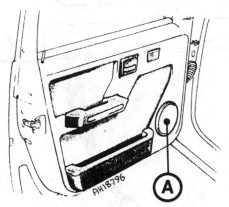

Fig. 12.13 Speaker unit location in front door panel (A) (5-door model) (Sec 33)

2   Irrespective of whether a radio is fitted from new or not, most cars are fitted with a roof-mounted aerial and coaxial aerial cable, normal interference suppression and radio connection wiring harnesses (including speaker harness on some models). Speaker housings are either located in each front door panel or the rear quarter panels.
3   To remove a standard type radio/cassette unit, detach the battery, pull off the radio control knobs and unscrew the mounting nuts. The surround can then be withdrawn and the radio removed after disconnecting the aerial and wiring.

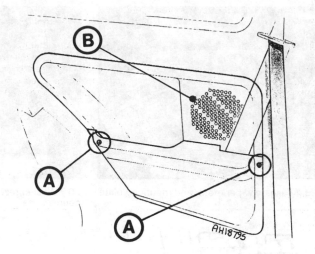

Fig. 12.12 Rear side panel and retaining screws (A) on 3-door models. Remove for access to speaker unit (B) (Sec 33)

4   An alternative and increasingly common radio or radio/cassette fixing is by means of concealed side clips, access to which is gained by inserting special release keys through the slotted holes in the front face of the unit each side. These keys are usually supplied with the radio unit so keep them safe, but not in the car. When removal is required, insert the keys into the release access holes each side, release the clips and withdraw the radio unit.
5   When the radio unit is withdrawn sufficiently, detach the wiring connections from its rear face.
6   Refit in the reverse order of removal. Where applicable, the release keys do not have to be used, simply press the unit into its housing until the retainer clips are felt to catch.

33   Speaker units – removal and refitting

1   The standard location for speakers is in the front door panels (5-door models) or in the rear quarter panels (3-door models). The removal and refitting procedures are much the same for both fixings.
2   Remove the door or quarter trim panel concerned as described in Chapter 11.
3   Disconnect the wiring connectors from the speaker unit.
4   Undo the four retaining screws and remove the speaker (photo).
5   Refit in the reverse order of removal.

34   Roof mounted aerial – removal and refitting

1   Remove the radio unit and detach the aerial from its rear face, Section 32.

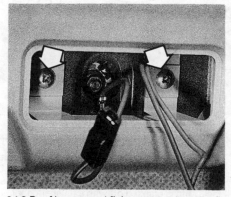

34.3 Roof lamp panel fixing screws (arrowed)

34.4 Aerial retaining nut and earth lead

2   Remove the interior roof lamp (Section 22).
3   Unscrew the two retaining screws and remove the roof lamp panel (photo).
4   Unscrew the aerial retaining nut and the earth lead nut (photo).
5   Attach a suitable length of cord to the radio end of the aerial. The cord must be at least as long as the aerial lead, so that when the lead is pulled through the body channels, the cord takes its place (and can subsequently be reattached to redirect the lead through the channels during the refitting procedures).
6   Detach and remove the parcel shelf on the passenger side.

7   Detach the trim from the front screen pillar on the passenger side. Also carefully detach the headlining at the leading edge on the passenger side.
8   Remove the aerial from the roof and withdraw the lead and cord, feeding them through the various body channels, then when the cord emerges through the hole in the roof panel, disconnect it from the radio end of the aerial.
9   Refit in the reverse order of removal. Ensure that the lead connections are secure and that the earth lead connection is clean.

35   Fault diagnosis – electrical system

Symptom	Reason(s)
Starter fails to turn engine	Battery discharged
	Battery defective internally
	Battery terminal leads loose or earth lead not securely attached to body
	Loose or broken connections in starter motor circuit
	Starter motor switch or solenoid faulty
	Starter brushes badly worn, sticking, or brush wires loose
	Commutator dirty, worn or burnt
	Starter motor armature faulty
	Field coils earthed
Starter turns engine very slowly	Battery in discharged condition
	Starter brushes badly worn, sticking or brush wires loose
	Loose wires in starter motor circuit
Starter motor noisy or excessively rough engagement	Pinion or flywheel gear teeth broken or worn
	Starter motor retaining bolts loose
	Blown fuse
Battery will not hold charge for more than a few days	Battery defective internally
	Electrolyte level too low or electrolyte too weak due to leakage
	Plate separators no longer fully effective
	Battery plates severely sulphated
	Drivebelt slipping
	Battery terminal connections loose or corroded
	Alternator not charging
	Short in lighting circuit continual battery drain
	Regulator unit not working correctly
Ignition light fails to go out, battery runs flat in a few days	Drivebelt loose and slipping or broken
	Alternator brushes worn, sticking, broken or dirty
	Alternator brush springs worn or broken
	Internal fault in alternator
	Regulator faulty

Failure of individual electrical equipment to function correctly is dealt with alphabetically, item-by-item, under the headings below

Horn

Horn operates all the time	Horn push either earthed or stuck down
	Horn cable to horn push earthed
Horn fails to operate	Cable or cable connection loose, broken or disconnected
	Horn has an internal fault
	Blown fuse
Horn emits intermittent or unsatisfactory noise	Cable connections loose

Lights

Lights do not come on	If engine not running, battery discharged
	Wire connections loose, disconnected or broken
	Light switch shorting or otherwise faulty

Symptom	Reason(s)
Lights come on but fade out	If engine not running, battery discharged
	Wire connections loose
	Light switch shorting or otherwise faulty
Wipers	
Wiper motor fails to work	Blown fuse
	Wire connections loose, disconnected or broken
	Brushes badly worn
	Armature worn or faulty
Wiper motor works very slowly and takes excessive current	Commutator dirty, greasy or burnt
	Armature bearings dirty or unaligned
	Armature badly worn or faulty
Wiper motor works slowly and takes little current	Brushes badly worn
	Commutator dirty, greasy or burnt
	Armature badly worn or faulty

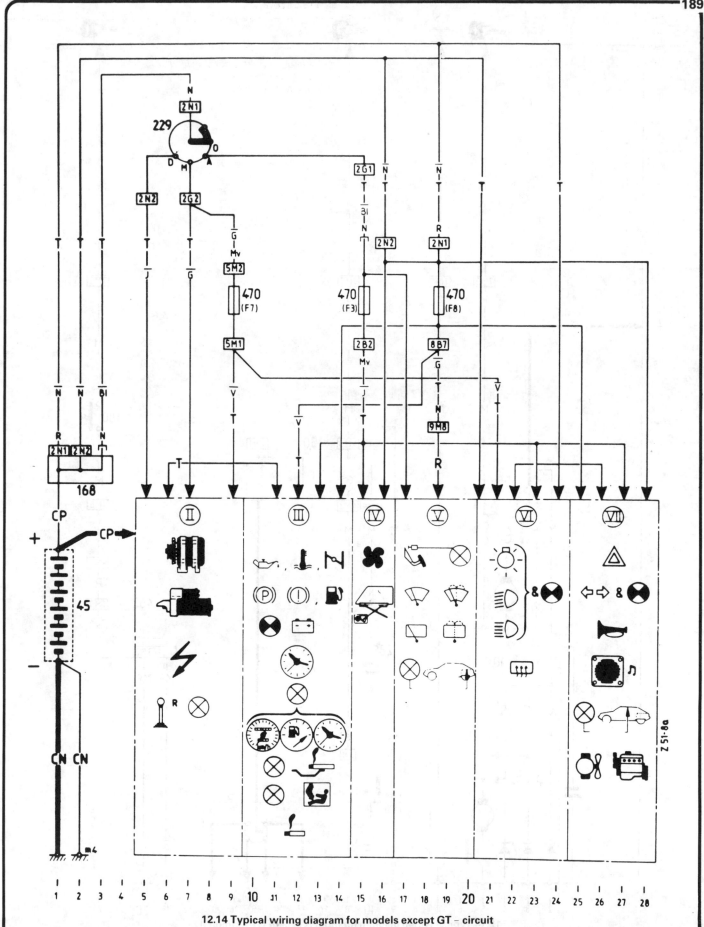

12.14 Typical wiring diagram for models except GT – circuit

12.14 Typical wiring diagram for models except GT – circuit II

12.14 Typical wiring diagram for models except GT – circuit III

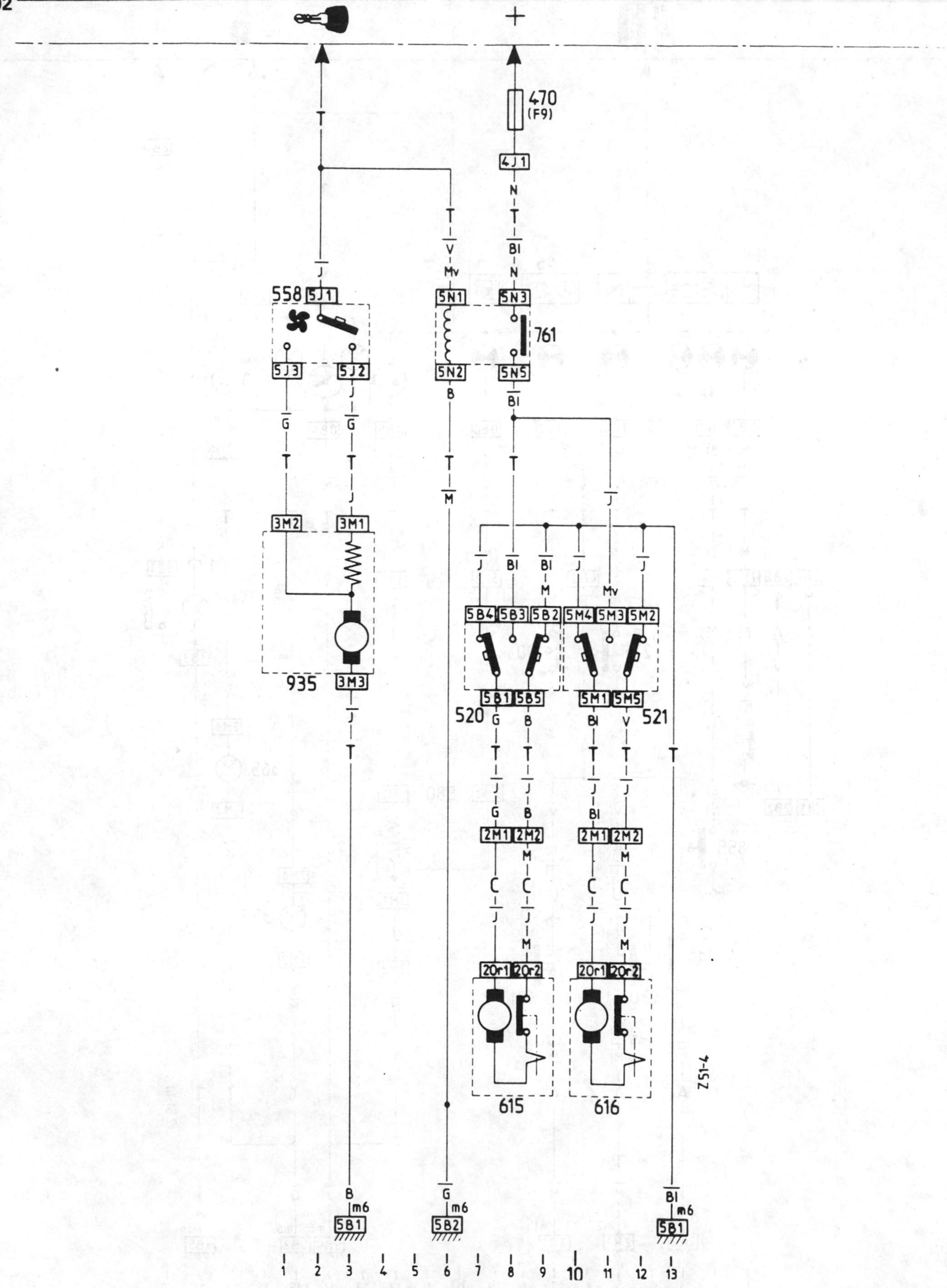

470
(F9)

558

761

935

520

521

615

616

Z51-4

1 1 2 3 4 5 6 7 8 9 10 11 12 13

12.14 Typical wiring diagram for models except GT – circuit IV

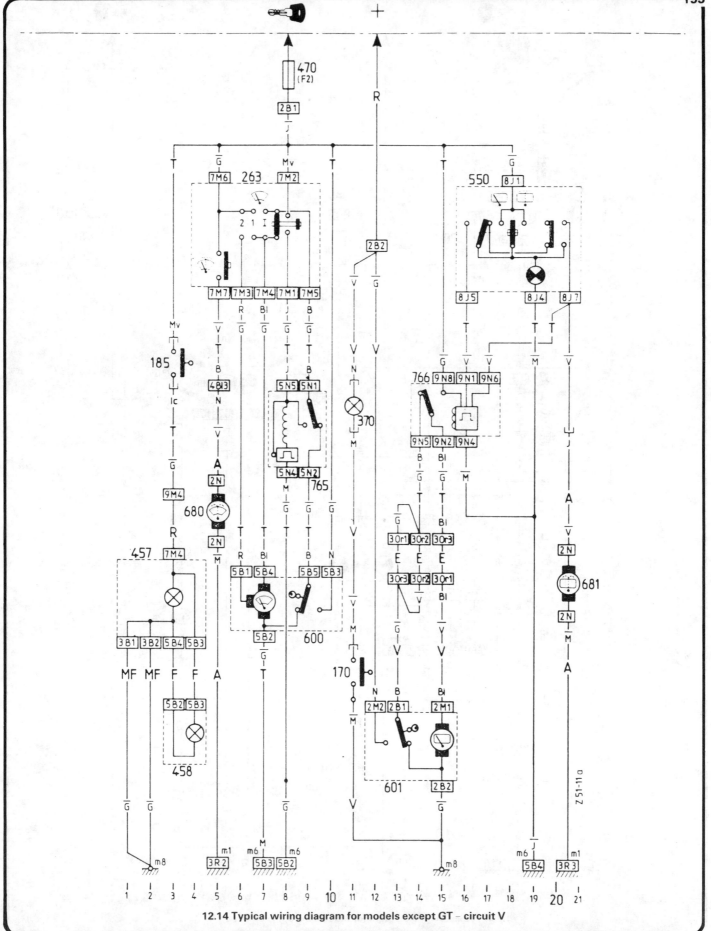

12.14 Typical wiring diagram for models except GT – circuit V

12.14 Typical wiring diagram for models except GT – circuit VI

12.14 Typical wiring diagram for models except GT – circuit VII

Key to Fig. 12.14

No	Description	No	Description
1	Cigar lighter	489	RH main and dipped beams
5	Ignition distributor	502	LH rear loudspeaker
10	Alternator	503	RH rear loudspeaker
25	Horn	511	Rear fog lamp switch
45	Battery	512	Long range lamp switch
46	Instrument panel	520	LH front window winder switch
50	Ignition coil	521	RH front window winder switch
55	Anti-pollution control unit	532	Heated rear screen switch
70	Monitoring unit (for horn, flasher, head lamps)	535	Driver's heated seat switch
75	Ignition module	536	Passenger's heated seat switch
84	Water level indicator unit	546	Interior spot lamp switch
85	Oil level control unit	550	Rear screen wipe switch
90	Centralised door lock control unit	558	Interior heater fan switch
130	T.D.C. sensor	570	Hazard warning switch
140	Distance sensor	580	Fuel gauge
145	Direction indicator unit	600	Windscreen wiper motor
168	Battery connector	601	Rear screen wiper motor
170	Tailgate switch	615	LH front window motor
180	Reversing lamp switch	616	RH front window motor
185	Stop lamp switch	625	LH front door lock motor
190	Handbrake switch	626	RH front door lock motor
225	Choke switch	627	LH rear door lock motor
229	Anti-theft/Ignition switch	628	RH rear door lock motor
230	Door switch (LH, front)	629	Boot door lock motor
231	Door switch (RH, front)	635	LH engine cooling fan motor
236	Brake hydraulic fluid level switch	640	Clock
237	Coolant level switch	650	Engine oil low pressure switch
260	Lighting/direction indicator/horn switch	660	On-board computer
263	Windscreen wiper/washer switch	680	Windscreen washer pump
285	Coil suppressor	681	Rear screen washer pump
300	Starter motor	682	Headlamp washer pump
302	Flowmeter	688	Throttle butterfly position potentiometer
331	Main actuator	690	Interior central lighting
332	Idling actuator	695	Interior spot lamp
333	Carburettor float chamber venting solenoid	720	Diagnostic socket
334	Canister electro-valve	721	Radio connections
336	Ignition distributor vacuum electro-valve	728	Carburettor heater
337	Butterfly opener electro-valve	729	Anti-pollution relay
355	Heater control lighting	736	Additional main beams relay
365	Ashtray lighting	737	Dipped beams relay
370	Boot lighting	755	Headlamp washer relay
385	LH rear No. plate lighting	760	Heated rear screen relay
386	RH rear No. plate lighting	761	Front window motor relay
430	LH front brake caliper	765	Windscreen wiper motor relay
431	RH front brake caliper	766	Rear screen wiper motor relay
440	LH front side lamp	767	Electric cooling fan timer relay
441	RH front side lamp	768	Electric cooling fan control relay
442	LH tail lamp	769	Electric cooling fan power relay
443	RH tail lamp	774	Engine cooling fan relay
445	LH rear lamp	780	Diurnal lamps relay
446	RH rear lamp	789	Diurnal lamps resistance
457	LH stop lamp	795	Lighting rheostat
458	RH stop lamp	810	LH side repeater
460	LH rear fog lamp	811	RH side repeater
461	RH rear fog lamp	822	LH heated seat
462	LH reversing lamp	823	RH heated seat
463	RH reversing lamp	833	Lambda probe
470	Fuses	835	Engine oil level sensor
480	LH front direction indicator	840	Water temperature sensor
481	RH front direction indicator	843	Oil temperature sensor
482	LH rear direction indicator	850	Cooling fan thermal switch
483	RH rear direction indicator	853	Air temperature switch
486	LH long range lamp	855	Engine coolant thermal switch
487	RH long range lamp	935	Blower motor
488	LH main and dipped beams	945	Heated rear screen

Harness code

A	Front
AE	Driving school
B	Water level indicator unit
C	Door
D	Emission control
CK	On carburettor
CN	Battery negative cable
CP	Battery positive cable
E	Tailgate window wiper
F	Rear light cluster inter-connection
H.P.	Loud speaker
J	Fuel gauge
K	Piloted carburation
M	Engine
MF	Lamp earth
MP	Interior lighting earth
P	Interior lighting
PR	Rear door
R	Rear
RC	Direction indicator repeater
SC	Heated seat
T	Instrument panel
TC	Carburettor warning lamp
U	Brake pad wear
V	Tailgate

Colour code

B	White
Bl	Blue
G	Grey
Ic	Transparent
J	Yellow
M	Brown
Mv	Mauve
N	Black
Or	Orange
R	Red
V	Green

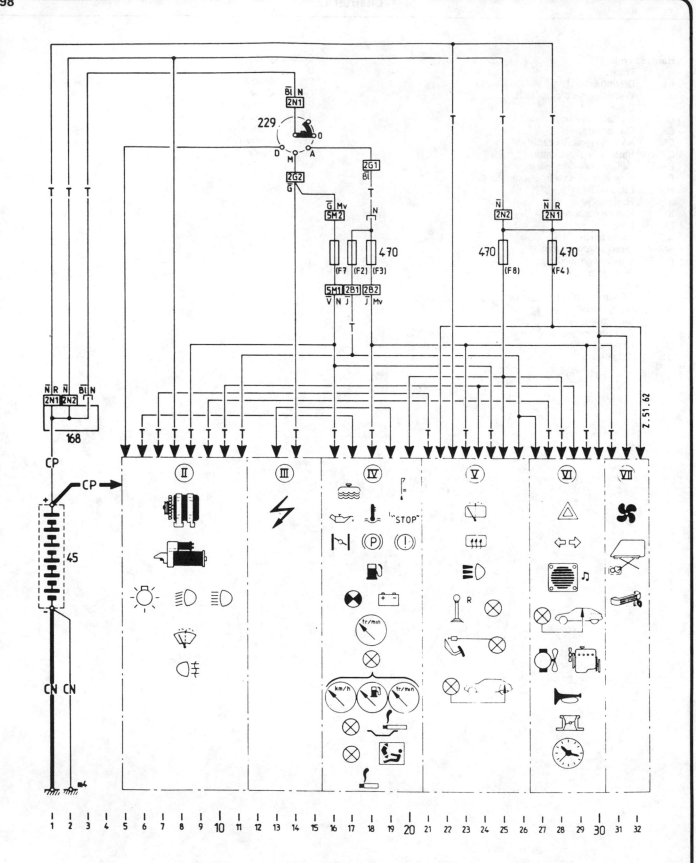

12.15 Typical wiring diagram for GT models – circuit I

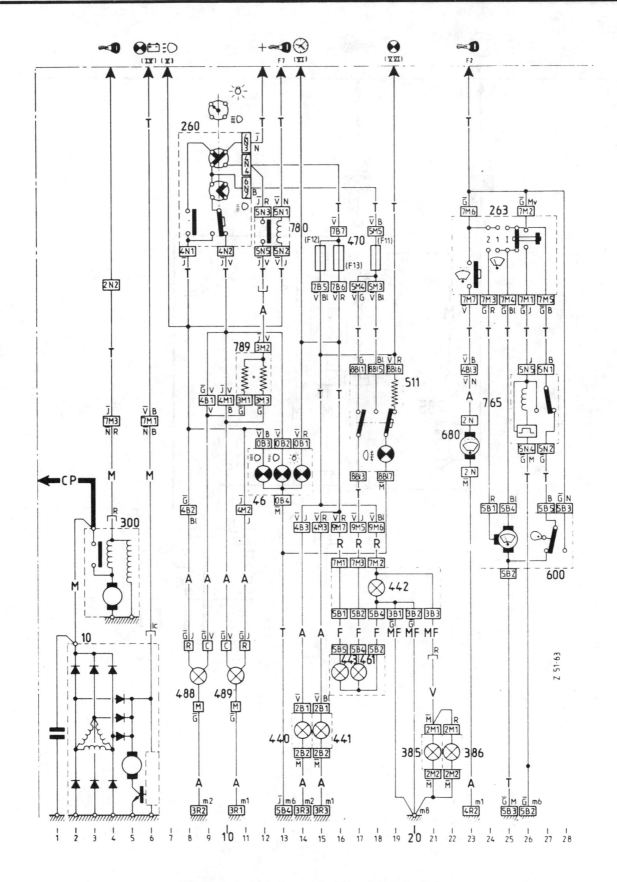

12.15 Typical wiring diagram for GT models – circuit II

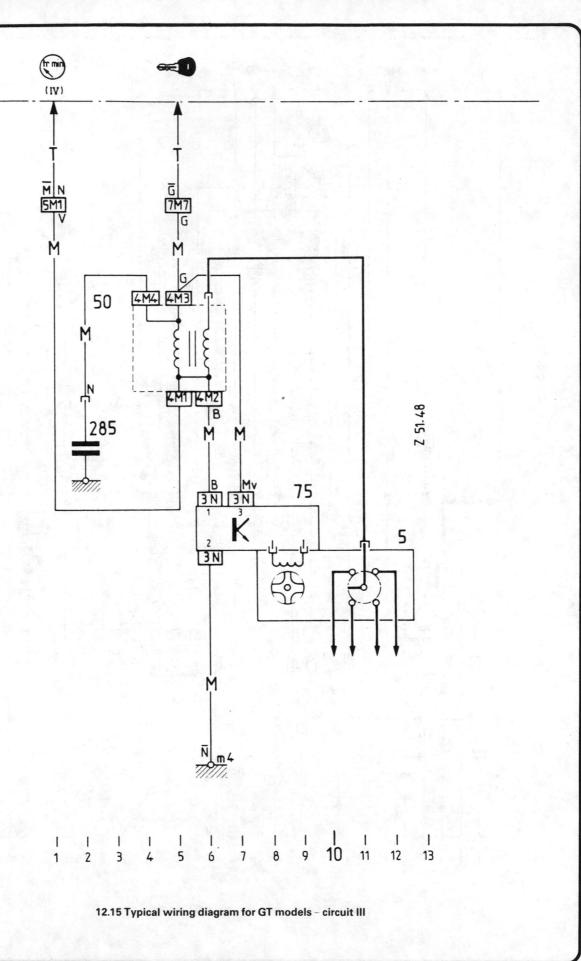

Z 51.48

12.15 Typical wiring diagram for GT models – circuit III

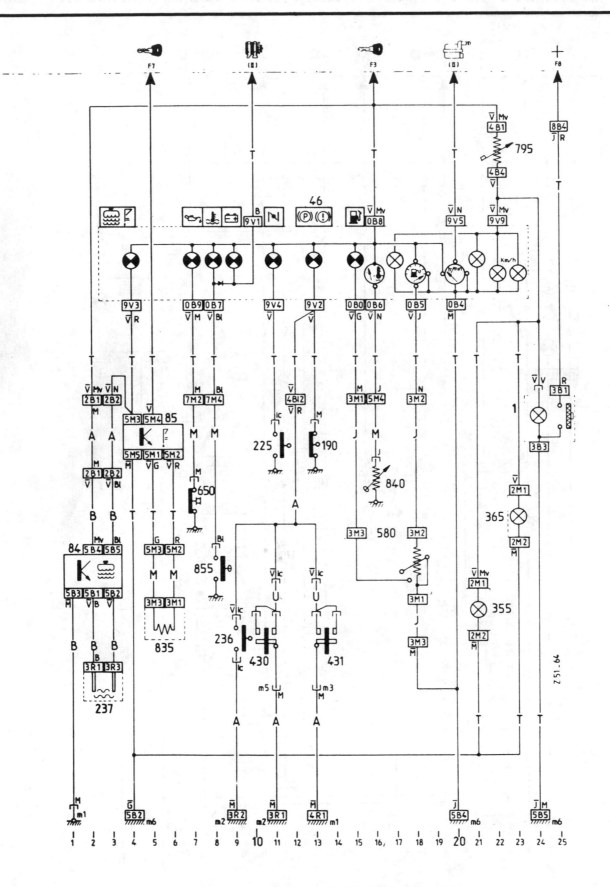

12.15 Typical wiring diagram for GT models – circuit IV

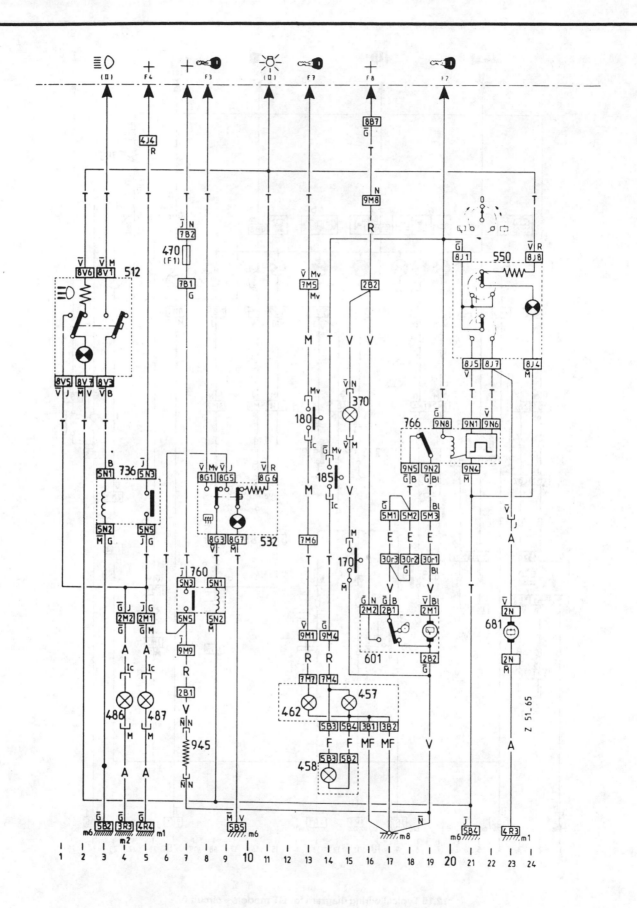

12.15 Typical wiring diagram for GT models – circuit V

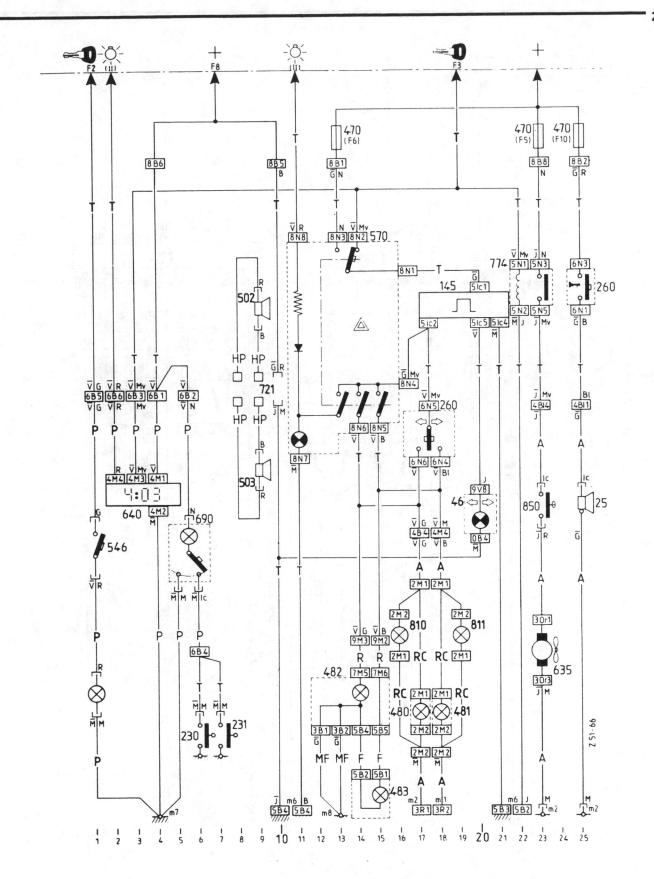

12.15 Typical wiring diagram for GT models – circuit VI

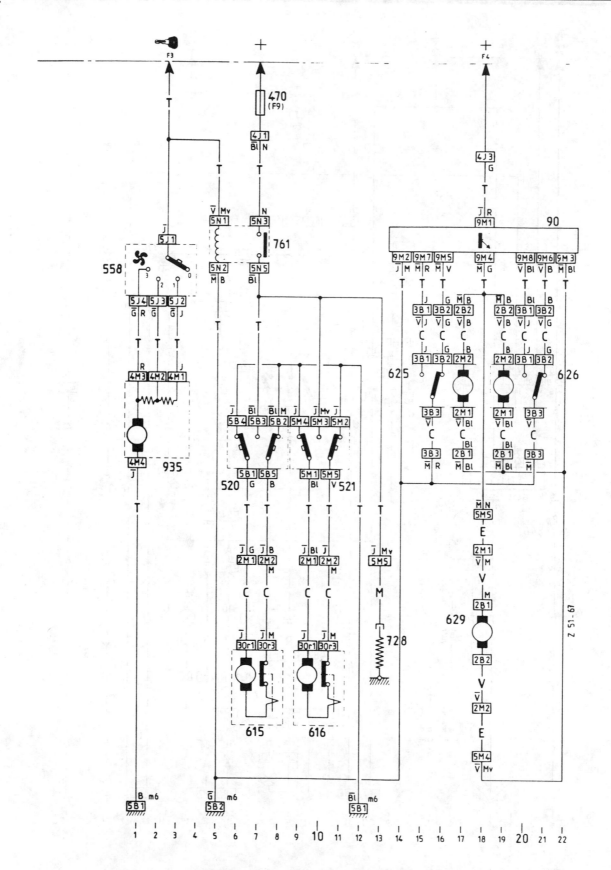

12.15 Typical wiring diagram for GT models – circuit VII

Key to Fig. 12.15

No	Description	No	Description
1	Cigar-lighter	570	Hazard warning switch
5	Distributor	580	Fuel tank gauge unit
10	Alternator	600	Windscreen wiper motor
25	Horn	601	Rear screen wiper motor
45	Battery	615	Front L/H window motor
46	Instrument panel	616	Front R/H window motor
46	Instrument panel	625	Front L/H door lock motor
46	Instrument panel	626	Front R/H door lock motor
50	Ignition coil	629	Boot door lock motor
75	Ignition module	635	Engine cooling fan (LH side)
84	Water level indicator unit	640	Clock
85	Oil level control unit	650	Engine oil low pressure switch
90	Door locking control unit	680	Windscreen washer pump
145	Direction indicator unit	681	Rear screen washer pump
168	Battery connector	690	Central interior lamp
170	Boot light switch	695	Interior spot lamp
180	Reversing light switch	721	Electrical supply for radio
185	Stop lamp switch	728	Carburettor heater
190	Handbrake switch	736	Long range lamps relay
225	Starter motor switch	760	Heated rear screen relay
229	Anti-theft/Ignition switch	761	Front window motor relay
230	Interior light switch (front L/H door)	765	Windscreen wiper motor relay
231	Interior light switch (front R/H door)	766	Rear screen wiper motor relay
236	Hydraulic brake fluid level switch	774	Engine cooling fan relay
237	Coolant level switch	780	Diurnal lamps relay
260	Lighting/direction indicator/horn switch	789	Diurnal lamps resistance
260	Lighting/direction indicator/horn switch	795	Lighting rheostat
263	Windscreen wash/wipe switch	810	L/H side repeater
285	HT coil suppressor	811	R/H side repeater
300	Starter motor	835	Engine oil level sensor
355	Heater control lighting	840	Water temperature sensor
365	Ashtray lighting	850	Cooling fan thermal switch
370	Boot lighting	855	Engine coolant thermal switch
385	LH rear number plate lighting	935	Interior heater fan
386	RH number plate lighting	945	Heated rear screen
430	LH front brake calliper		
431	RH front brake calliper		
440	Front L/H side lamp		
441	Front R/H side lamp		

Harness code

A	Front
B	Water level indicator unit
C	Door
CN	Negative cable
CP	Positive cable
E	Screen wiper-tailgate
F	Rear lamp interconnection
HP	Loudspeaker
J	Gauge
M	Engine
MF	Lamp earth
P	Interior lamp
R	Rear
RC	Direction indicator repeater
T	Instrument panel
U	Brake pad wear
V	Tailgate

No	Description
442	L/H tail lamp
443	R/H tail lamp
457	L/H stop lamp
458	R/H stop lamp
461	R/H rear fog lamp
462	L/H reversing lamp
470	Fuses F7, F2, F3, F8, F4
470	Fuses F12, F13, F11
470	Fuse F1
470	Fuses F6, F5, F10
470	Fuse F9
480	Front L/H direction indicator
481	Front R/H direction indicator
482	Rear L/H direction indicator
483	Rear R/H direction indicator
486	L/H long range lamp
487	R/H long range lamp
488	LH main and dipped beams
489	RH main and dipped beams
502	Provision for rear L/H loudspeaker
503	Provision for rear R/H loudspeaker
511	Rear foglamp switch
512	Long range lamp switch
520	Front L/H window motor switch
521	Front R/H window motor switch
532	Heated rear screen switch
546	Interior spot lamp switch
550	Rear screen wash/wipe switch
558	Interior heater fan switch

Colour code

B	White
Bl	Blue
G	Grey
Ic	Transparent
J	Yellow
M	Brown
Mv	Mauve
N	Black
Or	Orange
R	Red
V	Green

Index